The car and British society

MANCHESTER
UNIVERSITY PRESS

STUDIES IN
POPULAR
CULTURE

General editor: Professor Jeffrey Richards

The car and British society

Class, gender and motoring,
1896–1939

SEAN O'CONNELL

Manchester University Press

Manchester and New York

distributed exclusively in the USA by St. Martin's Press

Published by Manchester University Press
Oxford Road, Manchester M13 9NR, UK
and Room 400, 175 Fifth Avenue, New York,
NY 10010, USA

Distributed exclusively in the USA by
St. Martin's Press, Inc., 175 Fifth Avenue, New York,
NY 10010, USA

Distributed exclusively in Canada by
UBC Press, University of British Columbia, 6344 Memorial Road,
Vancouver, BC, Canada V6T 1Z2

British Library Cataloguing-in-Publication Data
A catalogue record for this book is available from the British Library

Library of Congress Cataloging-in-Publication Data
O'Connell, Sean
    The car and British society : class, gender and motoring 1896–1939
/ Sean O'Connell.
        p.   cm. — (Studies in popular culture)
    "Distributed exclusively in the USA by St. Martin's Press."
    ISBN 0–7190–5148–7 (hardcover) 0–7190–5506–7 (paperback)
    1. Automobiles—Social aspects—Great Britain—History.   2. Great
Britain—Social life and customs.   3. Social classes—Great Britain—
History.   I. Title.   II. Series: Studies in popular culture
Manchester, England)
HE5663.A6028   1998
303.48'32—dc21   98—18297

ISBN   0 7190 5148 7   *hardback*
        0 7190 5506 7   *paperback*

First published 1998

05 04 03 02 01 00 99 98   10 9 8 7 6 5 4 3 2 1

Typeset in Monotype Garamond by Lucy Morton & Robin Gable, Grosmont
Printed in Great Britain by Redwood Books, Trowbridge

For my Mum and in memory of my Dad

STUDIES IN
POPULAR
CULTURE

General editor's introduction

There has in recent years been an explosion of interest in culture and cultural studies. The impetus has come from two directions and out of two different traditions. On the one hand, cultural history has grown out of social history to become a distinct and identifiable school of historical investigation. On the other hand, cultural studies has grown out of English literature and has concerned itself to a large extent with contemporary issues. Nevertheless there is a shared project, its aim, to elucidate the meanings and values implicit and explicit in the art, literature, learning, institutions and everyday behaviour within a given society. Both the cultural historian and the cultural studies scholar seek to explore the ways in which a culture is imagined, represented and received, how it interacts with social processes, how it contributes to individual and collective identities and world views, to stability and change, to social, political and economic activities and programmes. This series aims to provide an arena for the cross-fertilization of the discipline, so that the work of the cultural historian can take advantage of the most useful and illuminating of the theoretical developments and the cultural studies scholars can extend the purely historical underpinnings of their investigations. The ultimate objective of the series is to provide a range of books which will explain in a readable and accessible way where we are now socially and culturally and how we got to where we are. This should enable people to be better informed, promote an interdisciplinary approach to cultural issues and encourage deeper thought about the issues, attitudes and institutions of popular culture.

Jeffrey Richards

Contents

Illustrations

General editor's foreword

The 1935 British film *The Last Journey* focuses on the pursuit of a runaway train by a swish sports car. It is a potent visual symbol for the rise and rise of the motor car in British society and culture. That rise is the subject of Sean O'Connell's book. He seeks to broaden the study of the car from the previously dominant emphases on manufacture and technology and to place it in the contexts of class, gender and consumption. He is particularly interested in how cultural norms, class perceptions and tastes shaped attitudes to the car and car ownership; in examining these areas, he challenges, interrogates and revises many existing interpretations.

O'Connell explores the application of notions of masculinity and femininity to the car, driving and ownership. He discusses the effect of motoring on the nature and patterns of leisure, legitimate middle-class outlets such as touring, and car clubs being complemented by the illegality of working-class 'joyriding'. He analyses the road safety debate, tracing the emergence of an influential *laissez-faire* ideology and a powerful pro-motoring lobby which blocked any attempt to resist the growing hegemony of the internal combustion engine.

One of the most notable developments in car culture was driving into the country and Sean O'Connell examines the mutually contradictory aims of rural preservationists, the middle-class leisure motorists and the country folk who variously saw the motor car as a nuisance and a boon. He concludes with an analysis of representations of the car in both visual and literary culture. The car and the motorist were used as both critiques and celebrations of modernity, but O'Connell uncovers a strong tendency to link the car with danger, death and misogynism. His fresh and stimulating study, enlivened by the use of new oral evidence, emphasises the complexity and ambivalence of the love affair with the motor car which has come to characterise British society during the twentieth century.

Jeffrey Richards

Acknowledgements

There are a number of people without whom this book could not have been written. Initially, I would like to thank Jeffrey Richards and Vanessa Graham at MUP, for providing me with the opportunity to write this book. Bill Lancaster helped with my application for an ESRC studentship award in the first place, so if you don't like this book blame Bill. Jim Obelkevich supervised my doctorate and endeavoured to propel the research down a number of interesting pathways. If I didn't always follow your advice Jim, sorry; if you don't like this book, blame me. A number of others have offered their encouragement and advice over the years and I would like to thank Kate Beaumont, Andy Davies, Alun Francis, Steve Koerner, Terry Gourvish, Gwynne Lewis, Ros Lucas, Tony Mason, Mike Tadman, Nick Tiratsoo, Steve Tolliday, Chris Reid, Carolyn Steedman and John Walton.

Wherever I have travelled in conducting my research I have found archivists and librarians extremely helpful. I wish to acknowledge the assistance of archivists at the Automobile Association, the Archive and Special Collections at the University of Liverpool, the Modern Records Centre at the University of Warwick, the Museum of Rural Life at the University of Reading and the Royal Automobile Club. I am also grateful for the many occasions on which the staff of the British Library (Bloomsbury and Colindale) and the staff at Manchester Central Reference Library dealt with my requests.

I also owe an immeasurable debt to Jill Greenfield whose love, support and intellectual guidance have seen me through the 'double whammy' of a thesis and a monograph with my sanity intact.

Introduction

In 1996 Britain celebrated a century of motoring. This was not the centenary of the first motor car, but of the Locomotives on Highways Act of 1896, which, by removing the famous regulation that motor vehicles be preceded by a person on foot carrying a red flag, ushered in the era of modern motoring. Business, labour and economic historians have busied themselves with investigations of the motor industry, the labour relations within that manufacturing sector and its role within the British economy. However, the consumption of the car, and its social and cultural impact upon British society, have rarely been explored. Thus the car's travels beyond the factory gates, and thereafter beyond the motor showroom, have been, in Bert Moorehouse's words, 'virtual *terra incognita* to the academic mind.'[1] This study deals primarily with that terrain, but it does not ignore the existing histories of the car's production.[2] The following analysis embraces a growing preference amongst scholars to move from explanations of consumption that study only one element of the entire process, towards more integrated accounts that consider the interrelated dynamics of production, distribution, marketing and consumer uses of the product.[3] In the case of a consumer durable such as the car which is also a transport technology, the role of the state must also enter the historical equation.

In following this path, it will be maintained that the car, like any technology, was subject to contestation amongst a variety of social, economic and political factors. The years between 1896 and 1939 saw the establishment of features of motoring which still influence the way the car is perceived to this day. By 1939 almost two million private cars were using Britain's roads. Motoring was by that date no longer seen as a luxury hobby: it had become a central factor in the lifestyles of approximately one in every five families. This study explains how this came to pass. It also sets that story, of how a developing technology changed lifestyles and consumption patterns, within a broad under-standing of the social relations which shaped these developments and were in turn influenced by them. In doing so it re-evaluates some questions, providing new insights into the historiographies of the dif-fusion of car ownership and the development of road-safety policy. It also examines questions about the car that have not been asked previ-ously by British historians. The enquiry into the relationship between the car, motoring and gender ideologies which is presented here repre-sents the first attempt to undertake this task in a British case study. Similarly, the material on rural Britain offers original analysis of the complex relationship between the car and the rural economy. This introduction will explain the foundations on which this study is built. First, it summarises the historiography of the car, both in Britain and in the USA. Second, it outlines the key themes that are addressed in this study.

Theo Barker's recent survey of the evolution of motoring research revealed a general paucity of literature, noting that historians have been slow to turn their attention towards the history of motor transport. Where they have done, the focus has often been upon manufacturing. Whilst company records and other sources familiar to the business historian are relatively accessible, the 'many-sided effects of the growing flood of motor cars as they poured on to the poor and limited roads of the early days [have] posed a much greater challenge to historians', which is 'far more difficult to analyse and discuss'.[4] In fact, only two studies of any depth, Harold Perkin's *The Age of the Automobile* (1976) and Kenneth Richardson's *The British Motor Industry 1896–1939: An Economic and Social History* (1977) have taken up this challenge.[5] As the first social histories of the car in Britain, both studies necessarily covered a great deal of ground in the interests of filling a gap in our knowledge. Important as it was to engage in this range of coverage, the breadth of the studies is also a weakness, as too many matters are treated in too little detail. Perkin's work suffers the most in this respect. Written to accompany a television series, it was an attempt to cover a century of automotive history. In the course of the narrative, the reader is not only informed of the social, cultural and economic history of the motor car and other motor vehicles; there are also chapters on the use of the tank in the First World War and the aeroplane in the Second World War. Clearly, such a vast survey inevitably left little room for either the detail or analysis which must form part of any historical endeavour.

Concentrating on a shorter period than Perkin, Richardson's study provided a number of empirically detailed surveys of different aspects of the car's history. Successive chapters offered coverage of the pre-history of the car, specialist manufacturers, the American challenge to the British manufacturers, the popular car and volume production, motor racing, sports cars, the arrival of middle-class motoring, before climaxing with a study of the petrol companies, garages and motor-car distribution. As his preface indicated, Richardson's intent was to write about the people who 'made the British motor industry'.[6] This accounts for what is an almost heroic portrayal of the events and personalities. It also explains the fact that two chapters are devoted to motor racing and sports cars, whereas coverage of the everyday user of the car is squeezed into a single chapter. Thus, Richardson's version of events is filled with positive, resourceful men: it is a world of impressive in-ventors, engineers, manufacturers and racing drivers. Even relatively unglamorous figures, such as William Letts and Charles Jarrott, motor-car importers and founding members of the Automobile Association are lauded. For Richardson they were of 'that excellent breed which establishes committees and gets the business of the world done'.[7] To summarise Richardson's contribution, it would be necessary to con-clude that he provided a good deal of empirical evidence, but failed to situate his narrative within wider historical events or identify the possible historiographical significance of much of what he found. Neither account offered any perception that technology is socially constructed through cultural and political factors as much as by technical necessity or scientific discovery. For example, Perkin and Richardson failed to explain why fewer women have held driving licences than men through-out the history of motoring. Furthermore, in offering scant analysis of the role of pro-motoring lobbyists, they failed to illuminate the process through which the car became established as the dominant form of transport in the UK.

The latter of these two developments was explored in some detail in William Plowden's study *The Motor Car and Politics in Britain* (1971).[8] Covering the period from 1896 to 1970, Plowden chose to concentrate on the development of government policy towards the car. A former journalist and civil servant, who became a lecturer in government at the London School of Economics, Plowden provided an informed interpretation of the competing claims of various interest groups that influenced government policy towards motor transport. The most instructive sections of the book are those that deal with the period up to 1939, his access to government papers being limited after that date. Plowden's account is a useful corrective for those historical studies which failed to fully investigate the notion of the car as a contested technology. Plowden provided an illuminating insight into unfolding attitudes towards the car within government and the civil service. In particular, he highlighted the role that the motoring lobby secured for themselves as advisors to the government on road-transport issues. Chapter 4 of this study will continue Plowden's analysis of the debate over road safety. In the process, the findings of Clive Emsley's recent contribution to this field will be queried.[9] Emsley argued that the development of road-safety policy was not inspired by class interest but was generated, instead, through an *ad hoc* process in which ministers, bureaucrats and technical experts endeavoured to find solutions to a number of intricate problems. However, by interrogating the records of the National Safety First Association (NSFA), the organisation favoured by government for the dissemination of road-safety policy, a different interpretation of events becomes necessary. Existing studies have left the NSFA unexplored and have therefore failed to record the organisation's links with motor manufacturers and motoring organisations. Once these are acknowledged, the activities of the NSFA and the direction of road-safety discourse and policy must be seen in a new context.

The scarcity of British historiographical material on the car, from which to draw inspiration, is partially offset by the amount of material available covering the automobile's impact in the USA. However, there too the earliest work on automobile history has recently been critiqued because it suffered from the same technological determinism that beset the historiography in Britain. Thus, the work of pioneers, such as John B. Rae and James J. Flink, has been accused of describing the automobile's progression as inevitable and unproblematic.[10] For example, Peter Ling suggested that historians who stressed 'the psychological appeal of the automobile as an instrument of autarky … independence and … personal power' were failing to analyse the 'less romantic' facets of automobility.[11] A younger generation of social historians has offered a re-evaluation of the automobile, posing new questions of, and providing new insights into, its role in early-twentieth-century America. Rather than having a history revolving entirely around individual liberty and mobility, it is clear that the design, marketing and uses of the automobile were often shaped by considerations of class, gender and race, with all the potential for inequality of opportunity thus entailed. The literature is growing, and offering history of an increasingly ambitious and sophisticated nature. Howard L. Preston's study of Atlanta analysed the effect of growing automobile ownership on the largely car-less African-American population. For them the automotive age increased their social and residential isolation, the car allowing more prosperous citizens, including the small middle-class African-American community, to retreat to the new suburbs outside Atlanta.[12]

Virginia Scharff has highlighted the gender-blindness of earlier work, producing a fascinating study that has revealed gender's centrality in the early American car culture.[13] Her study described the rough-hewn, masculine self-image of the developing automobile industry. That the automobile was so strongly associated with masculinity presented several problems once significant numbers of women began to become interested in motoring and gained access to automobiles. Scharff charts the problems faced by female drivers in a society whose gender expectations suggested that a woman's place was not at the wheel, in control of a dangerous and powerful technology, but in the passenger seat. Automobile manufacturers also 'shared the prejudices, desires, interests and insecurities of their gender, class and culture' and many of those involved within the motor industry expressed disquiet about the female influence on what they believed to be a masculine technology.[14] Thus the design, marketing and uses of the automobile in early-twentieth-century America were all heavily influenced by gender ideology.

The most recent contribution to American automobile historiography was made by Clay McShane.[15] McShane offered an account of how American society adopted the automobile which acknowledged that the process was one that cannot be explained simply in terms of technological

inevitability. Beginning by posing the question of whether the automobile as a technology could have been banned or rejected, he found
that the answer was yes. Indeed, Wolfgang Sachs's history of the automobile in Germany reminds us that there was a ban on cars in parts
of Switzerland until as late as 1925.[16] McShane argues that the American
automobile overcame any such threat because at the heart of its growing
popularity lay its symbolic qualities as much as its utilitarian ones: 'The
automobile triumphed because it was more than just a form of travel.
Rapid acceptance grew, not just out of mechanical superiority, but the
motor car's application as a status object and symbol of liberation. The
new machines cannot be evaluated just as a technology or another new
transportation mode.'[17] This insight, and others offered by recent
American work, have assisted many of the theoretical and methodological decisions taken during the course of research for this study of
the car's impact on British society. For, like much of the recent American
research, this book is written in response to the important omissions
in the existing British studies.

My own research has also been influenced and guided by several
insights gathered from recent historical and sociological research on
consumption and technology. The new sociology of technology, best
exemplified in the work of Judy Wajcman, was amongst these influences.[18] Her work offers a critique of the technological determinism of
previous sociological coverage of technology. Rather than simply
considering the effects of technology on society, it also examines the
effects of society on technology. This approach is a highly appropriate
one for this study, given the nature of the previous historiography,
which was largely concerned with mapping the car's impact on any
number of aspects of our lives without asking questions about how
notions of class, gender or other factors might have influenced the
car's technological development in the first place. A major aim of this
enquiry, therefore, is to provide a new perspective on the car's history,
identifying its dialectical relationship with social relations such as those
of class and gender. In exploring this perspective, the extent to which
these cultural and social influences brought a strong element of con-
tingency to the development of the car, as a technology and as a
consumer good, will be acknowledged.

Consumption is the other major theme which runs throughout the
study. As noted above, there is a substantial literature dealing with the

production of the car, but we also need to know the history of its 'modes of consumption and the ways these have been suffused with meaning.'[19] This aspect of our analysis has been informed by the evidence of a sample of seventy-six people whose experiences of motoring date back to before 1939.[20] It is not claimed that the set of respondents assembled as part of this research exactly replicates the actual demographic profile of motorists in the years between 1896 and 1939. Not surprisingly, the sample does not contain anybody with adult experiences of motoring before 1918. The eldest respondent was born in 1901 and the youngest in 1931, but the majority were born between 1901 and 1925. The vast majority of respondents fitted the anticipated profile of pre-1939 motorists, having emanated from either professional or commercial family backgrounds. However, a smaller number came from lower-middle- and working-class backgrounds, reflecting the complexity of the social composition of car owners by the late 1930s. The testimony from the respondents was gathered through a variety of means. Seventeen members of the sample were willing to have their life histories recorded in oral history interviews. A further twelve provided evidence through questionnaires that were distributed through Quicks Ltd, a Manchester-based Ford dealership, who were able to provide a database of pre-war motorists. The remaining members of the sample provided their testimony through detailed correspondence which they composed in response to appeals for information that had been placed in various local newspapers and national magazines. The majority of information collected from the respondents was qualitative in nature, providing valuable insights into the meaning placed upon car ownership by individuals and families. It was also possible to develop quantifiable data from the testimony of respondents on such matters as the gender and social background of car drivers and the methods by which ownership was achieved and financed. The information supplied by these respondents has been placed alongside a broad range of more traditional sources in order to present the fullest possible appraisal of the car's impact on British society between 1896 and 1939.

Testimony from members of the sample suggested that new questions should be asked of the traditional sources. In particular, their evidence indicated that any understanding of consumption and the diffusion of consumer durables must address the symbolic dimension of the world of goods. In pursuing this theme, the work of Mary

Douglas and Baron Isherwood, and Pierre Bourdieu have been influential in suggesting avenues of thought.[21] Douglas and Isherwood's *The World of Goods* provided an interesting critique of the assumptions economists make about consumption. In particular, they have called for greater weight to be given to the 'metaphorical understanding' of goods. It is only through this approach that 'we can come to a more accurate idea of why consumers buy goods'.[22] In particular the notion of the rational individual, commonly used in economic explanations of consumption, is an 'an impossible abstraction from social life'.[23] Furthermore it is 'absurd to aggregate millions of individuals buying and using goods without reckoning with the transformations they effect by sharing consumption together'.[24] Goods make physical, visible statements about the hierarchy of values subscribed to by their owner and they are read by those who know the codes and scanned for information. Bourdieu has argued that the structure of consumption is the key to the reproduction of social hierarchies and relations and that it provides a mechanism by which they can be analysed. Bourdieu places less emphasis on goods as such, preferring instead to concentrate on cultural capital and its expression in terms of taste. The perspectives offered by Douglas and Isherwood alongside those of Bourdieu provide a useful framework in which to seek an understanding of the car and its consumption in pre-1939 Britain. Douglas and Isherwood's work is most useful when evaluating econometric analyses of the historical diffusion of private cars. Bourdieu's concepts are of greater heuristic value when considering the uses to which cars were put. His empirical work on middle-class consumers has also highlighted the importance of recognising the intricate distinctions that can be made in the consumption process. Several historians have recognised the shifting and heterogeneous nature of the middle classes during this period, but this is the first attempt to establish the impact of that social diversity on the design, sales and uses to which the car was put.[25] The polymorphous nature of the middle classes was not simply due to income or occupational differences; it was also the result of carefully contrived distinctions that revolved around virtually every aspect of middle-class lifestyle. It will be suggested that the car as a very visible artefact became integral to the arena of middle-class distinction. As such the consumption of the car must be analysed in all its aspects, from the type of car chosen to how it was paid for to how and when it was used. Thus this analysis follows the car out of the factory gate and through the motor showroom to explore its impact on the lifestyles and experiences of British motorists. It examines how the consumption of the car, and its development as a technology, was inextricably linked with the gender and class ideologies of British society in the early twentieth century.

Notes

1 H. F. Moorehouse, *Driving Ambitions: An Analysis of the American Hot Rod Enthusiasm* (Manchester, Manchester University Press, 1991), p. 221.
2 See Chapter 1 for details of this area of the historiography.
3 See, for example, B. Fine and E. Leopold, *The World of Consumption* (London, Routledge, 1993); G. McCracken, *Culture and Consumption: New Approaches to the Symbolic Character of Consumer Goods and Activities* (Indiana University Press, 1988); Frank Mort, *Cultures of Consumption: Masculinities and Social Space in Late Twentieth-Century Britain* (London, Routledge, 1996).
4 T. Barker, 'Slow progress: forty years of motoring research', *Journal of Transport History*, 14 (1993) 142.
5 H. Perkin, *The Age of the Automobile* (London, Quartet Books, 1976); K. Richardson, *The British Motor Industry 1896–1939: A Social and Economic History* (London, Macmillan, 1977).
6 Richardson, *The British Motor Industry*, preface.
7 *Ibid.*, p. 217.
8 W. Plowden, *The Motor Car and Politics in Britain* (Harmondsworth, Pelican Books, 1973).
9 C. Emsley, '"Mother, what did policemen do when there weren't any motors?" The law, the police and the regulation of motor traffic in England, 1900–1939', *Historical Journal*, 36 (1993) 357–81.
10 J. B. Rae, *The American Automobile: A Brief History* (Chicago, University of Chicago Press, 1965); J. B. Rae, *The Road and the Car in American Life* (Cambridge, MA, MIT Press, 1971); and J. J. Flink, *America Adopts the Automobile, 1895–1910* (Cambridge, MA, MIT Press, 1970).
11 P. Ling, *America and the Automobile: Technology, Reform and Social Change* (Manchester, Manchester University Press, 1992), p. 170.
12 H. L. Preston, *Automobile Age Atlanta: The Making of a Southern Metropolis, 1900–1935* (Athens, University of Georgia Press, 1979).
13 V. Scharff, *Taking the Wheel: Women and the Coming of the Motor Age* (New York, The Free Press, 1991).
14 *Ibid.*, p. 112.
15 C. McShane, *Along the Asphalt Path: The Automobile and the American City* (New York, Columbia University Press, 1994).

16 W. Sachs, *For the Love of the Automobile: Looking Back into the History of Our Desires* (Oxford, University of California Press, 1992), p. 18.

17 McShane, *Along the Asphalt Path*, pp. x–xi.

18 J. Wajcman, *Feminism Confronts Technology* (Cambridge, Polity Press, 1991); D. MacKenzie and J. Wajcman (eds), *The Social Shaping of Technology* (Milton Keynes, Open University Press, 1985). See also W. E. Bijker et al. (eds), *The Social Construction of Technological Systems: New Directions in the Sociology and History of Technology* (London, MIT Press, 1989).

19 Moorehouse, *Driving Ambitions*, p. 222.

20 The names of all respondents have been changed to preserve their anonymity. It is hoped that all the material gathered from the respondents can be deposited in an appropriate archive.

21 M. Douglas and B. Isherwood, *World of Goods* (London, Lane, 1980); P. Bourdieu, *The Logic of Practice* (Oxford, Oxford University Press 1992); P. Bourdieu, *Distinction: A Social Critique of the Judgement of Taste* (London, Routledge, 1986).

22 Douglas and Isherwood, *World of Goods*, pp. 4–5.

23 *Ibid.*

24 *Ibid.*

25 R. Samuel, 'Middle Class Between the Wars', *New Society*, January–June 1981; A. A. Jackson, *The Middle Classes 1900–1950* (Nairn, David St John Thomas, 1991); A. Light, *Forever England: Femininity, Literature and Conservatism between the Wars* (London, Routledge, 1991).

1

'By their cars ye shall know them': class, status and the spread of car ownership

An elite activity in Edwardian Britain, car use by 1939 extended to approximately one in five families. This chapter identifies the significant factors in the diffusion of car ownership between 1896 and 1939, by which point there were two million private cars. The approach taken is influenced by both economic and cultural strands of historical debates about consumption. Existing historical interpretations of the development of motoring in Britain have very much focused on the economic conditions framing the behaviour of car manufacturers. It will be seen that these arguments are compelling but that they do not tell the full story. A hallmark of this study will be an assessment of the symbolic dimension the car possessed as an expensive and novel consumer durable. It will be argued that consumer behaviour has influences other than the purely utilitarian. Deeply rooted cultural values, which were themselves a product of, and producer of, economic behaviour, influenced the development of car ownership. An assessment of notions of taste and social status must enter the equation, alongside the economic variables. In the process significant new findings will be reported, including the extent to which socio-cultural factors affected the behaviour of consumers, credit-providers, manufacturers and motor agents, thereby limiting the speed of market growth.

The first section of this chapter relates the growth of the infant motor industry in the twenty years after 1896. The cultural, economic, legal, social and technical factors that shaped motoring's evolution are

BY THEIR CARS YE SHALL
KNOW THEM.

Sir Coupay and Lady de Ville.

Mr. and Mrs. "Popular Twenty."

Mr. Elwyn Poigninyn and his wife.

Sam and Sadie Severn

Enery and Liz.

1   Social distinction and the car,
as seen by *Autocar* in 1924.

considered. This section also delineates the development of distribution, marketing and production techniques within the industry.

The second part of the chapter examines the diffusion of car ownership in the inter-war years. Previous work has acknowledged the effect of middle-class taste on car design and on the proliferation of models. Here, significant new evidence will be presented indicating that similar notions also affected the ways in which the car was sold. In particular it will be shown that despite the apparent success of hire-purchase, this was a form of payment which was looked upon with a great deal of ambivalence. As a result manufacturers and dealers soft-pedalled their use of this method of payment. It was rarely featured in advertising, for example, and strict limitations were placed on its use by finance companies. The extent to which this previously unacknowledged factor may have limited market growth will be assessed.

The final section involves the first attempt to explore aspects of the market for second-hand cars. In particular, oral evidence is employed to reveal the extent to which a small, but significant, number of working-class people made use of the second-hand market to become car owners from the mid-1930s. Many of these working-class buyers were prepared to share cars between families or friends and often engaged in second jobs in order to obtain ownership of this prized consumer commodity.

The early years of the motor industry: 1896–1914

On 14 November 1896 Harry Lawson's one-year-old Motor Car Club organised a London to Brighton demonstration run for automobiles. This event took place on what became known as 'emancipation day', celebrating as it did the passing into law of the Locomotives on Highways Act. Until that time the advancement of motoring in Britain had been severely hampered by legislation. The Locomotive Act of 1865 had introduced the so-called 'red flag' legislation. Road locomotives were restricted to 4 m.p.h. in the countryside and 2 m.p.h. in urban areas, with the added stipulation that vehicles be preceded, at a distance of sixty yards, by a red-flag-carrying walker. Although the Highways and Locomotives Act of 1878 made it possible for local authorities to remove the red-flag regulations in their areas, there was little real prospect of significant advances in either motoring or in motor-vehicle manufacturing in such a legislative climate.

The 1896 act was the culmination of a concerted campaign by the embryonic motoring lobby, including Lawson's Motor Car Club, Sir David Salomons' Self-Propelled Traffic Association and the newly-founded journal *Autocar*. Perhaps the most significant moment in the crusade was the attendance of the Prince of Wales and other members of the royal family at a motor exhibition, organised by Lawson, at the Imperial Institute in February 1896.[1] As a result of the 1896 legislation the speed limit for motor vehicles was raised to 12 m.p.h., a figure which was increased again, to 20 m.p.h., by the Motor Car Act of 1903. Changing legislative conditions allowed the nascent British motor industry to take the first uncertain steps towards establishing itself.

However, the industry's early years were not straightforward, even after the legislation of 1896 and 1903. To begin with, British manufacturers had to make up for time lost to French and German competitors in the 1890s. In fact most early British cars, such as Daimler and Napier, were adaptations of French models. Moreover, by 1903 manufacturers in the USA were outproducing the French, and the British began to keep a watchful, and sometimes critical, eye on the American market. Early growth of the industry in Britain was not assisted by the lack of interest shown in motor manufacturing by large engineering firms.[2] The industry attracted a large number of speculators and company promoters, who did not enhance its financial respectability.

Despite his significant role in securing the 'emancipation' legislation, Harry Lawson quickly fell from grace following his disastrous involvement with Daimler and Humber.[3] His British Motor Syndicate invested large sums on patents in an attempt to corner the entire motor-car market. Lawson finally lost his patents-war in the High Court in 1903.[4]

Manufacturers also faced a choice between the relative merits of electric-, steam- or petrol-powered vehicles. Even by 1905, when there were sixteen thousand private cars on British roads, petrol-powered cars had not triumphed completely.[5] Furthermore, as the purveyor of a novel new technology, each individual car manufacturer had the task of convincing initially sceptical consumers that having left *A* their vehicle would actually reach *B*. For this reason an integral aspect of the early marketing of the car revolved around road races and reliability trials. The earliest and most important of the reliability trials was held in 1900, under the auspices of the proprietor of the *Daily Mail*, Alfred Harmsworth, and the Automobile Club (later the Royal Automobile Club). Amongst the drivers taking part were Herbert Austin, who drove a car he had built for Wolseley, and S. F. Edge, who was behind the wheel of one of his Napiers. The trial's purpose was described by *The Times* as being 'to prove that the motor car is, even in its present state of development, a serious and trustworthy means of locomotion; not a toy, dangerous and troublesome alike to the public and the owner.'[6] Most of the races, trials and stunts that were a hallmark of the first two decades of the motor industry were designed as spectacular events organised to demonstrate the reliability and utility of the car to potential buyers. Another of the most spectacular stunts, in terms of the sales that followed it, was organised by Percival Perry. In 1911 Perry, who was the man entrusted by Henry Ford with the task of establishing his cars in the UK, arranged for a Model T to be driven to the summit of Ben Nevis.

The early motor industry also had to evolve successful and efficient distributive and production strategies. Initially it was the norm to lay down the standard chassis of each model only on receipt of a deposit, of up to a third of the retail price, from the buyer. In return for their outlay car buyers could expect a degree of consultation in the building process.[7] This approach to retailing drew upon the origins in the engineering trade of many of the early car producers, who had experience of selling machine tools and domestic hardware rather than luxury items.[8] However, as companies began to move towards batch production they established agencies through which their vehicles were distributed.[9] Although many manufacturers would have preferred that their appointed agents sold only their cars, in reality most car showrooms displayed several marques. From the available production figures it is probably safe to conclude that the use of agents was normal practice amongst motor manufacturers by 1906 when the total number of cars on British roads stood at 23,000 and the largest companies Humber and Argyll produced 1,000 and 800 cars respectively.[10] As the agency system evolved, a distribution system emerged that borrowed a good deal from practices employed by the cycle trade. Indeed many of the first motor agents were also cycle agents. This correlation grew more marked as cycle manufacturers moved into motor-car manufacture in the middle of the Edwardian period. Companies, such as Rover in 1904, expanded into the new industry once it became clear that consumers and engineers had reached a general agreement about what were to be the dominant conventions in motor-car design.[11]

The next stage in the development of motor-car manufacture was a movement from batch production of a few dozen models at a time to annual-model production plans. This system allowed firms to implement a limited amount of standardisation within the production system. However, progress in this direction was slow. By July 1912, according to *Automobile Engineering*, only Sunbeam and, to a lesser extent, Wolseley had made substantial progress towards the introduction of new methods of production.[12] Greater rationalisation of production and distribution methods offered the prospect of reducing prices and thereby extending car ownership beyond the most affluent members of society. There has been some discussion amongst historians, however, about the speed at which motor manufacturers sought to extend the market by lowering prices. The two strands of this debate echo much of the contemporary commentary on the burgeoning motor industry. Writing in 1962, S. B. Saul accused the pre-1914 motor industry of a 'general backwardness' and conservatism, which was evidenced by the 'tentative and tardy nature of the changes away from traditional methods of the engineering industry' towards investment in the more standardised production of cheaper cars.[13] Saul drew support from a 1912 edition of *The Times* for his assertion that the leading manufacturers lacked commercial acumen. *The Times* wrote: 'To put it bluntly, the fact is that there is no firm at present which has been sufficiently enterprising to lay down a large enough plant to make small cars in sufficient numbers to make their production really cheap.'[14] In the following year *The Economist* was less critical of motor manufacturers: 'British manufacturers up to the present have proceeded very cautiously in the past, contenting themselves with a comparatively small production until their reputations were established against the older firms of the Continent. In the better-class vehicles, costing, say £400 or more, the British manufacturer fears no outside competition.'[15]

The term 'better-class vehicles' is revealing because there was certainly an element of self-congratulation amongst the British manufacturers that their cars, being more expensive than many of those on offer in America, were superior in design and engineering quality. They found support from the British motoring magazine *Autocar*, which, in 1912 congratulated 'our English makers' for maintaining 'their reputation for high grade work rather than cheapen their reputation by the use of the inferior material and workmanship they would be obliged to employ to compete with American manufacturers of cheap cars'.[16] Thus many voices in the motoring world were content to see British manufacturers follow a policy of what can be labelled conspicuous production.[17] For example, when Charles Friswell became chairman of Standard he vetoed the company's plans to manufacture cars for a 'less exalted market' than the one he prized.[18]

Moreover, the motor industry also acted comparatively early to impose price maintenance on motor dealers. In doing so it operated against the interests of many prospective car owners. In 1910 the Society of Motor Manufacturers and Traders (SMMT) welcomed the addition to its ranks of a Motor Traders' Association (MTA) whose task was to prevent retail-price cutting. It did so by the creation, in 1911, of a 'stop list' of price-cutting agents who were boycotted by SMMT and MTA members.[19] In January of that year, an edition of *Motor Trader* revealed that motor manufacturers had made it clear to the motoring press, burgeoning in large part due to income from motoring advertisements, that they did not appreciate discussion of price maintenance in their pages. The industry had noted that the cycle industry had previously lost sales through the public deliberation of what *Motor Trader* called 'a purely trade matter'.[20]

As we have already noted, the spectacular advances being made by the motor industry in the USA, led by Henry Ford, formed the back-drop to contemporary discussions of the relative merits of the early British motor industry. Recent appraisals of Saul's critique of pre-1914 motor manufacturers have sought to qualify his criticisms. Roy Church, for example, has argued that any analysis should locate the production policies of motor manufacturers within the context of British socio-economic circumstances.[21] Thus, it has been argued that the nature of the British market differed markedly from the American one. On the eve of the First World War, Ford's American plant produced 200,000 vehicles compared with the 5,000 of Peugeot and the 3,000 of Wolseley, the largest French and British manufacturers respectively.[22] The invest-ment necessary to achieve the economies of scale and subsequent price reductions reached by Ford was only possible because of relatively high levels of real income in a society where geographical distances were more significant and rail density was lower than in Britain, France or Germany.[23] Thus the limited size of the British market was a central impediment to the adoption of American mass-production techniques.

The willingness of British manufacturers to experiment, from 1911, with cyclecars has also been cited in response to Saul's critique. Cyclecars were essentially adapted motorcycles with three or four wheels and room for one or two uncomfortable occupants. They have been rather ingloriously described as 'combining the comfort of a cement mixer, the noise of a pneumatic drill and the directional ability of a chicken with its head cut off'.[24] The best-known example of these machines was the 1912 Humberette; selling at £125, it was the most popular of sixty makes of cyclecar at that time.[25] If the claim that the first issue of *Cyclecar* magazine in 1912 sold 100,000 copies is correct then a sense of the untapped demand for cheaper motoring can be clearly appreci-ated.[26] However, the poor quality and uncomfortable cyclecar was never going to be a substitute for a motor car proper. According to its his-torian, the cyclecar was looked down upon by those motorists with more expensive vehicles. Moreover the fact that manufacturers such as Armstrong-Siddeley were careful to keep the company's name off their cyclecar, which they called the Stoneleigh, suggests that manufacturers were keen to ensure that their more affluent customers continued to see a clear distinction between the two products.[27]

The absence of good quality cheap cars boosted the sales of the British motor-cycle industry. So much so, in fact, that motor-cycle registrations fell below those of cars only in 1925, the figures being 558,911 and 590,156 respectively.[28] Following that, however, the gap in registration figures widened rapidly and by 1938 motor-cycle registrations were below the 1925 figure, standing at 499,265, whereas private car registrations had soared to 1,984,430.[29] Steve Koerner has chronicled the history of the British motor-cycle industry. He argues that the industry was badly hit by the introduction, during the 1920s, of cheap 'baby' cars such as the Austin Seven and the 'Bullnose' Morris. Crucially, registration figures for motor-cycle combinations consistently deteriorated at a rate that was 'far more acute' than the fall in solo motor-cycle registrations.[30] Koerner maintains that the motor-cycle manufacturers did not match the technological advances that were made by the motor-car industry. In particular, motor cycles lost popularity because they offered less carrying capacity than even the smallest car, were inherently unstable and left riders and pillion passengers vulnerable to injury should an accident occur.[31]

However, it was not a British motor-car manufacturer that initiated the extension of the market away from its luxury image. Henry Ford's British managing director, Percival Perry, struck the most decisive blow in that process. In persuading Henry Ford to set up an operation at Trafford Park in 1911, to assemble parts shipped over from the USA, Perry recognised and exploited the market for cheaper cars. By 1913 Ford UK were producing 7,310 cars, more than double the figure for Wolseley, who were the biggest British manufacturer with a figure of 3,000.[32] At £135 for the basic Model T, Ford were offering by far the best value economy car on the market, a fact corroborated by the Model T's 60 per cent share of the market for cars valued at under £200 in 1913.[33] Given their relative size, production techniques, and the attractions of loftier market niches, few British companies attempted to compete with Ford in the low-priced car market. Of those who did, the most aggressive and innovative was Morris Motors who entered the fray in 1913 with the Morris Oxford, competitively priced at £175. Despite producing only 303 Oxfords in its first year, Morris attained lower production costs than its bigger British rivals. Morris achieved this by operating against the trend of vertical integration that was a feature elsewhere in the industry.[34] Morris cars were assembled entirely from bought-in components. In the process, the prices paid for components reflected the economies of scale secured by Morris's suppliers.

William Morris had been a cycle retailer before turing his hand to motor-car manufacture and his production policy was largely borrowed from the cycle industry.

So, in eighteen years the British motor-car manufacturing industry became the equal of the older French industry. It did not, however, match the amazing success of American producers such as Ford. It is clear that the fundamental differences between the two markets meant that it was unrealistic to believe that it could. However, despite the arguments that have been levelled against Saul's critique of the conservatism of the early British motor-car manufacturers, many aspects of his thesis still seem to have merit. British car producers were indisputably constrained by the size and nature of their market, but few took the sort of commercial initiatives that were to make Morris Motors the country's biggest car producer by the middle of the 1920s. Their innovative approach, inspired by the success of the Model T in the pre-1914 British market, was to begin the process of expanding car ownership beyond the wealthier echelons of society. Other manufacturers seemed locked into a self-fulfilling prophecy whereby the market could not be extended because cars could not be made cheaply enough. It is difficult not to be left with the impression that without the arrival of Ford at Trafford Park the extension of the market for private cars would have been slower than was the case. By 1914 car-ownership levels were still relatively low, although at 132,000 they were almost double the figure for 1911.[35] The car was beginning to be associated with utility as well as luxury uses. But it was the inter-war decades that were to witness Britain's first period of 'motoring for the million'. In these years ownership figures grew twentyfold, and it is to this important period that we now turn.

Selling cars in a middle-class market: 1918–1939

The inter-war years saw the arrival of Britain's first era of mass motoring. The number of private cars rose from just over 100,000 in 1918 to slightly over two million in 1939. There are a variety of explanations for this impressive growth. Most importantly, the retail price of cars fell markedly in real terms. For example, by 1936 average prices stood at 49.8 per cent of their 1924 level.[36] These reductions were the result of the production of smaller cars, most famously the Austin Seven and the 'Bullnose' Morris, together with increased rationalisation and efficiency in manufacturing methods. The rising levels of real income amongst the middle classes were also instrumental in extending the market, particularly following the recovery from slump in the early 1930s. Increasing use of hire-purchase is also widely believed to have had a significant impact on the market, being utilised in 'perhaps 50–60 per cent of all new car sales' by the end of the 1920s; a figure that had risen to 'perhaps 65–70%' by the late 1930s.[37] The tentative nature of these figures is a consequence of the motor industry's failure to record credit-sales figures.[38]

Despite its successes, the motor industry has not escaped criticism for its failure to introduce Fordist production methods in the inter-war years. Wayne Lewchuk has accused the largest motor manufacturers of conservatism in two respects. First, he alleges short-termism in respect to an apparent preference to finance shareholders' dividends rather than the investment necessary to develop a mass market.[39] Lewchuck also maintains that motor manufacturers failed to take full control of the production process, instead following a 'British system of production' that allowed trade unions to set production targets through the operation of piece-work.[40] Lewchuk's arguments have been repudiated on a number of counts. First, Steve Tolliday has cast serious doubt on Lewchuk's assessment of union influence.[41] Most tellingly, however, analyses of demand-side constraints have revealed the inadvisability of Fordist production. Adopting an econometric approach, centred on consumer-demand theory, Sue Bowden and Paul Turner have indicated three stages in the diffusion of car ownership.[42] The first stage, roughly covering the years up to the 1914–1918 war, involved the car being identified as a luxury with prices to match that association. The second stage, the inter-war years and the 1940s, is seen as being marked by technological changes and greater rationalisation of the production process. The lower prices that resulted enabled car ownership to filter down through Britain's professional and commercial middle classes, who began to identify car ownership as a necessity rather than a luxury. According to Bowden and Turner the car remained firmly within this second stage during the inter-war years due to the skewed distribution of income, which was much more marked in the UK than in the USA. As a result of these income differentials many consumers who might have met the cost price of a new car would have had difficulties in

Jean Rosolen's family proudly pose with their car in the mid-1930s. **2**

meeting the high running costs; Bowden has argued that these costs were potentially as high as a third of the cost price of a new car.[43] British car manufacturers were correct, therefore, to develop a system of production which met the conditions of the British market rather than gamble and fail with Fordist production policies. Finally, the third stage, mass ownership, was reached when increased economies of scale and technological improvements made further price reductions possible. This mass production stage occurred in the 1950s as British society entered a period of greater affluence.

The insights of business and economic historians of the industry are invaluable, but to present a fully nuanced account of the diffusion of car ownership it is necessary to employ the methodological and theoretical insights of socio-historical analysis. In doing so, the role that taste and social status play in the world of consumption must be addressed. Furthermore, their role should be analysed in every element of the consumption process, alongside the economic determinants, to allow a more integrated approach that takes account of production, distribution, marketing and uses of the car.

The role of taste and status in the developing market for cars has not been entirely ignored by economic and business historians. The influence of these factors on design and production strategies in the 1930s has been well documented.[44] In particular, the shift by the major motor manufacturers from a policy of price competition in the 1920s towards one of model/price competition and product differentiation in the 1930s has been widely reported. Two factors dictated this policy. First, throughout the inter-war years, fears of market saturation were continually being expressed. The SMMT felt that, given the skewed distribution of income in the British economy, ownership would be confined to the comfortably off professional and commercial classes. Their impression of market potential was enhanced during the economic downturn of the early 1930s, when the number of motorists buying replacements for existing cars overtook first-time buyers for the first time. In 1931, for example, replacement sales totalled 114,000 whereas sales to first-time buyers fell away to only 27,000.[45] In such a market regular design alterations offered the hope of inducing motorists to replace their existing car for the latest model. Second, manufacturers were responding to growing signs amongst consumers of an increased desire to express status and individuality through choice of motor car. This trend was demonstrated both by the poor sales of economy cars, such as the 1931 Morris Minor SV, and the increased employment, by individual buyers, of coach-builders who created special bodies for less expensive cars. In effect, what was happening was what David Gartman, writing about the American market of the 1920s, has described as the growing importance of car aesthetics as a corollary to the dilution of 'the social distinction of mere ownership', as ownership levels rose.[46]

The Morris Minor SV was introduced in 1931 at a cost price of £100. It was a spartan car, pared down to the absolute minimum with only a three-speed gearbox and a single windscreen wiper. It did not sell well at all, as Miles Thomas, sales manager at Morris Motors at the time, recalled in his autobiography. He claimed that orders in fact poured in for the more expensive and better equipped Morris Minor: 'It was an interesting exercise in consumer preference that although attention was undoubtedly attracted to the Morris Minor by the fact that one *could* be purchased for as little as £100, the actual buyers wanted something that showed that they had *not* bought the cheapest product. And so everybody was happy. No one wants to keep down with the Joneses!'[47]

By the late 1920s companies such as Thrupp and Maberley and designers like William Lyons were busily catering to desires for individuality in the motoring community, providing special bodies to glamorise cheap models such as the Austin Seven and Wolseley Hornet. By 1932, Wolseley were producing a Hornet chassis with no body to allow customers to have their own special bodies built to their own taste without the need to pay for two sets of bonnets, wings and running boards.[48] Morris and Austin went further, commissioning motor-body builders Gordon England, Mulliner and others to design production models for them.[49] Manufacturers became aware that the horsepower rating of various cars, which corresponded to the amount of annual road tax payable by the owner, took on great significance for many motorists. In consequence, the large manufacturers built a model in each category so as not to miss out on any particular market niche. A statement from Vauxhall motors explained their policy: 'This tax business has become an obsession in the mind of the motorist. An "eight", he realises, costs less in tax and insurance than a "ten" or a "twelve" and so on: and other factors have largely to be ignored. There is a class-consciousness in horsepowers, and the manufacturer has to build a model for every class, and to suit every purse.'[50] So, as Political and Economic Planning (PEP) observed, manufacturers produced a cheap, small model of seven or eight horsepower, hoping it would capture a large market whilst also offering a number of other models, designed to appeal to the better-off. Such a policy avoided the risk inherent in single-model production whilst enabling manufacturers 'to cultivate technical, aesthetic or snobbish appeal'.[51]

Certain marques also came to be identified with different social groups – as Graham Robson has noted: 'It would never have done, for instance, for a respectable bank manager to be seen in a sports car and certainly he would never have considered any type of imported car.'[52] 'Appropriate' cars for the gentry were Armstrong-Siddeleys, Bentleys, Lanchesters and Rolls-Royces, but they studiously avoided Humbers, which were seen as the cars of the staid middle-aged middle classes. As a conventional car, the Humber proved a safer choice than the SS.1, and its immediate successors, which had an unfortunate reputation that was very widespread. A string of negative appellations were applied to this car by oral interviewees and in motoring literature. The SS.1 was often referred to as 'a cad's car', or 'a promenade Percy's car'. It also had a reputation as a flashy car favoured by 'spivs' and 'shady traders'.[53] The SS.1 had its chassis designed by body-builders, who gave it an attractive and expensive appearance. *Autocar* described it as a £310 model that looked like a £1,000 car.[54] This discrepancy between looks and cost may explain some of the animosity towards the car. As has been cogently argued by Pierre Bourdieu, taste functions as a marker of class: 'taste classifies and it classifies the classifier.'[55] Thus, the hierarchical consumption of goods provides an insight into social relations: in the case of the SS.1 car its comparatively low cost allowed new social groups to enter the sports-car niche. Hence its buyers came to be viewed as intruders in a sphere of motoring they had previously been unable to join, with the result that they were classified – by the 'Bentley Boys' and others amongst motoring's cognoscenti – as a motoring *nouveau riche* whose sense of good taste had not caught up with their purchasing power. If the car were judged on looks alone today's visitor to transport museums might well decide that the SS.1 was more attractive than the Bentley.

Thus annual model changes, increased accent on styling, and accessories on even the cheapest cars, together with production of models in all price and horsepower categories, kept unit costs high, inevitably hindering the industry's ability to reduce retail prices.[56] By 1938, the six largest producing groups were turning out forty different types of engine, and in the case of twenty-six of these engines fewer than a thousand units were being manufactured annually.[57] So, in effect the nature of the market, with strong demand for cars that demonstrated status and discrimination, contributed to the creation of a self-fulfilling prophecy. Manufacturers' beliefs that the market for cars would remain stubbornly within the higher income brackets were reinforced by the production costs inherent in meeting the desires of their existing market. This much has been recognised before, but this mixture of the cautious approach to market development by the manufacturers and status concerns amongst middle-class consumers also affected another important aspect of the diffusion of car ownership – the instalment selling of vehicles.

A survey of the motoring magazines of the pre-1939 era leaves a puzzling impression about attitudes towards hire-purchase. In the absence of any significant provision of bank loans for those purchasing a car, hire-purchase was the major form of credit available to prospective car buyers and its role in extending car ownership in inter-war Britain has been acknowledged.[58] However, a sampling of car manufacturers' advertisements placed in *Autocar* and *Motor* between 1919 and 1938 indicate that hire-purchase facilities were mentioned in only 4 per cent of advertisements.[59] Even then, references to instalment-payment plans were often to be found only in the small print. This would suggest that manufacturers found hire-purchase a somewhat delicate subject to broach with their middle-class public. This impression is reinforced by a statement made in *Motor Trader* during 1936 by the chairman of the Motor Finance Corporation, a leading hire-purchase provider: 'So far as I am aware, no manufacturer and no dealer has, as yet, attempted to use hire-purchase facilities as an advertising stunt to sell his vehicles to the public.'[60] That public shared the same reticent outlook. In fact a 1931 book on direct marketing which offered advice on 'delicate' subjects listed the discussion of 'deferred terms' alongside such matters as 'intimate personal hygiene'.[61] So, notwithstanding the increasing numbers of car buyers who made use of what were dubbed 'out of income systems', it was done with great discretion, as was recalled by Graham Robson: 'Although there was a good deal of hire purchase activity, even at the beginning of the 1930's, it was always a rather hole-in-the corner and furtive way of raising the money. Somehow (and such were the fiscal standards of the day) hire-purchase was always considered to be a "not quite nice" way of financing one's purchase and it was never talked about.'[62]

Discussion of hire-purchase was also something of a rarity in motoring magazines. The leading motoring journal, *Autocar*, regularly featured items on such subjects as buying new or second-hand cars and motor insurance. However, in the inter-war years, they produced only one small article directly referring to hire-purchase. Even this brief piece, written in 1937, was tucked away inside the back cover, and described hire-purchase as a 'little known side of the automobile industry'.[63] *Autocar* itself had certainly done little to make it better known. This circumspection would seem to have been derived from attitudes towards hire-purchase demonstrated by middle-class motorists, many of whom were reported to be prepared to go to great lengths to conceal their use of instalment payments. In 1924 *Garage and Motor Agent* reported that motorists using instalment plans were 'shy of putting their orders in the hands of local agents'. London car showrooms were popular for this reason, offering 'the privacy the provincial purchasers feel is their's when far from their homes'. The article concluded by conjecturing that the 'shame' attached to the use of deferred payments would pass in time. In the meantime, dealers were advised to cultivate the 'utmost security and secrecy', in order to secure this type of business. At the same time, details of hire-purchase schemes should be placed in the footnotes of trader's advertising, so as not to risk the loss of cash customers.[64] The inference was clearly that such clients liked it to be very apparent that they were indeed cash buyers.

If the 'shame' of buying via hire-purchase was dying down, as *Garage and Motor Agent* suggested it would, it was still strong enough in 1935 for that journal to describe the continuing 'old-fashioned but powerful prejudice against hire-purchase on the part of the very class of people who are most justified in employing it'. Again the popularity of London motor marts was mentioned, as was that of provincial centres, which could also offer the 'hire-purchaser the impersonality and privacy that belong to crowds'.[65] Dealers were advised to use advertising to stress that deferred payment schemes were carried out in the strictest confidence. The Society of Motor Manufacturers and Traders also noticed the phenomenon of the attraction of London for hire-purchase buyers. They reported that in 1938, 34 per cent of new cars sold within the London region were purchased by customers whose homes were outside the area.[66] It is possible that London was popular amongst car buyers because it offered a wider choice of models. But, if that was so, trade insiders did not make reference to it, focusing instead on the anonymity offered to hire-purchase buyers by the capital's car showrooms. The experiences of our sample of pre-1939 motorists is also interesting in this respect. They provide further evidence indicating the ambivalent relationship between car buyers and hire-purchase. Several members of the sample, from a variety of backgrounds and regions, recalled that buying on the 'never-never' was just not done. Welshman Roger Gibbs emphatically asserted that his farming father had not made use of hire-purchase when buying cars in the 1930s: 'I can safely say that my father would not buy anything – much less a luxury such as a car – without first having the money to pay for it, and this was true of the great majority of people in those days. The pleasure of possessing a car was the thought that they really owned it. If you had reached the status of being a car owner it was taken as an indication that your business was successful, and how successful, by the grade of car. This theory was absolutely foolproof.'[67]

William McAvoy, a London-born senior civil servant, told me: 'every car I paid cash. I was brought up by a very strict Scots father who taught me the only thing you bought on tick was a house.'[68] Mary Breck, whose father was a manager in a Liverpool hardware store, recalled that he always bought his cars with cash: 'he saved up until he could pay cash. He wasn't keen on hire purchase and that kind of thing.'[69] Slightly more than a quarter of respondents offered information on the financing of car buying, but only three recalled the use of hire-purchase. In contrast sixteen respondents remembered cars being bought by cash payments. Obviously this evidence is at odds with what is known about the widespread use of hire-purchase. Perhaps the sample drawn upon here is simply unrepresentative? It might also be possible, particularly in the case of female respondents, that they were actually uninvolved in the financial side of the purchase and remained unaware of how the deal was transacted. However, by scrutinising attitudes held by motor traders, manufacturers and the financial establishment towards hire-purchase, it might prove possible to solve the discrepancy between our sample and the estimated figures for the role of hire-purchase in the diffusion of car ownership in the 1920s and 1930s.

Motor dealers greatly preferred cash-paying customers for several reasons. First, cash in the bank was preferable to waiting for out-standing payments. There was also much confusion, particularly in the 1920s, about the legal situation with regard to hire-purchase. Many dealers feared fraud by unscrupulous buyers, who might be tempted to resell a car just acquired under the hire-purchase system. When this did occur, it was very often the trader who was left with the financial consequences. The United Dominions Trust (UDT), the largest finance house involved in motor-related hire-purchasing, ensured that all agree-ments were drawn up between the customer and the trader.[70] These business concerns created a degree of insecurity around instalment payments and contributed to an atmosphere of ambivalence towards hire-purchase which paralleled that demonstrated by car buyers. Doubts also emanated from the same concerns that determined the behaviour of middle-class consumers. Most obviously, as has already been inti-mated, fears of offending the economic and social sensibilities of potential customers led dealers to soft-pedal on the issue of hire-purchase. So, although dealers appreciated that the future of their business involved embracing hire-purchase, that embrace was at times a little tentative.

Motor dealers were particularly suspicious of schemes suggested as a means of expanding the market beyond those with high incomes. On occasions when such initiatives were submitted they were met with criticisms which carried more than a hint of class prejudice. In 1924 Ford's 'Weekly Purchase Plan' was greeted with hostility by 'Ford Dealer', in an article in *Motor Trader*. For a minimum weekly payment of £1 over two and a quarter years, the plan enabled customers to take delivery of a Ford car once all instalments had been settled. 'Ford Dealer' believed it was 'really very difficult to examine the scheme seriously as it appears to be so obviously unsound and impossible'. However, it was admitted that dealers had earlier considered hire-purchase itself to be unworkable. The language of the article then becomes very revealing:

> To turn down the scheme because it is *undignified* is also unwise be-cause we do many things in everyday life that our grandfathers would not have touched for this reason … The understanding of the scheme – that it enables a man of small means (say from £250–600 per annum) to purchase a car – might have a grain of substance in it if it were not for the fact that *any man who is so financially weak in this way has no business to buy a car at all* … a man who cannot pay … this small sum [the £25 deposit on a Ford hire-purchase deal] must be in a very bad way and *an undesirable customer*.[71]

The language used here is very interesting because it illustrates a dis-trust, not only of the Ford scheme, but also of those who might have used it. The whole concept was viewed as the type of new American business method with which past generations of British businessmen would not have sullied their ledgers. Such schemes did carry an increased element of risk for traders, but arguments opposing the extension of hire-purchase frequently articulated fears about greater risk in terms of the potential dishonesty of customers attracted by innovations in in-stalment buying. An argument grounded entirely on economic rationale might have been expected to raise instead the subject of high running costs and the ability of less wealthy motorists to meet them. This would have been particularly relevant in the case of the Model T, which attracted the very high horsepower tax rating of £23 per annum.

Ironically, in the United States of America, the Ford Weekly Plan had been established because Henry Ford disapproved of the concept of hire-purchase. By June 1924, 80,000 Americans had received delivery of their car by this means, and a further 170,000 were in the process of paying for one.[72]

In 1929 *Garage and Motor Agent* argued against the extension of hire-purchase payment plans. It urged that eighteen months be the maximum time allowed for the completion of payment. Such a scheme would attract 'those who *can* afford to run a car, although they have little capital', whilst repulsing 'the undesirable element which has little hope and less intention of ratifying the agreements into which it enters'.[73] In a well-known comment on British car buyers of this era, cited earlier, Miles Thomas suggested that their motto was: 'No one wants to keep down with the Joneses!' It would seem that many dealers were reluctant to do business with the Joneses in the first place. In effect they were engaged in what could be described as conspicuous retailing. A solidly upper-middle-class market provided motor dealers with a lucrative trade in accessories, repairs and fuel. For this reason dealers were content with the policy of price/model competition which developed in the 1930s. In fact, in 1934 *Motor Trader* advocated formal price fixing, arguing that the vast majority of dealers were 'not anxious to see any reductions in prices, especially in the case of small and inexpensive cars'. Moreover, they would have welcomed 'an informal agreement' amongst the leading manufacturers that raised prices by '5 or 10 per cent'.[74]

As Martha L. Olney has revealed, manufacturers initially viewed hire-purchase as a means of ensuring a smoother cash flow.[75] This was particularly the case in Britain, where throughout the inter-war period large numbers of cars were bought in late spring, or following the Motor Show in October and November. Dealers were also forced into dealing with finance companies in order to pay in advance for the stock they were to receive from the manufacturers. Hire purchase was not, therefore, simply introduced as an aid to extending the market, but also as a means of regulating cash flow. There is no doubt that the extension of hire-purchase facilities was extremely important in the growth of the motor vehicle market, but the ambivalent attitude of consumers towards its use does seem to have reinforced both dealers' resistance to projected extensions of the instalment principle and manufacturers' reluctance to trumpet hire-purchase in advertising campaigns. One 1934 article in *Motor Trader* made this point explicitly, citing trader reluctance for the absence of a campaign to push this form of sale.[76] It remains questionable whether or not a campaign to publicise and de-stigmatise hire-purchase might have increased sales of new cars in the 1920s and 1930s, or whether the social sensibilities of middle-class consumers were simply too resistant for such a policy to have worked. Many buyers were clearly prepared, out of necessity, to make use of hire-purchase when purchasing a family car, but they were extremely reluctant to acknowledge it. If a manufacturer had broken ranks and trumpeted their hire-purchase facilities it is conceivable that they would actually have lost as many customers as they gained through this approach.

The role of the UDT must also be considered when analysing the history of hire-purchase and the motor car. By 1929 the UDT ran hire-purchase schemes for Austin, Chrysler, Crossley, Darracq, Dodge Bros., Essex, Fiat, Hudson, Lea Francis, Morris, Renault, Rhose, Singer, Sunbeam, Talbot and Wolseley.[77] The managing director of the UDT, J. Gibson Jarvie, was a familiar figure to readers of the motor-trade press where he campaigned on behalf of his company and hire-purchase. Innovative as the company was, they were careful to appeal to traditional banking virtues, as the bulk of their financial backing emanated from City institutions. When they received further backing from the Bank of England, in January 1930, they felt that they had achieved full respectability within the City. Montagu Norman, the governor of the Bank of England, had been under pressure from the Labour government to set a lead for the financial sector in the reorganisation of British industry. He chose to back the UDT because of its combination of innovation and traditional virtues and, importantly, because it insisted that it did not finance luxuries.

This last point sat uneasily with the fact that cars were very much seen as leisure items in this period. For example, Winston Churchill's raid on the Road Fund in his 1926 budget was justified as the taxation of a luxury hobby in a time of national need.[78] The UDT underscored the utilitarian and respectable nature of its motor-car business by a variety of measures. As early as 1927 Jarvie had urged traders to dismiss notions of no-deposit hire-purchase, arguing that if people couldn't raise the necessary 25 per cent they couldn't 'by any stretch of the imagination be considered desirable hire purchasers'.[79] Furthermore, the UDT, and other finance houses, imposed a system of qualitative and quantitative credit rationing. The preferred hire-purchaser was a householder who owned a business and was married with children. Such types were seen as having the greatest incentive to complete payments. It is known that this qualitative and quantitative credit rationing served to discourage sales to some groups who, though professionals, were in receipt of irregular incomes.[80] It would be interesting to learn how many other potential buyers were turned down through any of the more subjective elements of this rationing. For instance, potential women buyers do not seem to have featured in Jarvie's vision of model hire-purchasers. Moreover, how many potential male hire-purchasers, who perhaps did not look the part as they entered the car showroom, were dealt with summarily by dealers who misjudged their potential respectability in hire-purchasing terms? And how many others, either through suspicion or embarrassment about hire-purchase, decided not to contemplate ownership until cash reserves were sufficient? Of course these questions are unanswerable, but it is interesting to note that the econometric analysis of the market suggests a lower incidence of car ownership amongst the lower middle classes than might have been anticipated.[81] Furthermore by 1938, despite the continual fears of market saturation, there were still 500,000 salaried employees identified by the SMMT as potential car owners who remained non-owners.[82]

These deliberations return this discussion to the apparent discrepancy between use of hire-purchase facilities by our sample of pre-1939 motorists and the estimates of its actual usage. In the context of the preceding discussion, their limited experience of hire-purchase appears less surprising. It seems necessary to make two comments about those estimates. First, it is possible that they have overstated the contribution played by hire-purchase in the extension of car ownership in the interwar period. Suggestions by James Foreman-Peck et al. that hire-purchase was involved in 65 to 70 per cent of new car sales by the late 1930s appear difficult to square with the fact that by the early 1960s the proportion of new cars sold via hire-purchase was estimated to be as low as 21 per cent.[83] However, given the stress laid on the utilitarian uses of cars purchased through hire-purchase, the same authors are surely correct to maintain that a high proportion of cars bought via hire-purchase were used for 'trade purposes'.[84] PEP estimated that as many as 40 per cent of sales by 1939 were to business users.[85]

The evidence presented here indicates that hire-purchase was a less straightforward option for the leisure motorist. Many of those who made use of hire-purchase clearly felt some unease about doing so. Manufacturers and dealers responded to this with an element of discretion, which may have exacerbated the problem. By not attempting, through greater publicity, to legitimise credit use amongst their middle-class clientele, manufacturers and dealers may have inadvertently placed a check on the growth of car ownership.

Economic and business historians have supplied extremely valuable perspectives on the diffusion of the motor car in inter-war Britain. This discussion has attempted to fuse these perspectives with a more social-historical analysis in order to initiate a new interdisciplinarity to the question at hand. In the process, it has become clear that cultural norms, class perceptions and taste were all factors in the spread of such a significant consumer good as the car. Just as a mixture of middle-class culture and taste fashioned the way a car looked, it also defined the ways in which it could be sold. In the process, areas where growth in ownership could have occurred were limited. Valuable as the econometric analysis of the market for cars before 1939 has been, at its heart is the notion of the rational economic actor. As has been repeatedly argued, such a concept is ultimately an untenable abstraction from social life.[86] The example of the car indicates that it is clearly impossible to aggregate millions of individuals buying and using goods without reckoning on the social and cultural aspects of their consumption. In the case of hire-purchase and the car, many consumers' decisions were based on more than rational economic calculations.

The second-hand car market

Business and economic histories of the motor industry have focused on the new car market. However, the evidence provided by the sample of seventy-five pre-1939 motorists has indicated the importance of the second-hand car market. A significant proportion of respondents came from backgrounds that did not meet the accepted criteria of the pre-1939 car-owning family. Their story deserves to be told, in order that the full complexity of car ownership by the 1930s be acknowledged.

The evidence presented below also indicates that Steve Koerner's analysis of the motor-cycle industry in the 1930s accurately suggested that a growing used-car market 'seriously undercut the economy appeal of the motor cycle' and hit that industry's registration figures.[87] Data provided by our sample suggests that by the 1930s consumers, from both the lower middle and skilled working classes, were exploiting the growing availability of cheap second-hand cars to become owners through a variety of financial routes. For some their car ownership was transitory, but it was no less significant for that. Equally significantly, their behaviour has parallels with that identified by research conducted into post-1945 consumerism.

Many working-class consumers, in particular, were willing to share the purchase or running costs of a car within the extended family, or amongst friends – they thereby brought traditional working-class cultural and spending patterns to the sphere of motoring. For example, the Critchley brothers, both employed in the Coventry motor industry, shared the cost of a second-hand Standard Big Nine, bought for £47 from a workmate in 1936.[88] Another Coventry car-worker, Chris Newlove, owned a variety of cars towards the end of the 1930s including the rather flashy SS.1.[89] As in the case of the Critchley brothers, Chris Newlove shared some of the costs of ownership with his brother. At another point he shared a car with a friend; the partnership only breaking up when Chris's friend barred women from the car. Chris had wanted to offer a young woman a lift home from a dance, so he asked his friend to oblige by sitting in the dickey seat – an exposed and uncomfortable pull-out seat at the rear of the vehicle:

> We were at the Dun Cow pub and I met this girl and I was gonna take her home to Coventry – and asked him if he would get in the back and he said 'Not bloomin likely!' So, I just went and told the girl I weren't taking her home. So that was what started him off. All the way home we argued, not enough to fight one another, but that was when it started. We had an understanding then: I said 'Now, Tom we'll flog the car.'

In other cases, friends or associates offered financial help in meeting the prohibitive running costs of a car in return for its use on occasional weekends or family holidays. John Nickle recalled his London childhood, in the 1920s, during which his lorry-driver father often borrowed an open-tourer Austin Seven for family outings: 'I gleaned in later years that in order to borrow the car my father helped his friend, who owned the car, with the cost of the insurance and road-fund tax and always returned the car with a full tank of petrol.'[90] In all, six respondents provided examples where car ownership had been facilitated by some form of car sharing between friends or brothers.

Another possible path to car ownership involved husband and wife both being employed in relatively well-paid jobs, or one or the other securing employment in a second job. The sample includes at least five examples in which a wife's wage contributed to the finances of a car-owning family. In a further five cases income provided by a working daughter or son provided a family with the extra capital that made car ownership attainable. In another three cases fathers were engaged in some form of second occupation. Gaylord Goulding recalled his father working simultaneously as a cinema projectionist and insurance agent, thereby financing the purchase of a second-hand Clyno in the 1930s. His mother was ambitious to own the car, but less pleased when it frequently required maintenance on the street outside the house, a task in which a mechanically minded friend aided Mr Goulding senior.[91] In several of these cases there was an overlap between fathers working in second jobs and some of the other factors identified here, suggesting that several of these families sought ways of financing a lifestyle they might not otherwise have been able to realise. Thus, Harold Radlinski, a bus driver, whose purchase in the mid-1930s of a Humber was in part financed by the wages of his wife, exploited his new-found mobility to further supplement his income by trading in spare car-parts.[92] Mark Shaw was a local government officer earning only £200 a year but he still managed to buy a family car. The purchase was facilitated by the cash he earned playing in a dance band at weekends and through having a working son living at home.[93]

A further striking trend amongst the sample was the number of occasions in which respondents mentioned some form of connection with the motor industry. In at least sixteen cases car owners worked in a job connected with motoring and transport or had friends or relations who did so and were therefore in a position to help with costs, advise on purchasing, or otherwise facilitate the chances of car ownership. Extrapolating from this, it would seem highly likely that the incidence of lower-middle- or working-class car ownership was appreciably higher amongst those with such affiliations. This is surely no coincidence, as their proximity to motor vehicles enabled them to amass the knowledge that made a foray into the largely middle-class pastime of motoring a possibility. For them the automobile, of one sort or another, bore no great mystique and the fact that others around them began to take up motoring placed it on their agenda of possible leisure activities. Most importantly, a knowledge of the technology, a familiarity with establishments where cheap cars could be bought, and an ability to maintain the car may well have made the difference between buying a cheap second-hand car or not. Chris Newlove described the process by which he chose a car in the 1930s:

> Well, most of the time I would look … at the car sales in the paper … or we also used to go to the car sales occasionally. There was one at the Motor Mart years ago … once a week, you'd go there and have a look, see if there's any bargains going. But the scrap merchants used to sell second-hand cars … I bought a big Austin Cambridge once from a scrap yard. I don't think you'd give above £10 for it, and I took all my relations down to Bournemouth for a week's holiday and went back the next week and brought them home in it, so it wasn't a bad old car that one. I kept it for perhaps a few months and then I would change it again for something else.[94]

Employed as a clerical worker in the motor trade, Tony Craven was equally at ease buying or selling cheap second-hand cars:

> Before the war I was living in the Worthing area … There was a marvellous breaker's yard, run by a man called Percy Vokes – he was quite well known and you could get almost anything from him. And I remember, in the 1930s, I had bought an Austin Seven Swallow, quite cheaply, and I hadn't had the opportunity to collect it and when I was visiting Percy Vokes' breakers yard I saw something like the end of a cigar sticking out and I said 'What's that Percy?' 'Oh' he said, 'its a French car, an Amilcar. It's a French sports car. Driving wheels are stripped. Apart from that it's alright.' So, I said 'How about swapping it for an Austin Seven Swallow?' 'Oh, don't mind', he said 'yes' … Yes, it was really what was available against what took your fancy.[95]

An occupational analysis of the sample corresponds with the econometric indicators, which suggest that the professional and commercial middle-classes were prominent amongst car owners by the 1930s. Approximately four in every seven respondents came from these groups. However, one in seven motorists discovered by the sample were employed in lower-middle-class or white-collar occupations. Most arresting was the revelation that one in eight of our pre-1939 motorists were from working-class backgrounds. If this sample is anywhere near representative, it suggests that by the end of the 1930s car ownership was a possibility for many amongst the working class who were in well-paid jobs or were in a position where some form of car-sharing was possible, and preferably both. It is also important to note that these working-class owners bought cheap second-hand cars and may have drifted in and out of ownership according to their ability to finance running costs. Car-sharing between working-class brothers or friends may have come to end, for instance, if one of the partners in the endeavour got married or began saving for their wedding. Many amongst the lower-middle-class owners might also have experienced this pattern of intermittent ownership.

The 1939–1945 war and subsequent austerity brought the motoring of these members of our sample to a halt, but post-war studies of working-class consumerism suggest that motorists in our sample were foreshadowing aspects of the behaviour of the next generation. Writing about working-class car-ownership in the 1960s, Ferdinand Zweig made three points which tally with the findings reported here. First, he found that ownership levels were greatest amongst the Vauxhall workers he studied, as opposed to workers in other industries. Second, he identified single men or married men with no children as more likely to have a car. Finally, he found car-sharing was a significant practice, with as many as four workers having part-ownership of a car.[96]

Contemporary observers were not totally unaware of car ownership amongst the working classes. Reporting on a London Transport Strike in 1937, *The Hampstead Gazette* visited pickets at the Edgware bus depot and found that they had set up a system for taking people to hospitals or other urgent business: 'quite a few of the busmen have their own cars and these are used to convey the working-class members of the public to their destinations.'[97] Whilst in 1939 Herbert Parker, the Member of Parliament for Romford claimed that amongst Ford employees at their Dagenham factory there were '1,500 to 2,000 who possess motor cars of their own'.[98] In 1935, when the journalist Ivor Brown made a tour of England, he noted that

A journey along the main road from the East Coast to London on a Sunday evening in summer is a tedious business, owing to the density of traffic, but instructive. Myriads of East Enders, packed seven or eight in an antiquated car which has been bought for a few pounds and seems almost to be held together by string and straps, are jogging home from a day at Clacton or Southend … the cars are … heavily charged with conglomerate uncles and aunts, children bunched like bananas … Thirty years ago these people never left the town, except perhaps for one week in the year. Saturday night was spent in the gin-palace and Sunday morning was spent in sleeping it off. [But such is] the new democratic week-end, even if it be mainly devoted to covering decent sand with orange peel and cigarette cartons.[99]

Conclusion

Brown's patronising tone offers one more reminder of the importance of class and social status in the diffusion of car ownership. An appraisal of their role suggests that a number of important provisos should be attached to the existing consensus about the diffusion of car ownership before 1939. Cultural norms, class perceptions and taste were all factors in the spread of such a significant consumer item. Middle-class culture and taste fashioned the way a car looked, and to some extent they also defined the ways in which it could be sold. Concerns about hire-purchase, emanating from cultural and economic sources, produced an uneasiness about this form of financing a move into car ownership. However, it is impossible to say how many potential middle-class car buyers allowed the stigma surrounding hire-purchase to delay or prevent their entry into motoring, although Bowden and Turner's surprise at what they believe were low levels of ownership amongst the lower-middle classes might be partly explained by the evidence and arguments submitted here. It should also be recalled that the quantitative and qualitative credit rationing employed by finance houses such as the UDT did restrict sales. It would be interesting to learn what proportion of applicants for hire-purchase were turned down through one of the more subjective elements of this rationing. Jarvie's stipulations about solid, respectable hire-purchasers were intended to establish his company's form of instalment paying as 'quite distinct from the working-class "tick" system of accounts',[100] but they also ensured that even some professional groups, who were not recipients of a regular income, were deemed a credit risk. The proponents of econometric analysis are, of course, correct to stress the essentially middle-class nature of the market, but the question they pose and the model constructed to answer it, drawn from consumer demand theory, is essentially tautological. Of course, a consumer has to have enough money in order to buy something at the prevailing price and, as in this instance, to meet the running costs. But what if, as in cases cited here, consumers were prepared to share the costs of such a prized commodity? Alternatively, what if technological knowledge or connections with the motor industry provided them with valuable information on where cheap models could be picked up, or enabled them to cut costs by doing their own repairs? The findings outlined here suggest that the diffusion of cars cannot simply be represented in a pyramid-shape, where upper-class ownership is followed by a trickle-down effect through the middle classes until working-class ownership becomes a possibility in the final mass-market stage. Of course, this image reflects the general pattern, but it is clear that many in the working classes were car owners earlier than others in middle-class groups who might have been expected to be ahead of them in the waiting list. The same qualification would also apply to those in lower-middle-class occupations, such as Tony Craven, whose connection with the motor industry also enabled him to find bargain-basement cars and to maintain them on a modest salary.

The evidence submitted here indicates the need to construct an explanation of the diffusion of car ownership that goes beyond the 'rational economic actor' model. This chapter has begun this process; the remaining chapters will continue it. In particular it will be necessary to ask why the car became a 'necessity' for the professional and commercial middle classes. Moreover, we must ask where a line should be drawn between the utility and symbolic values of a consumer good such as the car. It will prove equally enlightening to chart the gender ideologies that shaped and were in turn influenced by the onset of large-scale car ownership. Finally, the relationship between the car and discourses of national identity will be explored. The latter proved central in framing the debates about the car's impact on the countryside and in the controversy over road safety. In all of these areas the values of the comfortably off middle-class motorists, who formed the overwhelming majority of car owners, were very much to the fore.

Notes

1 W. Plowden, *The Motor Car and Politics in Britain* (Harmondsworth, Pelican Books, 1973), pp. 8–9.
2 R. Church, *The Rise and Decline of the British Motor Industry*, Studies in Economic and Social History (London, Macmillan, 1994), p. 1.
3 S. B. Saul, 'The motor industry in Britain to 1914', *Business History* 5 (1962) 22.
4 H. Perkin, *The Age of the Automobile* (London, Quartet Books, 1976), p. 40.
5 J. Foreman-Peck, S. Bowden and A. McKinlay, *The British Motor Industry* (Manchester, Manchester University Press, 1995), p. 13; B. R. Mitchell, *Abstract of British Historical Statistics* (Cambridge, Cambridge University Press, 1962), p. 230.
6 R. Church, 'Markets and marketing in the British motor industry before 1914', *Journal of Transport History*, 3 (1982) 5.
7 Foreman-Peck et al., *The British Motor Industry*, p. 29.
8 Church, 'Markets and marketing', p. 6.
9 Foreman-Peck et al., *The British Motor Industry*, p. 28.
10 Saul, 'The motor industry in Britain to 1914', Table 2; Mitchell, *British Historical Statistics*, p. 230.
11 Saul, 'The motor industry in Britain to 1914', 24; Church, *The Rise and Decline of the British Motor Industry*, p. 1.
12 Cited in Saul, 'The motor industry in Britain to 1914', 39.
13 *Ibid.*, 40.
14 *The Times*, 20 August 1912; cited in Saul, 'The motor industry in Britain to 1914', 43.
15 *The Economist*, 22 November 1913.
16 *Autocar*, 21 September 1912.
17 This term is borrowed from D. F. Davis, *Conspicuous Production: Automobiles and Elites in Detroit, 1899–1933* (Temple University Press, Philadelphia, 1988).
18 R. Church, *Herbert Austin: The British Motor Car Industry to 1941* (London, Europa, 1979), pp. 187–8.
19 K. C. Johnson-Davies, *The Practice of Retail Price Maintenance: With Particular Reference to the Motor Industry* (London, Iliffe and Son, 1955), pp. 1–4. See also J. Levy, *Retail Trade Associations: A New Form of Monopolist Organisation in Britain* (London, Kegan Paul, Trench, Trubner and Co. Ltd, 1942).
20 *Motor Trader*, 4 January 1911.
21 Church, 'Markets and marketing'.
22 Church, *The Rise and Decline of the British Motor Industry*, p. 5.
23 *Ibid.*
24 G. Bishop, *The Age of the Automobile* (London, Hamlyn, 1977), p. 146.

25   A. B. Demaus, and J. C. Tarring *The Humber Story 1868–1932* (Glouces-
     ter, Alan Sutton Publishing Limited, 1989), p. 52. Foreman-Peck et al.,
     The British Motor Industry, p. 20.
26   M. Worthington-Williams, *Automobilia* (London, Batsford, n.d.) p. 47.
27   M. Worthington-Williams, *From Cyclecar to Microcar* (London, Beaulieu
     Books, 1981).
28   S. Koerner, 'The British motor-cycle industry during the 1930s', *Journal
     of Transport History*, 16 (1995) 55–76.
29   *Ibid.*, Tables 2 and 3.
30   *Ibid.*, 63.
31   *Ibid.*, 62.
32   Foreman-Peck et al., *The British Motor Industry*, p. 14.
33   Church, *The Rise and Decline of the British Motor Industry*, p. 6.
34   Church, 'Markets and marketing', 6.
35   Mitchell, *British Historical Statistics*, p. 230.
36   Society of Motor Manufacturers and Traders, *The Motor Industry of
     Great Britain* (London, SMMT, Annual).
37   Foreman-Peck et al., *The British Motor Industry*, pp. 71–2.
38   Committee on Consumer Credit, *Consumer Credit: Report of the Commit-
     tee* (London, HMSO 1970), Cmnd. 4596, p. 450.
39   W. Lewchuk, 'The motor vehicle industry', in B. Elbaum and W.
     Lazonick (eds), *The Decline of the British Economy* (Oxford, Clarendon
     Press, 1986), p. 147.
40   W. Lewchuk, *American Technology and the British Vehicle Industry* (Cam-
     bridge, Cambridge University Press, 1987).
41   S. Tolliday, 'The failure of mass production unionism in the motor
     industry, 1914–39', in C. Wrigley (ed.), *A History of British Industrial
     Relations, Volume II* (Brighton, Harvester, 1987).
42   S. Bowden, 'Demand and supply constraints in the inter-war UK car
     industry: did the manufacturers get it right?', *Business History*, 33 (1991)
     241–67; S. Bowden and P. Turner, 'Some cross-section evidence on
     the determinants of the diffusion of car ownership in the inter-war
     UK economy', *Business History*, 35 (1993) 55–69; S. Bowden and P.
     Turner, 'Demand for consumer durables in the interwar period', *Journal
     of Economic History*, 53 (1993) 244–57.
43   Bowden, 'Demand and supply constraints', 258–9.
44   See, for example, R. Church and M. Miller, 'The big three: competition,
     management and marketing in the British motor industry 1922–1939',
     in B. Supple (ed.), *Essays in British Business History* (Oxford, Clarendon
     Press, 1977).
45   Society of Motor Manufacturers and Traders, *Motor Industry of Great
     Britain 1932* (London, SMMT).
46   D. Gartman, *Auto Opium: A Social History of American Automobile Design*,
     (London, Routledge, 1994), p. 62.

47 M. Thomas, *Out on a Wing* (London, Michael Joseph, 1964), p. 168.
48 *Autocar*, 22 April 1932.
49 T. R. Nicholson, *The Vintage Car 1919–1930* (London, Batsford, 1966), p. 254.
50 Cited in Political and Economic Planning, *Motor Vehicles* (London, PEP 1950), p. 65.
51 *Ibid.*
52 G. Robson, *Motoring in the Thirties* (Cambridge, Stephens, 1979), p. 35.
53 See, for example, R. Sutton, *Motor Mania: Stories from a Motoring Century* (London, Collins & Brown Limited, 1996), pp. 11–12.
54 *Autocar*, 9 October 1931.
55 P. Bourdieu, *Distinction: A Social Critique of the Judgement of Taste* (London, Routledge, 1986), pp. 1–2.
56 Bowden, 'Demand and supply constraints', 263.
57 P. Bagwell, *The Transport Revolution from 1770* (London, Batsford, 1974), p. 212.
58 Even by the 1960s the proportion of sales financed by bank loans was negligible. Committee on Consumer Credit, *Report of the Committee*, p. 451.
59 One issue of *Autocar* or *Motor* was sampled for each year between 1919 and 1938. Hire purchase was featured in only 15 of the 417 advertisements surveyed.
60 *Motor Trader*, 26 February 1936.
61 M. Rittenberg, *Direct Mail and Mail-Order (Principles and Practice)* (London, Butterworth and Co. 1931), p. 122.
62 Robson, *Motoring in the Thirties*, p. 35.
63 *Autocar*, 10 September 1937.
64 *Garage and Motor Agent*, 26 January 1924.
65 *Garage and Motor Agent*, 2 March 1935.
66 Society of Motor Manufacturers and Traders, *Motor Industry of Great Britain 1940*, p. 85.
67 Respondent 32, Roger Gibbs: born South Wales (date unknown).
68 Respondent 17, William McAvoy: born London 1901.
69 Respondent 37, Mary Breck: born Liverpool 1916.
70 Bowden and Collins, 'The Bank of England, industrial generation and hire purchase between the wars', *Economic History Review*, XLV (1992) 124.
71 *Motor Trader*, 26 March 1924; emphasis added.
72 M. L. Olney, 'Credit as a production-smoothing device: the case of automobiles, 1913–1938, *Journal of Economic History*, 49 (1989), 389.
73 *Garage and Motor Agent*, 17 August 1929.
74 *Motor Trader*, 11 July 1934.
75 Olney, 'Credit as a production-smoothing device', pp. 383–6.
76 *Motor Trader*, 10 October 1934.

77 Bowden and Collins, 'The Bank of England', 125.

78 Plowden, *The Motor Car and Politics*, ch. 9.

79 *Garage and Motor Agent*, June 1927.

80 Bowden and Turner, 'Demand for consumer durables', 253.

81 Bowden and Turner, 'Some cross-section evidence', 66.

82 In 1938 the SMMT calculated that a salary of £250 p.a. was necessary for the motorist to meet purchase and running costs of a new car. In that year 2.5 million salaries met that criteria and car ownership hovered on the 2 million mark.

83 Committee on Consumer Credit, *Report of the Committee* p. 455.

84 Foreman-Peck et al., *The British Motor Industry*, p. 72.

85 PEP, *Motor Vehicles*, p. 58.

86 See, for example, M. Douglas and B. Isherwood, *World of Goods* (London, Lane, 1980), pp. 4–5.

87 Koerner, 'The British motor-cycle industry', 62.

88 Respondent 14, Reg Critchley: born Nottingham 1907.

89 Respondent 13, Chris Newlove: born Hampshire 1914.

90 Respondent 24, John Nickle: born London.

91 Respondent 20, Gaylord Goulding: born Gravesend 1931.

92 Respondent 2, Harold Radlinski: born 1904.

93 Respondent 6, Keiran Shaw: born Stockport 1912 (son of Mark Shaw).

94 Respondent 13, Chris Newlove: born Hampshire 1914.

95 Respondent 23, Tony Craven: born London 1913.

96 F. Zweig, *The Worker in an Affluent Society* (London, Heinemann, 1961), p. 104.

97 *Hampstead Gazette*, 7 May 1937.

98 *Hansard*, House of Commons Debates, fifth series, 2 May 1939: cols 1816–27.

99 I. Brown, *The Heart of England* (London, British Heritage Series 1935), p. 75.

100 Bowden and Turner, 'Demand for consumer durables', 253.

2

'A myth that is not allowed to die': gender and the car

The opening chapter demonstrated that it was not simply matters of technical efficiency, income and utility that determined the design, marketing, sales and uses of cars. The values and realities of a class-based society had a crucial role in shaping this process. This survey of the emerging car culture continues by examining the ways in which beliefs about gender, consumption and technology influenced motoring and the motor car. The developments described here had an influence on British society long after 1939. In the years between 1896 and 1939 the car arrived as a new technology, available by the end of our period to millions of people. The agency that gender came to have in shaping ideas about car use has ultimately prevented millions of women from taking to the driving seat. On the other side of the equation, an identification of driving skill with masculinity has encouraged many a young male to learn to drive. Even by the mid-1960s only 13 per cent of women held a driving licence, in comparison with 56 per cent of men.[1] By the late 1970s the gap was narrowing steadily but continued to be appreciable. At that point 30 per cent of women held licences, compared with 68 per cent of men.[2] Furthermore, in one-car families women have seldom been granted use of the car for any significant periods.[3]

Previous histories of the motor car have failed to address this issue. Of course, as Joan Scott has argued, historians are susceptible to the gendered notions that are current within the society in which they work;[4] Kenneth Richardson's *The British Motor Industry 1896–1939* being a clear example of this phenomenon. Richardson's study is an illustration of how the car has come to be identified very largely with masculinity. When the narrative does leave the 'masculine' world of the motoring engineers, entrepreneurs and manufacturers to examine some of the uses to which cars were put, it is singularly unrevealing about gender issues and the car. At only two points is there any indication that women had a role in the development of motoring. The first of these is appended to the end of a discussion of motor sport, where the reader is offered, in one paragraph, a list of names which 'deserve to be recorded' of the women who took part in motor races.[5] The second is an uncritical narration of a Birmingham urban legend about a woman motorist who could not do a three-point turn and had passers-by pick her car up and turn it around so that she could return home.[6]

This chapter will begin the analysis of the relationship between gender and the car with an assessment of which members of motoring families drove. It will emerge that, even by the late 1930s, the majority of car-owning families were without a female driving-licence holder. Traditional gendered notions about separate spheres and the control of technology ensured that the car came to be identified with masculinity. This association was not absolute, however, and increasing numbers of women did obtain driving licences in the years following the 1914–18 war. As the number of women drivers rose, many male motorists, car dealers and manufacturers began to express their concern about what they believed was a feminisation of the car. It will be argued here that this belief was too simplistic an explanation of a complex process. The alleged feminisation of the car must be re-examined, with a fuller focus on the role of masculinity and the male consumer in the process. Furthermore, our discussion of gender must itself be set in the context of the issues surrounding class, consumption and social status which have already been discussed. This approach will indicate that masculinity and men were every bit as involved in the aesthetic side of the car as femininity and women.

Gender, technology and the car

At this point it will be useful to relate some of the arguments that have emerged from what has been called the 'new sociology of technology'. A major figure in this movement is Judy Wajcman, who argues that only by acknowledging technology as a social construct can we accurately measure its effects on society, as well as the effects of society on technology.[7] Rather like Joan Scott, and other gender historians, Wajcman maintains that our notions of femininity and masculinity are constantly under contestation and reconstruction. She has attempted to describe the part technology plays in this process, concluding that women are often reluctant to enter into many areas of technology because the language and symbolism of that technology is masculine. Thus, for women control of technology 'is not simply a question of acquiring skills because these skills are embedded in a culture of masculinity that is largely coterminous with the culture of technology. In the school and the workplace this culture is incompatible with femininity. To enter this world, to learn its language, women have first to forsake their femininity.'[8] Thus, the social and cultural construction of much technology as masculine serves to alienate women from it. Once this is understood it becomes possible to see how technology can be analysed as 'a culture that expresses and consolidates relations among men'.[9]

As a new and potentially powerful and liberating technology, the car was extremely susceptible to the type of gendering process described by Wajcman. Its arrival at the time of great controversy over the issue of women's role in society, with the debate over women's suffrage raging, made the woman driver a powerful symbol of potential equality. However, given the dominant gender ideology of the late nineteenth and early twentieth centuries, the driver's seat was seen as a naturally male position. There were also other aspects of this emerging technology that facilitated the car's identification with masculinity. In the first instance, the car's association with the engineering industry implanted the car in a world of masculine language of engineers and entrepreneurs. Second, the pioneering spirit of its early protagonists also lent itself to a sense of masculine endeavour. Writing in 1904, Rudyard Kipling celebrated this masculine enterprise: 'any fool can wait to buy the invention when it is thoroughly perfected, but the men to reverence, to admire, to write odes and erect statues to, are those Prometheuses and Ixions (maniacs, you used to call us) who chase the inchoate idea to fixity up and down the King's Highway with their red right shoulders to the wheel.'[10]

Meanwhile, many physical aspects of early motoring, such as the tricky and exerting task of using a starting handle to start the engine or the ability to fix a puncture at the roadside, were offered as reasons for the car being an essentially male tool. This did not prevent many younger women, in particular, from venturing out at the wheel of a car, but from their very earliest endeavours they were the subject of disparaging comment. On seeing his first woman driver, in 1905, one *Autocar* reader castigated what he called 'these would-be men' and expressed the hope that 'the controlling of motor cars will be wrested from the hands of such persons'.[11] These were not simply the prejudices of an idiosyncratic motorist. It was widely felt that the control of a dangerous technology like the car was best left to men. For example, in 1907 *The Times* motoring column argued that it was 'difficult to reconcile the right practice of motor-driving with the feminine lot and temperament'. One reason for this being that, 'Feminine nerves, too, finely responsive to great occasions, are sadly liable to lapses through such prolonged trials as ambitious motor-driving entails.'[12] This sort of essentialist argument was to be reiterated throughout the period under investigation and beyond. Thus traditional ideas about femininity, masculinity and the control of technology were extremely influential in the way the car was perceived and used by men and women.

An initial difficulty in assessing the role of gender in the car culture's formative decades is the severe shortage of quantitative data. For example, it is not possible to calculate with any authority the numbers of each sex holding driving licences in the period. Only one official survey, conducted by the Ministry of Transport in six 'representative' areas during 1933, provides statistical information on this question. It suggested that 12 per cent of all driving licences were held by women.[13] Small though this figure may be, it was certainly a great increase compared with the numbers of women who drove in the years before 1914. In a 1938 issue, *Good Housekeeping*'s motoring editor, Gillian Maud, argued that the woman driver was non-existent before 1911: 'Women, even at the beginning of motoring were itching to "take over", but I will defy anyone to provide a picture, published prior to the coronation of King George V, showing a woman in control of a car. No man would admit that any woman *could* drive.'[14] In fact the first reported woman driver, Baroness Campbell de Lorentz, had taken to British roads in 1895.[15] However, as Maud's comment suggests, she and others like her remained a rarity for many years.

In the very earliest years of this century, female drivers were rare enough to receive press coverage whenever they undertook more than the most mundane trip. In 1901, for example, *Autocar* reported the news that Miss Vera Butler was driving in France with her father. Even more noteworthy was the news that she had passed the driving test which motoring tourists were called upon to undertake.[16] In 1905, the same magazine offered an account of Miss Dorothy Levitt's London–Liverpool–London drive, which she completed in two days. This was the longest known drive by a woman driver at that point.[17] Levitt was arguably the best known of the early women drivers. Formerly a noted horse-rider, she became the first British woman to compete in motor races in 1903. She had a number of victories and became an amateur driver in S. F. Edge's Napier cars. In 1909, her book *Woman and Her Car: A Chatty Little Book for Women who Motor or Want to Motor* was published.[18] It dealt with the practicalities of motoring from a female perspective, but it is also interesting for what it reveals about gender and the early car culture. It offers instructive insights into the relationship between gender, socio-economic freedom and the car. For, as we shall see, when it comes to access to the driving wheel it is economic independence that has always been a woman's best guarantor of gaining that position.

The reader of Levitt's book quickly learnt of her atypical and privileged 'bachelor girl' lifestyle, waited on by two servants, in her flat in London's West End.[19] She was clearly a woman of significant independent means. She did not, however, have the masculine physique many commentators believed was required by the motoring pioneer. Thus, the preface to the original edition may have surprised many readers with its description of Levitt: 'The public, in its mind's eye, no doubt figures this motor champion as a big strapping Amazon. Dorothy Levitt is exactly, or almost so, the direct opposite of such a picture. She is the most girlish of womanly women.' Furthermore, she was described as 'slight in stature, shy and shrinking, almost timid'.[20] Nonetheless she was not prepared to accept what was rapidly becoming the customary female position in the passenger seat, asserting that there might 'be pleasure in being whisked around the country by your friends and relatives, or … chauffeur; but the real intense pleasure comes only when you drive your own car.'[21] She also challenged many of the widely held conceptions about gender and the car by arguing that although the engine of a car might look 'horrid', it could be 'easily mastered' by women with only a 'few hours of proper diligence.'[22] As for the difficulty of starting the engine, she admitted there was a 'great knack' involved, but 'this, once overcome, ceases to be hard work.'[23] Of course, such behaviour went beyond the bounds of what most upper-middle-class men and women would have seen as acceptable feminine behaviour. However, Levitt was not prepared to forsake her ascribed femininity completely, acknowledging that although it was 'possible for a woman to repair a tyre' she was sure that 'not one woman in a thousand would want to ruin her hands in this way.'[24]

Further evidence that the pioneer women motorists were very much an elite grouping can be derived from an assessment of the first female motoring club – the Ladies Automobile Club of Great Britain and Ireland. The club's origins are obscure, but it seems likely that it was formed in response to the decision of the Automobile Club (from 1907 the Royal Automobile Club [RAC]) to refuse admission to females.[25] The inaugural meeting of the Ladies Automobile Club, in April 1903, attracted an attendance of just 17, but by 1909 membership had risen to 400.[26] It was organised by Lady Cecil Scott Montagu to provide members with a social club, technical information, a hotel booking service and motor efficiency trials or races. It also arranged driving lessons for members and their servants. Their original London club rooms were in the Hans Crescent Hotel, with parking facilities at Harrods department store.[27] In contrast to the Automobile Club, the less stuffy and more aggressive defender of motoring the Automobile Association (AA), formed in 1905, did admit female members after a degree of soul-searching, which was described years later by the AA's Secretary Stenson Cooke:

> We shuffled a little uneasily in our seats when we had the first application from a woman driver of a car. We thought in those days that no one except a quick-thinking resourceful man ought to be at the wheel. As men will do we pondered thoughtfully over this daring intrusion – and as men invariably do, we decided to let the women have their own way. I must admit we were inclined to believe that there would be a snag somewhere, and that since the day when the first woman joined our organisation, we have watched carefully in case our early-formed theories proved correct.[28]

As in many other aspects of gender relations, the 1914–18 war was a critical phase in the evolving relationship between femininity, masculinity and the car. The shifting of gender roles during the war led to women being called upon to perform numerous tasks previously defined as masculine and beyond their capabilities. One of these areas was motor driving, where women were heavily involved both in France and on home soil.[29] With a shortage of drivers in 1914 the government was indebted to the four-year-old British School of Motoring, which provided the services of its instructors. Initially, its courses were available solely to men, but by 1916 women were also receiving tuition.[30] By the end of the war large numbers of women were engaged in driving duties, with, for example, five thousand serving in the Women's Legion Transport Section.[31] The work of these women received essentially positive coverage both during and immediately following the war, although, as was the case with women's war work generally, their employment as ambulance drivers, for instance, was described as having allowed men to be released for 'more important work'.[32]

Following the war, however, attitudes towards these women mirrored those expressed elsewhere in the world of work, as a cacophony of voices called for a return to 'normal' peacetime gender and work patterns. Thus, by February 1919 letters were appearing from readers of *Autocar* describing the continued employment of women drivers in the Auxiliary Service Corps as a scandal. In the following September the army announced its decision to replace these women with male drivers.[33] Meanwhile the Metropolitan Police were responding to calls from London taxi drivers to proscribe the licensing of female motor-cab drivers. Four such licences had been granted in 1917, despite the opposition of male taxi drivers. However, in replying to their petition the chief constable described that decision as an exceptional act, 'a war-time measure based on the shortage of manpower', and it was not proposed 'to revert to it in normal circumstances.'[34]

It is conceivable that many of the women who learned to drive during the war never had the opportunity to drive again, but their experiences nonetheless gave greater confidence to the next generation of potential female motorists. As the writer Viola Meeking put it in *Autocar* during 1921, the war had led many women to discover the pleasures of motoring. Previously they had been at a disadvantage because childhood socialisation had left them ignorant of technology, 'the use of even the simplest of tools' having been discouraged.[35] The wartime achievements of women drivers should have made objections to, and jibes about, female drivers less tenable, but they were offered with increasing frequency as the number of women drivers increased in the 1920s and 1930s.

Attitudes towards women motorists during the inter-war decades also need to be understood in the context of the wider debate about gender roles, which was a frequent source of controversy.[36] Legislation passed during the ten years following the war did much to improve the position of women. Significant amongst these reforms were the Parliamentary Qualification of Women Act (1918) and the Equal Franchise Act (1928) which extended the right to vote in parliamentary elections, first to women over thirty and then to those over twenty-one. Also of importance was the Sex Disqualification (Removal) Act of 1919, which abolished all existing restrictions upon the admission of women into the professions and civic positions.[37] There were also changes in the social sphere. The immediate post-war years saw a great deal of attention focused upon the 'new freedom' of young women, and the car was accorded an important symbolic role in growing female emancipation. As Ray Strachey put it: 'With one bound the young women of 1919 burst out from the hampering conventions, and with their cigarettes, their motor-cars, their latch-keys, and their athletics they astonished and scandalised their elders.'[38] Not everybody was content with the shift in gender relations, and there were many advocates of traditional models of masculine and feminine behaviour. The women's magazine *Home Chat* welcomed the end of the war and the consequent call upon female labour, recording a sense of relief at the return to the home environment: 'Now we are feminine again'.[39] A new domestic ideology emerged which emphasised traditional gender roles in the context of the socio-economic conditions of the time. The middle-class woman's place was very definitely in the home, but her role was now to be one of professional housewife, trained and educated to run her increasingly servantless household along the lines of a domestic scientific management. Magazines such as *Good Housekeeping*, which was first published in Britain in 1922, represented the epitome of this development.[40] On the other side of this equation, traditional models of heroic masculinity, so popular amongst the pre-1914 middle classes, had been severely jolted by the emasculating realities of trench warfare. However, as exemplified by the extraordinary popularity of T. E. Lawrence, re-configurations of this form of masculinity continued to prove attractive to many in the post-1918 generation.[41] It is within this atmosphere of contested gender relations that the developments surrounding femininity, masculinity and the car must be assessed. For the woman driver provided a powerful, and often controversial, symbol of changing gender relations.

As has been illustrated, car ownership in the 1920s and 1930s was largely confined to the professional and commercial middle classes. The SMMT calculated that only those with comfortable salaries were capable of meeting both purchase price and running costs of a new car: in 1938, for instance, their estimated necessary salary was £250.[42] It is hard, therefore, to disagree with *Advertiser's Weekly*, which argued in 1934 that the 'number of women who can afford to run a car for their exclusive use provides a very limited market'.[43] Despite the advances made following the Sex Disqualification Removal Act, women were still very much in the minority in most professions. For example, the census of 1931 recorded only 133 women solicitors compared with 19,081 men.[44] By far the biggest group of professional women were employed as teachers. Women teachers earned up to £254 in an elementary school in 1930, whereas their male counterparts could earn £334.[45] This salary put the female teacher into the SMMT's bracket of potential motorist only by the end of the 1930s, and she still faced potential difficulties in convincing a finance house of her suitability as a hire-purchaser. Moreover, the widespread application of the marriage bar meant that she would be asked to leave her position if she wed. Interestingly, in the context of the discussion of car sharing in the previous chapter, there is some evidence of the adoption of this practice amongst female teachers.[46]

Further evidence of the small proportion of female owner-drivers amongst pre-1939 motorists was gleaned from the histories of the twenty-three female drivers that were narrated by our respondents. Only three of these women – a doctor, a farmer and the proprietor of a hairdressing salon – were owner-drivers. The remaining women drove either the family car or a car bought for them by family finances. The family car was usually purchased through a father's or husband's income. Women in the family were therefore technically reliant on the permission of a man before they could occupy the driver's seat. However, the low proportion of driving licences held by women – only 12 per cent of total licences in 1933 – indicates that in the majority of car-owning families it was a man, not a woman, who took the wheel. Having noted that the number of female licence holders was only 12 per cent of the total, the obvious question to pose is why wasn't the figure much closer to 50 per cent? Why weren't women also driving the family car? For example, in Manchester in 1938 there were 45,875 cars, motor cycles, goods vehicles and taxis on the city's streets, with 50,912 persons licensed to drive them.[47] It seems clear from this example that very few private cars were driven by more than one family member – a male.

Given some of the prevailing notions about gender, it is not surprising to find that, as ownership grew, the car became the site of increasing debate about shifting aspects of femininity and masculinity. Here was a rapidly diffusing technology, the control of which had been a largely male province before the war. Now it had the potential to become a very powerful symbol of feminine equality, presenting the opportunity of equal mobility, speed and independence to all who had access to the driving wheel. Many men clearly felt a challenge to their dominant position, both as drivers and in society more generally, and a plethora of letters, articles and comments by men in the motoring journals throughout the 1920s and 1930s portrayed the car and motoring as masculine concerns. Of course, many women also shared traditional notions about femininity, masculinity and technology. One result of this was a tendency to identify aspects of the car and motoring along gendered lines. This position was never more explicitly stated than in a 1929 *Morris Owner* article, entitled 'Women's Work in the Garage'. It was written by Mrs Victor Bruce, well known for her motoring exploits, which included a round-the-world trip.

> Where Phyllis is unable to drive – and it is much to the public good that she should not be urged to learn against her will – there is no reason why she should feel excluded from some part of the joy of ownership; the part that returns, in time and labour, service for willing service … in regard to the motor house, I do think it may be regarded as the woman's part to see that it is spick and span. Think how irritating it is, after a hard day at business and a long drive home in the traffic stream, to have to clear away the litter of the morning's operations before it is possible to put the car away for the night; and what a relief, after dreading the task, to find the garage spotless and a model of orderliness!
>
> Such matters as the making of loose covers for the seats clearly fall to the woman's share … If there is a man about … I do not consider

it a woman's task to attend to the rough washing of the car but women should supervise as they have a natural aptitude.[48]

So, although 'Phyllis' may simply have been not cut out to drive she did have instinctive talents which could make a second home of the car. Even those who did believe women could drive as well as men were imbued with this type of thinking. Writing in *Practical Motorist* during 1934, 'Cylinda' advised those women drivers whose 'menfolk sit with closed eyes, waiting for the crash', to let the men do the 'easy part – that is the actual driving'. 'Cylinda' urged the lady passenger to 'swallow your pride' and to carry out a number of 'humble jobs' that were nevertheless necessary for 'happy motoring'. These tasks included map-reading, ensuring adequate supplies of cigarettes and matches, and making advanced hotel and meal reservations, the reward for which would be 'the sweetness of her lord's temper and the smoothness of the tour'. Echoing the advice given by Mrs Victor Bruce, 'Cylinda' advised female readers to 'buy the most elaborate and scientific "gadgets" and make the home garage resemble a motor beauty-parlour'. In conclusion, the author maintained that women had 'done a great deal for the comfort of the motorist, so why should any of us care a jot when we hear men grow uncomplimentary about the woman driver. Let them drive. We can do the rest.'[49]

There were certainly a lot of opportunities to hear uncomplimentary comments about women drivers. Driving skill was constantly identified as a natural masculine quality and the act of driving was often fetishised as something of an art form. As such, it was something to be savoured. Driving could re-energise a man. As an *Autocar* columnist put it in 1927, 'manhood is restored by swinging into the seat of something one can drive with precision and dexterity.'[50] According to a driving instructor, who wrote to *Motor* in 1934, women did not 'think enough' about their driving or look upon it 'as an art'.[51] A regular stream of contributors to the popular and motoring press expressed a firm belief in the incompatibility of 'feminine' traits and driving. They employed conventional images of women as delicate creatures who were less rational than men and not always capable of handling some of the situations that arose in the more masculine world outside the home. The following example, written in 1927, is from the pen of the motoring writer Chandos Bidwell:

The tradition of womanhood is against their being competent drivers. In the past they have been brought up to fear rather than to face, to have things done for them rather than to do them for themselves. All that is changing, but tradition tells to a certain extent and, when the car, running at forty miles an hour, is within ten yards of a precipice, the woman driver is apt to say, 'John what shall I do?'

The word *concentration* is the great difference between a man and a woman learning to drive. He only has to be told things once. She will ask lots of unnecessary questions and then become interested in the horn or the colour of somebody else's car.

Bidwell went on to contend that men had the right psychological make-up to make a good driver: 35 per cent judgement, 25 per cent nerve, 20 per cent consideration, 20 per cent presence of mind. He concluded by informing his readers that women he had taught to drive were particularly nervous when changing gear, which is hardly surprising, given his attitude.[52]

This pseudo-biological argument was elucidated even more explicitly by a correspondent in *Autocar* during 1936:

I maintain that women as a class, omitting a few notable exceptions, are not and never will be as proficient drivers … as men because:–

1. All down the ages man has striven to protect and provide for his womenfolk, and the instinct to receive and to be served is so deeply ingrained into woman that a mere twenty years of motoring experience has by no means eradicated this trait; thus we find that a woman is naturally and fundamentally inconsiderate and selfish on the road.
2. The mind of the woman motorist is governed largely by instinct and environment, whereas that of man is subservient to reason. Thus if a woman wishes to stop suddenly or change her course she does so at once with no thought for any unfortunate who may be behind her.
3. Woman has not man's power to concentrate as she is continually being mentally sidetracked by such burning questions, prompted by an inflated vanity, as 'How do I look?'
4. Woman generally is a weaker vessel than man and is physically unfit to have control over such a dangerous instrument as a car if the maximum degree of safety for one and all is to be a feature of a good driver.[53]

Another correspondent, writing in 1927, explained how he loathed reporting other motorists to the police, but he made an exception where women were concerned: 'for the simple reason that I class them among the dangers of the road. I will not allow any of my friends of the fair sex to drive my car, because I respect and value it. Women are splendid in other ways but in car driving they are laughable.'[54]

These examples are taken from the motoring journals and represent the views of some of their contributors and correspondents. It is clear these opinions were founded in established notions of femininity, masculinity and the control of technology. The annual motor show editions of the leading journal, *Autocar,* produced for a wider audience the amusing stories circulated during the show. Many of these stories also reiterated traditional concepts of gender in the context of the car. For example, in 1927 Mrs Victor Bruce repeated the tale she had heard, and evidently believed, about the woman who had sent a jumper to the Rover company requesting a car in matching colours.[55] The same pattern of jokes and folklore has been identified for America by Michael Berger.[56] He maintains that the perceived threat to the social order posed by large numbers of mobile female motorists touched a raw nerve in the male psyche, setting off a reaction that was given expression through jokes and stories belittling women drivers. Many such stories have been etched in motoring folklore, reappearing in motoring literature or in interviews with elderly motorists. For example, one of my respondents Tony Craven, who has been motoring since the 1930s, explained why the notion of the 'woman driver' had emerged. He believed that the first women motorists were accustomed to gentlemen opening doors for them and they consequently expected right of way on the roads as well, with disastrous results.[57] In conveying this opinion he was replicating an explanation which had appeared in an article in *Morris Owner* almost sixty years earlier:

> [Women have been used to] a homage amounting to – shall we say – a 'right of way'. Man has stood aside for her to pass, held open doors for her, given up his seat to her in buses and trams. She has learnt to accept this deference as her right – and she sometimes trades on it. She quite unconsciously expects this same deference to be shown her on the road.[58]

Clay McShane has recently discovered that similar explanations were offered in the formative years of American car culture, but there is absolutely no evidence, in Britain or in the USA, to support this assessment.[59] Another of my respondents, John Rogers, claimed that, as a boy in the 1920s, he had watched a woman drive her car up a hill in a zig-zag fashion because that is what she had formerly done with her horse and carriage.[60]

Attitudes about femininity, masculinity and car driving were not shaped solely by prevalent ideas about the control of technology. As in other areas of gender relations, legal arguments were offered, explaining why men, rather than women, should take the driving wheel. Of course, such arguments also owed a great deal to traditional gendered notions.[61] A 1932 article in *Garage and Motor Agent* reminded readers that married women still held a subordinate legal position. It advised garage proprietors to confirm with husbands, fathers or employers of women, sons, daughters or chauffeurs, when they ordered goods or work. This was due to what they described as the legal problems that could arise should the car's owner later dispute the bill.[62] Another article which appeared in the *Autocar*, in 1929, warned male readers that they were responsible for any claims for legal damages brought against their wives for breach of contract or for any damages entailed as a result of an incident when their wives were driving the family car.[63] In this case, male reluctance to see women at the wheel can, in part, be explained by gender ideology institutionalised in law by an earlier generation. However, for men to see this as an excuse to keep their wives or daughters from driving would indicate a propensity to accept that their female relatives were more likely to come to grief in the family car. In 1935, the Law Reform (Married Women and Tortfeasers) Act finally ended a husband's responsibility for the civil liabilities of his wife.[64]

Scientific sources reinforced prevailing pseudo-biological accounts of women's unsuitability as drivers. In 1938 *Autocar* quoted from a piece in the *Psychologist* which dealt with three types of neurotic women drivers. It is worth quoting at some length because its language demonstrates how its scientific conclusions were reached within a discourse of gender ideology. In turn, these scientific assertions must have bolstered many readers' preconceived notions of gender difference.

> The aggressive women drivers comprise the first type. They are afraid that this is a man's world and all women are discriminated against by men. The open road and a powerful car under their hands give them an apparent opportunity to prove that they are as good as any man.

In their effort to prove this, these aggressive women take a fiendish delight in weaving in and out of traffic, frightening poor male drivers by their recklessness and verve. Many a woman takes out her hate of her husband, or her sexual dissatisfaction, in reckless driving.

Driving is, in a certain sense, a tremendously valuable emotional safety-valve. Many a woman who would like to use the axe on her husband or her boss, takes out her homicidal instincts on her car. The cost is only a few gallons of petrol, and is far preferable to a term in prison.

From this point of view, fast driving probably keeps a great many women out of asylums, but it would be better if we had special race-tracks where both men and women who wanted to blow off emotional steam could do so without endangering the lives of other motorists.

The second type of women neurotics comprises the ladies who are so imbued with a sense of their own worthlessness that they become completely helpless in any traffic situation which requires independence of judgement or action, self-reliance or ingenuity. These are the women who tangle traffic by their ineptitude, their over-cautiousness, their indecision. It is pretty safe to say that a woman who cannot plan a meal, design a dress, or decide where her children shall go to school will not make a good driver.

The third type of woman neurotic does not drive from the wheel, but from the back seat. This is the throne from where many a woman revenges herself for the slights of the kitchen. As in every neurosis, back-seat driving gives them a maximum of subjective power and a minimum of objective responsibility. Nagging, super-critical, worrisome and hysterical women often gain a tremendous sense of power by nullifying the objective superiority of their husbands by the use of caustic comments from the back seat.[65]

Thus, the idea of the driving seat as a masculine domain gathered credence from every conceivable angle and women's driving abilities were continually questioned. However, the woman driver was not without her defenders. Motoring magazines provided an obvious forum in which women motorists could defend themselves. Reading their words today confers a tangible sense of their frustration. Writing in *Morris Owner* in 1930, Dorothy Ashwell responded to an attack on women drivers in an earlier issue by calling for drivers to be divided into good and bad, with various degrees in between, instead of the customary point of reference whereby 'Men drivers are usually referred to as drivers, and women drivers always have the sex prefix attached.'[66] In the same year, and magazine, E. Spencer Cooper contended that some men still viewed being driven by a woman as 'a confession of weakness':

Do you sir, consider that your wife is a congenital idiot? Presumably not! ... The truth is that much of this insistence on the poorness of women's driving is rooted in jealousy. Put plainly, that is what it amounts to. It is the fighting of a rearguard action against the invasion of man's province ... It was true, once, that women, as a whole drove badly. Now that is a myth that is not allowed to die.[67]

Despite often being a site for the stereotypical depiction of women's relationship to the car, *Autocar* occasionally offered support for women drivers. In June 1927, an editorial defended women drivers, describing them as careful and considerate.[68] This only served to summon forth another flurry of letters on this contentious subject and in November the editor announced that no more letters would be printed on the subject for the foreseeable future.[69]

Analysis of accident figures by insurance companies and others also revealed the flaws in the cruder arguments about the car, gender and driving ability. In July 1935 the *Daily Express* featured an insurance broker's analysis of the ability of various categories of motorist. Women drivers emerged well from his appraisal, the broker remarking: 'Do not smile. The woman driver, generally speaking, is a very good risk.' Women, he went on to say, were a better risk than men because they drove more slowly and carefully, a factor which was particularly valid in the eighteen to twenty-one age group. In this connection, the broker was critical of sports cars that were 'in many cases ... driven by young men whose main ambition is to keep their feet hard down on the accelerator irrespective of road conditions.'[70]

The introduction of the driving test in May 1935 also provided a potentially objective criterion by which to judge the ability of individual drivers. As such, its introduction may well have encouraged many women to take up driving for the first time. Moreover, its arrival encouraged the growth of driving schools, whose experienced instructors offered less stressful tuition than was often the case for those women who had their first lessons with a male relation or boyfriend. Janet Powell, for example, explained in a somewhat understated manner the family tensions that arose during her first driving lessons: 'I went out with my father, for a time, but didn't find that very satisfactory because he was always rather worried that I was damaging the gears.'[71] The insurance broker, cited above, also appreciated the potential disadvantages faced by women who were taught to drive by their husbands and

Schoolteacher Mollie Farrell at the wheel of her Bullnose Morris in 1928.   **3**

However, a significant minority of women did take the wheel, either with the agreement of a husband, or father, or following a good deal of familial altercation. Christine Paul, for example, reported her belief that women from farming families, like herself, were more often to be seen in the driving seat than their urban and suburban counterparts. She first registered this belief when, in 1940, she found herself the only car owner amongst thirty-five women teachers. Only one other member of the all-female staff could drive.[83] The economic and spatial realities of country life ensured that even the most chauvinistic of farming men had potentially compelling motivations for encouraging a wife, but perhaps more frequently a daughter, to drive. Respondents mentioned the cases of a total of twenty-three female drivers who drove cars in their families, and, although the sample is small, it is interesting that six of these women were from farming families.

Other women, in danger of being denied a place at the wheel, took steps to outmanoeuvre a reluctant male. For example, in 1926 Tom Taylor's mother learned that her husband had bought a car and arranged, as was frequently the case, to receive basic driving tuition from the retailer. Mrs Taylor immediately informed the dealer that she, too, was to receive instruction. For the Taylors it was to be the beginning of many arguments about who drove the car.[84] Another respondent, Janet Powell, narrated the personal history of a friend, barred by her husband from driving the family car, who exhausted her savings to buy her own vehicle. However, her stand proved fruitless as without a personal income she was unable to meet the car's running costs.[85]

Of course, it is likely that many women happily accepted ideologies of separate spheres, as they were reinscribed in the car culture. As noted earlier, *Practical Motorist* recognised that pride of place in the front passenger seat, as map-reader and picnic organiser, offered women an obvious extension of the feminine role with which many middle-class women were content. However, this particular attraction of being a non-driver was touched upon by only one female respondent. It is far likelier that the 'masculinity' of the car, together with the widespread derisory comments made about women motorists, not least by fathers and husbands, must have combined to knock the confidence of many women who thought about, and decided against, taking up driving. Even the respondent who took some pride in the position of a navigator really hankered to be in the driving seat, and both she and her husband were, decades later, to suffer inconvenience caused by the adoption of traditional gender roles within their marriage. Marjorie Sculthorpe was asked if she had ever learned to drive:

> No. And I have to say I was not allowed to. My husband said to me: 'You're a dreamer, you watch the scenery.' He said: 'You'd have your eyes off the road.' He said: 'No.' And yet our Michael, who was ham-fisted if anybody ever was – driving lessons at 17 – you know that sort of thing. I was a bit resentful really, but he said 'I'll take you wherever you like, you want to go'; he was very good. And he said: 'You can be the navigator.' And I enjoyed being a navigator ... the only thing was, you see, when he didn't have such very good health I would have been a help then, if I'd driven. And as somebody said: 'What's the use of a car in the garage, your husband in hospital and you messing about on buses?' And I've been messing about on buses ever since really.[86]

Countless women must have had similarly unfulfilled desires. In her narration of these events, she was not bitter about her husband's actions, far from it. She accepted his opinion because it was shared widely throughout society, and in many ways seemed natural.

Clearly, both in the realm of public debate and within the family, control of the car was often seen as best left to a male who was deemed qualified to control this powerful, liberating and potentially dangerous new technology through possession of traditional masculine traits. Cars were defined as a masculine technology and they were operated in a space outside of the feminine sphere of the home. However, the increasing use of cars by women clearly threatened the masculine identity of many men, who fought to identify the car and motoring with traditional notions of masculinity. Developments in another aspect of motoring also threatened the car's identification with rugged, down-to-earth and utilitarian masculinity – the aesthetics of the car. It is this facet of the relationship between gender and the car that will now be addressed.

Gender, consumption and the car

If long-standing beliefs about gender and technology were enormously influential in the evolving car culture, established assumptions concerning consumption and gender were equally important. Moreover, these assumptions reinforced those about technology, as women's interest in the car was deemed to be largely about aesthetics and status rather than utility. With the middle-class family economy clearly divided in ideology, if not always in reality, between the woman's world in the home and the man's role of breadwinner, the female was identified as the prime mover in family consumption decisions. Thus historian Thomas Richards has asserted that by the end of the nineteenth century consumption had become 'something that women undertook on behalf of men'.[87] Such a maxim does not do justice to the complexity of the domestic economy, certainly not those of the middle-class family of the early twentieth century, where it was common for the husband to manage the entire family's finances.[88] Richards' comment also fails to acknowledge the active involvement of men and masculinity in consumption. Men were often just as attracted by the pleasurable side of consumption as their female contemporaries.[89] Moreover, their desires, tastes and concerns about expressing both status and appropriate masculine codes were manipulated by increasingly sophisticated advertisers and retailers. However, attempts to promote male consumption were circumscribed by the established association of femininity with consumption.[90] For example, by the turn of the twentieth century women's magazines were an established source whereby advertisers sought to stimulate demand for consumer goods.[91] The male consumer, however, could not be approached in such a direct manner. By 1939, when there were fifty women's magazines, there was only one men's lifestyle magazine – *Men Only*.[92] However, there were a myriad consumer magazines catering for the hobbies and pastimes of the male consumer, motoring being a prime example. Thus magazines such as *Autocar* and *Motor* were forums in which a largely male readership could be addressed by motor manufacturers, anxious to stimulate demand for their latest model.

As has been indicated, from its inception the car was far more than a utilitarian device; it was also heavily implicated in its owner's expressions of taste and status. This was particularly true for men, who in the clear majority of cases drove the family car. For the middle-class male engaged in professional or commercial activity, the model of car he drove made a statement about his success in the masculine world of work. For this reason it is noteworthy that medium and larger-sized cars sold best in areas with large numbers of professionals.[93] Furthermore, consumer surveys have consistently indicated that the male consumer has taken a 'disproportionate interest' in those forms of consumption upon which status has most closely depended.[94] This has been particularly true of the car. Post-1945 studies indicate that it was only when the numbers of married women gaining employment outside the home increased in the 1950s and 1960s that women achieved a significant input into car-purchasing decisions.[95] Nonetheless, taking their lead from dominant ideologies of consumption and gender, many of those involved in motoring prior to 1939 increasingly spoke of what they felt was a feminisation of the car. Thus in motoring magazines, the motor-trade press and amongst manufacturers, the female consumer was often depicted in stereotypical terms as fundamentally different from her male counterpart. This process had two predominant characteristics. First, the female consumer was often targeted because it was widely felt that wives and daughters of salaried men had the crucial say in the purchase of a car. Second, different aspects of the car were associated with femininity or masculinity. It was commonly felt that men used cars for utilitarian and business reasons and they were therefore presumed to be attracted by cost, economy, ruggedness and reliability. Less 'masculine' facets of the car were often associated with a growing feminine interest in motoring as a leisure pursuit, and women were adjudged to be attracted largely by styling, colour and comfort. No doubt many early motoring pioneers were fascinated by the mechanisms of their cars, but as ownership spread in the years before 1914 to take in families who were used to comfortable travel by train or coach, motor manufacturers had new demands to cater for. Yet those involved with motoring consistently depicted these developments as the result of growing female involvement. For example, the secretary of the AA, Stenson Cooke, recalling Edwardian motoring, described how 'John' was 'generally more concerned about the mechanism than comfort in riding', whereas 'Mary' insisted upon comfort if she was to ride in the new car.[96] As was intimated in the introduction to this chapter, such thinking had been instigated within the car culture by the association developed by motoring's pioneers between masculinity and the car.

Although such thinking was well established by 1914, it was articulated more frequently in the inter-war years for two interrelated reasons. First, the increasing numbers of women drivers induced manufacturers to consider the female consumer and her possible motivations with increasing regularity and, often, apprehension. Second, as described in the last chapter, the inter-war years saw the development of a large middle-class market which increasingly sought to display distinction through the choice of model. One way in which manufacturers responded was through regular design and styling changes. This increasing concentration on the aesthetic side of the car did not sit comfortably alongside the vision of rugged and masculine motoring handed down by motoring pioneers. Consequently, it was often alleged by many of those involved in motoring that the car was being subjected to a process of feminisation.

Women were widely credited with the deciding vote in selecting the family car. In 1919 the Scottish motor manufacturers Arrol-Johnston sought motor dealers for their vehicle in the trade magazine *Motor Trader* by explicitly citing their reasons for advertising in women's magazines:

> The 'Lady of the house' usually has a good deal to say in the choice of a car. And, having the gift of extempore eloquence and the time to think up reasons why, she often wheedles or bullies her poor old husband into buying the car SHE wants. Everybody knows that. The

firm of Arrol-Johnston Ltd., recognises the power of woman in this matter. They advertise the A.J. in several ladies' journals (between blushful frilly announcements and pictures of pearl pendants) and they never let up on telling the ornamental sex why they ought to have a tame vehicle from Dumfries concealed about the buildings.[97]

Entreaties such as this one reinforced popular stereotypes in the minds of car dealers and encouraged further quips about female consumers in their masculine world. For example, a 1926 edition of *Garage and Motor Agent* satirised women's influence in car buying, suggesting the creation of a new magazine called *Ladies' Own Lingerie and Car Repairer Weekly*.[98]

As Gail Reekie's work on sales literature in the early twentieth century has indicated, the burgeoning marketing industry offered a similar perspective on the relationship between gender and consumption; the female consumer being depicted as 'other' in retailing literature.[99] One marketing text book, published in 1931, advised motor manufacturers targeting women to ensure that their product was 'stylish and different from the cars owned by her neighbours'. Moreover, if her husband could be convinced that the car's running costs were reasonable, the 'choice of the car would ... be left largely to the woman'.[100] Such simplistic portraits of the middle-class family economy presented an image of a nation of men powerless to resist their wives' feminine wiles. Nonetheless, it was a portrait that was widely accepted and rarely questioned by the motor trade. In 1933, for example, the *Blackpool Gazette and Herald*'s motoring column claimed that 'ninety per cent. of cars in use to-day were designed and sold to please the lady motorist ... whose views on the subject are naturally restricted to considerations of colour and comfort.'[101] This perspective remained the dominant one within motoring circles throughout the inter-war period. Thus, in 1938 *Advertiser's Weekly*, in an article announced by the legend 'Women wear the trousers when it comes to buying cars', related Vauxhall Motors' opinion on this matter. Vauxhall's advertising department believed it had been proved to its 'satisfaction' that 'women to-day have a tremendous say in the purchasing of a car'.[102] However, no data was provided to support this conviction.

Between 1919 and 1939 *Motor Trader* paid serious attention to the subject of women buyers on only four occasions. The infrequency of this analysis should in itself cast serious doubt on the theory of an all-pervading feminine influence. On the occasions that *Motor Trader* explored this topic, business considerations were marred by an inability to understand the female consumer. The magazine's reflections were clouded by a fear of the damage that a perceived feminine faddishness could wreak on the car. In 1925, for example, *Motor Trader* remarked that, although in 'a great many respects the influence of women will be all to the good', chassis designers must beware of 'spoiling good engineering by some fashionable fad' and introducing 'freakish designs in bodywork' in order to 'appeal to a few notoriety seeking women'.[103] *Motor Trader* returned to the subject two years later, noting in an editorial that in the American market 'mere man is beginning to take rather a back seat … especially when it comes to buying. The woman buys: the man pays.' The editor believed that Britain had not yet reached 'that stage of feminine dictatorship in automobile matters, but there is no mistaking the direction in which things are tending'. In the same issue, *Motor Trader* made its first attempt to tackle the issue of women and the car in any detail. It advised the trade to 'take into account the psychological fact that women are very imitative'. Thus 'every woman driver seen on the road by another woman is as provocative of imitation as is the leader of a new fashion in hats or frocks.' A 'fashion for driving cars' had 'set in amongst women', and whether it was to be a 'long-lived or a short-lived fashion' there would be 'a big harvest for the trade to reap'.[104] A clear message emerged from this article: for women, motoring was merely a fad. By extension, women themselves were not to be taken seriously as motorists or consumers of cars. Women's interest in motoring was superficial, prompted by a love of display and leisure, rather than business or utility. *Motor Trader* advised dealers to study fashion shops in order to understand women's mentality. In the light of such sentiment within the motor trade, it is easy to comprehend how the growing trend towards model differentiation was laid at the door of the female consumer. Speaking in 1934, Herbert Austin bemoaned what he felt was the negative influence of consumer-led design on the car. He fondly recalled building his first vehicles, thirty years previously, when design 'was governed by practical considerations'. He had been able to take 'little interest in the shape of the body', but since the 1920s that early simplicity had gone and Austin bemoaned the fact that 'the woman's influence has come in'.[105] Accordingly, Austin Motors and other companies began to design cars with the female consumer in mind. One of the more successful of these attempts, the

Austin Seven Ruby saloon, appeared in 1935, the company describing it as 'possibly the most elegant baby car yet offered to the public'.[106] Other initiatives were less successful and involved fairly crude estimations of what might attract female consumers. One such effort was the 1933 Humber Vogue. The advertising for the Vogue informed potential buyers that the dress designer Captain Molyneux had been involved in planning the car.[107]

It is impossible to assess the success or failure of moves designed to court the female consumer. Undoubtedly by the 1920s and 1930s, as the minority of women car owners and drivers grew larger, their influence in the car showroom became more pronounced than it had been before 1914. However, as studies of the post-1945 period indicate, choosing a car was to remain very much a male prerogative until the late 1950s and 1960s. Attempts to woo the female consumer in the inter-war decades, therefore, were something of a double-edged sword. Giving a car a name designed to attract the female consumer was hardly likely to prove a successful ploy in itself. Female as well as male consumers were far more likely to be attracted by a car that met particular specifications in terms of price, running costs, reliability and so on. Furthermore, such a policy carried great risk of disenchanting many male consumers, particular those who believed that manufacturers were capitulating to female consumers. For example, in 1936 V. G. Townsend of Croydon wrote to *Autocar* to censure manufacturers for their 'tendency to pander to the feminine motorist', which he felt was 'only too noticeable in modern design'. As a result, 'the needs of experienced male motorists' were 'being ignored by manufacturers'. His letter concluded with the rather pathetic appeal: 'please, Mr Manufacturer, do not assume that every car is driven and owned by a woman or a nitwit.'[108]

It can be seen that elements of the design and operation of the car that did not correspond to notions of a rugged, unfussy masculinity were attributed to a feminine influence which was portrayed as largely outside of male control. But it was men who designed cars and men who formed the great majority of buyers. In some ways, notions of femininity enabled car owners and manufacturers to excuse aspects of motoring, such as annual model changes, by attributing them to fashion-conscious and influential female motorists and motorists' wives. It also served to preserve their sense of masculinity by allowing them to deny the existence of 'feminine' traits in their own behaviour. It was, after all, male consumers who most frequently paid the sort of fetishistic attention to each year's new models that *Motor Trader* accused the female consumer of giving to a new season's hats or frocks. Tied up with masculinity, in this case, were many of the issues highlighted in the last chapter. The purchase of stylish new cars was an expression of social status for both sexes, with men, as the actual buyers in most cases, the prime movers in this area of middle-class consumption. Late-nineteenth- and early-twentieth-commentators too readily depicted consumption as solely the province of women. As has been shown here, there was a strong tendency to make this claim for such an obviously 'male' product as the car. But it should be recognised that the middle-class male was as heavily implicated in consumerism as the female. In fulfilling his breadwinner role, he had potentially more social contacts with those above or below him in a heavily stratified social hierarchy. As such, he had cause to take precise care over his selection of goods. Lacking any developed market research on what women wanted from a car, manufacturers and dealers fell back upon traditional stereotypes. This does not mean that it was bad business sense to sell cars to women on the basis of comfort, looks and style, but it was a misunderstanding to conclude that these factors were not also a major consideration when men came to buy a car. In often attributing the desire to have the latest and most fashionable car to female members of the family, motoring commentators were ignoring the fact that the car played an important role in the display of status for all the middle-class family, male and female, in the caste-like atmosphere of inter-war Britain.

In the USA, the leading innovator in the car's aesthetics was Harley Earl. Although many of his actions were framed by a very masculine work environment, his success was based on an acknowledgement of the role of irrationality in the choice of a motor car. Earl mistrusted market surveys which consistently indicated that consumers put factors such as dependability, more headroom, less chrome and greater safety rather than speed at the top of their priorities when purchasing a car. Finally piqued into a response by the nagging of General Motors' Sales Department, Earl declared: 'By God, we'll design exactly what they want!' The result was the unsuccessful, high-roofed and big-windowed 'box cars' of 1939, which sold poorly and provided a victory for Earl's stylists over the market surveyors.[109] For as David Gartman has shown in his study of the American automobile before 1939, consumers confronted with sober questionnaires about car design responded with a sober inventory of preferences, but when confronted with glamorously styled automobiles the response was non-rational and emotional. This was equally true of men and women.[110]

Conclusion

This chapter has attempted to indicate the extent to which gender informed the culture of the car at a point in time where the 'masculinity' of this particular piece of technology was an arena of debate. The triumph and hegemony of the 'maleness' of the car is well known, but the agency of gender within this process has been poorly documented.

Ideologies of femininity and masculinity play a crucial role in the introduction and consumption of new technologies. Pre-existing attitudes ensured that the car was identified as a masculine technology, a process which deterred many women from seeking a place at the driving wheel. Others like Marjorie Sculthorpe sought to take their place in the driver's seat but were denied it for reasons clearly founded in gender ideology. This is not a story of brutish men denying women their freedom – although women's autonomy and mobility were limited in these cases. What has been explained is the role of gender ideology in the normative regulation of men and women; a process in which men and women regulated the behaviour of others of the same gender as well as that of the other gender. Thus many women were very happy to have their husbands fulfil the 'manly' role and chauffeur them around – whilst they were pre-eminent in organising the family's domestic life – and were equally susceptible to commonly held prejudices about the 'woman driver'.

Manufacturers and dealers were also influenced by similar notions about gender. In their case, ideas about gender and consumption led to what appears to have been an overestimation of the role of the female consumer in the diffusion of car ownership and design. At times this led to angst-ridden meditation on the negative effects some faddish female consumers might have on the car. On another level, such thinking allowed men to divert attention away from developments in automotive technology that did not fit well with more rugged visions of male identity. In the process, women became associated with an almost frivolous side of the car, being most frequently held responsible for developments in comfort or aesthetics. Men, on the other hand, were viewed as serious motorists; understanding how a car worked, they appreciated the intricacies of improvements in engineering. These developments masked the true complexity of the relationship between masculinity and the car. Many men were interested in the technical aspects of the car, but this was certainly not the case for all men. The car became central to the display of a variety of masculine identities, from the successful professional in his tasteful Armstrong-Siddeley or Rover, to the sporty owner of an MG or the plethora of flamboyant models that appeared from the 1920s onwards.

Each of these developments has had long-term consequences. Women are still the recipients of regular jokes and jibes about their driving ability, even though statistics have always shown that they are involved in fewer accidents. Women are still less likely to drive than men, even in motoring families. In one-car families where women do drive they usually have second call upon the car and are, in consequence, more frequent users of public transport. Thus, the modern transport system, dominated by the car, restricts the mobility of many women and exacerbates their confinement to the home and its immediate locality.[111] The first to experience this detrimental aspect of the car must have been wives in the army of middle-class suburban families that multiplied most rapidly in the 1920s and 1930s. For women in car-owning families who did not drive themselves, the notion that the car brought liberation and mobility must have seemed more than a little ironic.

For men, the legacies of the car's formative decades are equally important. For ever-expanding numbers of men, the car has had a significant role in the expression of masculinity, passing a driving test being something of a rite of passage for the young male. Whilst this can have many enjoyable aspects, the less attractive side involves the significant risks taken by the numerous young men who perennially associate enjoyable and skilful driving with risk-taking and speed. The next chapter returns us to this theme, as it is best explained as part of a thorough analysis of the multiplicity of uses to which the car was put in the years from 1896 to 1939.

Notes

1 Ministry of Transport, *National Travel Survey 1964: Part One – Household Vehicle Ownership and Use* (London, HMSO, 1964).

2 L. Pickup, 'Hard to get around: a study of women's travel mobility', in J. Little, L. Peake and P. Richardson (eds), *Women in Cities: Gender and The Urban Environment* (London, Macmillan, 1988), p. 98.

3 L. Pickup, *Housewives' Mobility and Travel Patterns* TRRL, Report LR 971 (Crowthorne, Transport and Road Research Laboratory, 1981).

4 J. Scott, *Gender and The Politics of History* (New York, Columbia University Press, 1988), ch. 2.

5 K. Richardson, *The British Motor Industry 1896–1939* (London, Macmillan, 1977), p. 168.

6 *Ibid.*, p. 182.

7 J. Wajcman, *Feminism Confronts Technology* (Cambridge, Polity Press, 1991), pp. 9–19.

8 *Ibid.*, p. 19.

9 *Ibid.*, p. 22.

10 Cited in R. Sutton, *Motor Mania: Stories from a Motoring Century* (London, Collins & Brown, 1996), p. 16.

11 *Autocar*, 2 June 1905.

12 *The Times*, 11 July 1907.

13 Ministry of Transport, *Report on Fatal Road Accidents which Occurred during the Year 1933* (London, HMSO, 1934), p. 7. There are no remaining licensing records of any significance. Until the creation of the Driving Licence Vehicle Centre in 1972 all licences were issued by local authorities. In 1972 each licensing authority forwarded their licensing records to the DVLA at Swansea. Shortly afterwards these records were returned to their district of origin and destroyed.

14 *Good Housekeeping*, October 1938.

15 *Automobile Association Archives*: Women Drivers File.

16 *Autocar*, 27 April 1901.

17 *Autocar*, 8 April 1905.

18 D. Levitt, *Woman and Her Car* (London, Lane, 1970), p. 8.

19 *Ibid.*, preface.

20 *Ibid.*, p. 4.

21 *Ibid.*, p. 16.

22 *Ibid.*, pp. 31–2.

23 *Ibid.*, p. 42.

24 *Ibid.*, p. 72.

25 H. Barty-King, *A History of the Automobile Association* (Basingstoke, Automobile Association, 1980), p. 35.

26 *Autocar*, 9 May 1903; Levitt, *Woman and Her Car*, foreword.

27 *Autocar*, 5 September 1905.

28 *Automobile Association Archive*, transcript of speech by Stenson Cooke, 6 May 1930.

29 The First Aid Nursing Yeomanry (FANY) helped the Territorial Army raise ten companies of 150 drivers for the army. The 5,000-strong Women's Legion Motor Transport Section did a similar job for the RAF. D. Mitchell, *Women on the Warpath: The Story of Women in the First World War* (London, Cape, 1966), pp. 221–2. M. Izzard, *A Heroine in Her Lifetime: A Life of Dame Helen Gwynne-Vaughn* (London, Macmillan, 1969), p. 281.

30 Richardson, *The British Motor Industry*, p. 169.

31 Mitchell, *Women on the Warpath*, pp. 221–2.

32 *Autocar*, 21 December 1918.

33 *Autocar*, 8 February 1919.

34 *Public Record Office*: HO 45/11164.

35 *Autocar*, 16 April 1921.

36 For a fuller discussion of this question, see A. Light, *Forever England: Femininity, Literature and Conservatism between the Wars* (London, Routledge, 1991); D. Beddoe, *Back to Home and Duty* (London, Pandora, 1989); B. Melman, *Women and The Popular Imagination in The Twenties* (London, Macmillan, 1988); M. Joannou, '"Nothing is Impracticable for a Single Middle-Aged Woman with an Income of Her Own": The Spinster in Women's Fiction of the 1920s', in S. Oldfield (ed.), *This Working-Day World: Women's Lives and Cultures in Britain 1914–1945* (Basingstoke, Macmillan Education, 1994).

37 M. Pugh, *Women and The Women's Movement in Britain 1914–1959*, (Basingstoke, Macmillan Education, 1992), p. 108.

38 J. Laver, *Between the Wars* (London, Houghton, 1961), p. 105.

39 Cited in Pugh, *Women and the Women's Movement*, p. 72.

40 J. Greenfield, 'The ideology of domesticity in popular women's magazines in the 1930s', unpublished M.A. dissertation, University of Warwick, 1991.

41 G. Dawson, 'The blond bedouin: Lawrence of Arabia, imperial adventure and the imagining of English–British masculinity', in M. Roper and J. Tosh (eds), *Manful Assertions: Masculinities in Britain since 1800* (London, Routledge, 1991). See also Pugh, *Women and the Women's Movement*, ch. 4.

42 S. Bowden, 'Demand and supply constraints in the inter-war UK car industry: did the manufacturers get it right?', *Business History*, 33 (1991), 256.

43 *Advertiser's Weekly*, 15 March 1934.

44 *Census* 1931.

45 Beddoe, *Back to Home and Duty*, p. 81.

46 F. Widdowson, '"Educating Teacher": Women and Elementary Teaching in London, 1900–1914', in L. Davidoff and B. Westover

(eds), *Our Work, Our Lives, Our Words*, (London, Macmillan Education, 1986), p. 112.

47 *City of Manchester Watch Committee: Statistical Returns* 1939. Vehicles in each category were: cars 28,759; motor cycles 5,998; goods vehicles 9,689; taxis 1,429.

48 *Morris Owner*, June 1929.

49 *Practical Motorist*, 19 May 1934.

50 *Autocar*, 27 May 1927.

51 *Motor*, 6 November 1934.

52 *Morris Owner*, February 1927.

53 *Autocar*, 21 August 1936.

54 *Autocar*, 4 November 1927.

55 *Autocar*, 21 October 1927.

56 M. L. Berger, 'Women drivers!: the emergence of folklore and stereotypic opinions concerning feminine automotive behaviour, *Women's Studies International Forum*, 9 (1986), 257–63.

57 Respondent 24, Tony Craven: born London 1913.

58 *Morris Owner*, January 1934.

59 C. McShane, *Along the Asphalt Path: The Automobile and the American City* (New York, Columbia University Press, 1994), pp. 149–72.

60 Respondent 17, John Rogers: born Christchurch 1919.

61 See, for example, Wajcman, *Feminism Confronts Technology*, pp. 1–25, on the gendering of scientific discourse.

62 *Garage and Motor Agent*, 15 April 1922.

63 *Autocar*, 12 April 1929.

64 C. W. Evans and D. S. Dannreuther, *Law for the Private Motorist* (London, Pitman, 1936).

65 Cited in *Autocar*, 29 July 1938.

66 *Morris Owner*, February 1930.

67 *Morris Owner*, November 1930.

68 *Autocar*, 3 June 1927.

69 *Autocar*, 4 November 1927.

70 *Daily Express*, 24 July 1935.

71 Respondent 19, Janet Powell: born Essex 1912.

72 *Daily Express*, 24 July 1935.

73 *Autocar*, 15 November 1935. Between 6 May and 26 October 1935, 17,300 of the 80,650 driving-test candidates were women. As in the case of driving licences, a more satisfactory and longer run of data does not exist.

74 Wajcman, *Feminism Confronts Technology*, p. 145.

75 *Autocar*, 12 March 1937.

76 *Autocar*, 11 June 1937.

77 Respondent 35, Jean Rosolen: born Leamington Spa 1924. Respondent 40, Rod Hendrie: born Sutherlandshire 1926.

78 Respondent 72, Betti Mansson: born Bebbington (date unknown).

79 Respondent 58, Molly Day: born Lancashire (date unknown).

80 Respondent 17, William McAvoy: born London 1901.

81 Respondent 16, John Rogers: born Christchurch 1919.

82 Respondent 16, John Rogers: born Christchurch 1919.

83 Respondent 49, Christine Paul: born Wiltshire (date unknown).

84 Respondent 56, Tom Taylor: born 1920.

85 Respondent 18, Janet Powell: born Essex 1912.

86 Respondent 21, Marjorie Sculthorpe: born Warrington 1915.

87 T. Richards, *The Commodity Culture of Victorian England: Advertising and Spectacle 1851–1914* (London, Verso, 1991), p. 206.

88 J. Benson, *The Rise of Consumer Society in Britain 1880–1980*, (London, Longman, 1994), p. 185.

89 See, for example, the discussion of men and fashion in C. Breward, *The Culture of Fashion: A New History of Fashionable Dress* (Manchester, Manchester University Press, 1995).

90 For full exposition of this subject, see V. de Grazia and E. Furlough (eds), *The Sex of Things: Gender and Consumption in Historical Perspective* (Berkeley and Los Angeles, University of California Press, 1996).

91 M. Beetham, *A Magazine of Her Own?: Domesticity and Desire in the Woman's Magazine, 1800–1914* (London, Routledge, 1996).

92 J. Greenfield, S. O'Connell and C. Reid, 'Gender, consumption and the interwar middle classes', in A. Kidd and D. Nicholls (eds), *Gender, Culture and Identity: The British Middle Classes, 1780–1940* (Manchester, Manchester University Press, forthcoming).

93 S. Bowden and P. Turner, 'Some cross-section evidence on the determinants of the diffusion of car ownership in the inter-war UK economy', *Business History*, 35 (1993), 67.

94 Benson, *The Rise of Consumer Society in Britain*, p. 195.

95 R. Scott, *The Female Consumer* (London, Associated Business Programmes, 1976), pp. 139–40.

96 *Automobile Association Archive*, Speech by Stenson Cooke, 6 May 1930.

97 *Motor Trader*, 5 May 1920.

98 *Garage and Motor Agent*, 18 December 1928.

99 G. Reekie, 'Impulsive women, predictable men: psychological constructions of sexual difference in sales literature to 1930', *Australian Historical Studies*, 24 (1991), 359–77.

100 P. Redmayne and H. Weeks, *Market Research* (London, Butterworth, 1931), pp. 151–2.

101 *Blackpool Gazette and Herald*, 6 May 1933.

102 *Advertiser's Weekly*, 28 April 1938.

103 *Motor Trader*, 26 September 1925.

104 *Motor Trader*, 10 August 1927.

105 Cited in R. Church and C. Mullen, 'Cars and corporate culture: the

view from Longbridge 1905–1989', in B. Tilson (ed.), *Made in Birmingham: Design and Industry 1889–1989* (Studley, Brewin, 1989).

106 *Austin Magazine*, September 1934; cited in Church and Mullen, 'Cars and corporate culture', p. 198.

107 *Advertiser's Weekly*, 28 September 1933.

108 *Autocar*, 8 May 1936.

109 D. Gartman, *Auto Opium: A Social History of American Automobile Design* (London, Routledge, 1994), p. 108.

110 *Ibid.*, p. 108.

111 For more on this, see Wajcman, *Feminism Confronts Technology*, p. 126.

3

'The right crowd and no crowding': leisure and the car

This chapter will examine the wide variety of uses to which the car was put during our period. Even by the late 1930s the majority of cars were bought for leisure and, as such, were extremely important as symbolic goods. Sales to commercial travellers, doctors, farmers and other professional and business users were, by the mid-1930s, estimated to stand at between 25 and 40 per cent.[1] Thus, as many as three in every four cars sold were used primarily for leisure. It will be argued that pre-1939 car owners existed in a social world which judged people by their capacity to consume as much as by their capacity for production. The car offered owners a chance to express their social position and good taste, setting them apart symbolically and physically from non-owners. Leisure pursuits will be seen as social practices by which individuals announced and established their position within the social world. Thus, this chapter reiterates the argument that it was not simply matters of utility or cost price which propelled the growth of car ownership.

Attending to this theme will involve a return to many of the class and gender issues examined in the previous chapters. It will be seen that as car ownership diffused it became an important and expressive commodity, fulfilling a variety of roles from the public demonstration of social standing through to the more interior, but interrelated, world of the individual's experience of motoring. Furthermore, as ownership diffused through a diverse range of social groupings, each set of owners mediated their relationship to the car in the context of their own discrete economic and social position. The vast majority of owners throughout the period under investigation were middle class, but it must be emphasised that there were many 'middle-class' identities and, importantly, budgets. This will be illustrated in this chapter through the diversity of uses to which the car was put, from those who travelled on the Continent to the motorists for whom the costs of car ownership severely restricted holiday expenditure. We will also meet, for the first time, some of the numerous criticisms of the car and its owners, many of which could be attributed to perceptions of the car's modernity. Two areas provide the focus for this account of the leisure uses of the car before 1939. First, the role of the car in redefining the leisure patterns and concomitant budgetary arrangements of motoring families will be explored. Second, some of the rituals engaged in by individual car owners or amongst groups of like-minded motorists will be explored. These pursuits were varied, sometimes being mutually antagonistic, and they changed over time. This aspect of our discussion will include an analysis of the role of motoring magazines and clubs, motor sport, and even the emergence of the joyrider. In the process, some of the rituals that have become identified with motoring culture will be explored. In particular, this area of the discussion involves a return to the relationship between masculinity and the car, for it seems that it was in motoring's various subgroups that this relationship was most ardently celebrated. The leisure uses of the car are central to any explanation of the development of the British car culture. Leisure also provides a further strand in our attempt to explain the consumption of the car in its entirety. Indeed, the popularity of the car cannot be explained without a detailed explication of the symbolic value of car ownership. For, from its earliest days, the car became fundamental to peoples' aspirations and desires about themselves as well as their impressions of their contemporaries.

'In the company of people of their own kind': pleasure motoring

John Urry has argued that the cultural practices of tourism are constituted by a set of preferred social activities which are highly structured by distinctions of taste. He writes that 'such practices lead people to want to be in certain places, gazing at particular objects, in the company of specific other types of people'.[2] Urry associates what he calls the 'romantic gaze' with scenery, being on your own, and the middle class; as opposed to the 'collective gaze', a classic example being the working-class seaside holiday.[3] Furthermore, in some cases 'the gaze we experience is structured by pre-existing cultural images in which the physical object is barely "seen" at all.'[4] A survey of motoring maps and accounts of motor tours published in newspapers and motoring magazines in the first four decades of the twentieth century provide a great deal of evidence in support of Urry's argument. Early motoring behaviour and manners were highly dependent on the prevailing tastes of the social groups who became car owners. The car offered owners the chance to express their status and their distinction from less wealthy groups in society. It provided this not only in terms of its own existence as a sought-after consumer product, but also in the opportunity it gave to owners to translate the social space between them and 'social inferiors' into geographical space. This was most clearly expressed in advertising for the socially exclusive Brooklands racing track, which carried the legend: '[T]he right crowd and no crowding.'

The car gave its owners a degree of independence that rival forms of transport could not match. Its mobility and speed meant it contrasted sharply with the train and other forms of public and private transport. These attributes of the car dovetailed neatly with the values of middle-class society, as *Autocar* pointed out in 1929: 'public transport, no matter how fast and comfortable, inflicts a sensation of serfdom which is intolerable to a free Briton. It dictates the time of starting, the route, the speed and the stoppages.'[5] The car, even more than the bicycle before it, provided the traveller with a sensation that was markedly different from that experienced through train travel. John Ruskin had bemoaned the railway's transmutation of a traveller 'into a living parcel'; the car offered liberation from this sense of commodification.[6] Instead, car ownership provided the opportunity to continue another form of commodification, that of selected aspects of 'English' heritage and landscape begun by the late-nineteenth-century cycling boom. The car, with its greater range, speed and comfort, increased the range of what Urry terms the 'romantic gaze' of the early-twentieth-century upper and middle classes.

A September 1905 edition of *The Times* offered readers a perspective on this aspect of the car; producing a breathless account of one afternoon's motor trip which reflected the new spatial and temporal rhythms that the car could offer. The article set out to explain the 'fascination it exercises upon its votaries' by recounting how the car enabled its occupants to travel to and through a number of culturally valued places whilst simultaneously ensuring that less esteemed sites were rapidly dismissed from view. The journey commenced in Abingdon and took in elevated views of Oxford, although the party did not stop to take in the perspective. They welcomed the speed of the descent from their vantage point because their route took them past 'rows of modern tenements so commonplace that the normal pace of a powerful car was no disadvantage.' Eynsham was described as 'the first place of any importance reached'. It was traversed at 'a moderate pace' and the 'impression left' on the travellers

> was really almost as complete as if one had been afoot, and far more rapid. It was an impression of substantial cottages, and houses, mostly of stone, *old but not very old*; and we should have found little more to detain us had we halted; for the Benedictine Abbey only the site can be traced on the spot – its history is in books – and the church, pleasing as it is generally, does not repay particular investigation into details.[7]

A highlight of the journey was the Cotswolds village of Burford, which was approached with eager anticipation: 'The upland air was exhilarating; the sensation of those who travelled was as of gliding through space.' The motorists paid Burford the tribute of actually descending from their vehicle, as it was judged 'a place for a sojourn, not for a rushing visit'. Without a trace of irony, given the author's means of transport, Burford was praised for its 'complete freedom from any suspicion of modernity' and its 'ancient streets' and associations with Charles II and William Lenthall (speaker of the Long Parliament) were lauded. The party then moved breathlessly on to Bilbury, described by William Morris as 'surely the most beautiful village in England', but the motorists did not stop: 'Upon its loveliness we did but glance in passing, and none of us had ever looked upon it, or anything equal to it before.' The sights of Cirencester, Fairford, Buscot and Faringdon were all viewed before the trip was completed.[8]

Thus the car facilitated what could be called a partial discovery of the nation, for which motorists could equip themselves with maps such as Bartholomew's *Contour Motoring Map of the British Isles* of 1907, which included a small inset map identifying industrial areas to avoid.[9] Industrial regions were not avoided for aesthetic reasons alone, as Ronald Gene recalled when narrating memories of a family trip in the 1920s. Being the family's junior member he was placed in the dickey seat of their Morris Cowley as the family set off from Great Sutton, near Chester, on route to Stratford-on-Avon. The journey was exciting; however, his most vivid memory was of being 'exposed to a variety of horrid industrial smells' as the car passed through Birmingham.[10]

The troublesome presence of industrial areas on the major roads taken by touring motorists was not the only inconvenience faced by late-Victorian and Edwardian car owners. The railway age had taken its toll on the infrastructure which had once supported coach travel. Roads and inns off the major routes were not ready to meet the new demands of motoring. Moreover, the luxury image of the car ensured that inn- and hotel-keepers often took the opportunity to charge motorists excessive prices for meals and accommodation, anticipating richer pickings from this class of business than could be expected from cyclists.[11] Furthermore, concerns about safety and the damage to rural roads caused by motorists resulted in the introduction of speed traps to ensnare motorists travelling at more than the 20 m.p.h. limit set down by the 1903 Motor Car Act. The two largest motoring associations, the RAC and the AA, did a great deal to defend the interests of motorists. Indeed, the AA was formed in 1905 to frustrate police road traps by employing scouts on bicycles to warn motorists of upcoming speed traps.[12] By 1909 the AA had 10,000 members, a figure that had risen to over 82,000 (50,000 car owners and 32,000 motor cyclists) by 1914.[13] The AA's membership fee was £2 2s a year, a sum that covered all legal costs in the event of prosecution.

The RAC and the AA echoed measures that had been taken earlier by the Cyclists' Touring Club (CTC) in respect of accommodation and meals in hotels and inns. Increasingly numerous from the 1880s onwards, cyclists were initially unwelcome visitors at inns that were no longer catering for road traffic. The cyclists' unfamiliar apparel, which was often dusty or muddy, did not improve matters. The CTC campaigned to persuade local authorities to improve roads and erect signposts, whilst it also negotiated fixed accommodation and meal rates at hotels for cyclists.[14] The RAC and AA made similar arrangements. By 1910, the latter's Hotel and Agents Scheme had signed up 1,000 hoteliers and repairers who offered AA members favourable rates.[15] Despite their efforts, articles and letters in *Autocar* and *Motor* were still denigrating the standards in British inns and hotels well into the 1920s. The problem of the roads was addressed, with significant effect, through the formation of the Road Board in 1910. This committee oversaw the distribution of a Road Fund, raised from direct, progressive taxation on motor vehicles, to rural authorities who were thereby able to place tarmac on the roads under their control. By 1915 the Road Board had spent £2.25 million for this purpose.[16]

The other great problem faced by the pioneering automobilists was the design and technical limitations of early motor cars. Every journey involved the strong possibility of a breakdown or puncture. One of the earliest motoring enthusiasts was Rudyard Kipling, whose letters kept friends and family informed of his adventures in a series of 'Coughing Janes'. Writing to his mother-in-law in 1901, he offered a colourful account of a very public breakdown: 'You won't know Brighton or Brighton seafront, so you will never understand the joy of breaking down for lack of fuel under the eyes of 5,000 Brighton Hackmen and about 2,000,000 trippers.'[17] Of course, there were far more inconvenient spots for a breakdown than Brighton, and the professional chauffeur was a necessity for many of the earliest motorists, who were without the know-how or desire to engage in dirty and tricky roadside repairs.

By 1914 the motorist could expect to be within reach of a garage or repair shop with at least rudimentary knowledge of motor mechanics.[18] But it was not until the inter-war years that they could be truly sanguine about undertaking lengthy drives in the rural areas of Britain. In these years cars became more reliable, garages more numerous, and the AA and RAC 'get you home' services, complete with networks of approved mechanics and phone boxes for the use of members, became more widespread. The AA had begun installing roadside telephone boxes for the use of its members in 1914.[19] During 1926, 7,500 of the RAC's members made use of its roadside phone boxes, a figure that rose to 11,000 by 1929 when there were 421 RAC phone boxes available for members' use and 2,000 official RAC repairers.[20] Partly as a result of such schemes, membership of the motoring organisations rose rapidly. The AA, which regularly released its membership figures, claimed over 82,000 members by 1914 and over 600,000 by 1937.[21] However, membership of a motoring organisation could not protect

During her girlhood, just after the First World War, Antoinette Duncan   **4**
experienced the high and low points of motoring.

cars or their owners from the vicissitudes of the British climate or
dusty roads. Mary Tye recalled motoring in her family's first car, a
GWK tourer, bought in 1920 and christened 'Daisy'. All occupants of
the car were exposed to the weather, and Mary reflected on encounters
with inclement weather: 'many times unless we were over the rubicon
my father turned round and headed for home.' No matter what time
the family returned home they 'had to leather Daisy down and cover
[her] with sheets.' The Tyes were clearly attached to 'Daisy', and when
the car was sold they 'all cried'.[22]

Saloon cars did not arrive in any great number until 1926, when
new patents facilitated mass production of pressed-steel bodies. By the
end of the 1920s, open-tourer models were a rare sight in the car
showroom.[23] The limited protection offered by tourers meant that many
motorists confined their expeditions to the spring and summer months.
This was particularly the case for longer journeys. Betti Mansson, from
the Wirral, recalled winter trips in her family's Bullnose Morris during
the 1920s as being 'very uncomfortable' even with the aid of cushions
and hot-water bottles. A 'muff' or old blanket was also required in
order to prevent the radiator freezing over.[24] If the car went any length

of time without use, the radiator had to be drained. Starting the car in the first place could present the appreciable inconvenience of pouring hot water over engine parts, taking out the warming plugs, stuffing rags into air intakes and, if all else failed, pushing or towing.

Cars could be licensed on a quarterly basis and many motorists protected their cars from the elements during the winter months and avoided the attendant problems of starting a car in cold weather, or driving on winter roads, by taking advantage of this facility. Of course, part-yearly licensing also allowed some motorists to cut the costs of car ownership. Indeed, the available licensing figures indicate that the pro-portion of car owners who engaged in this practice actually grew in the 1920s and early 1930s. Whereas in 1924 virtually three cars in every four were licensed on an annual basis, by 1931 the figure had dropped to virtually one in two.[25] March 25th, the first day of the spring-licensing period, was known amongst motorists as the 'Glorious 25th'. It was an eagerly anticipated date for those like the Rosolen family of Birmingham. Jean Rosolen recalled her 'mother crossing the days off on the calender until we could have the car again.'[26]

The greater comfort and reliability of inter-war cars, together with improving facilities for touring motorists, ensured that the inter-war decades, and in particular the 1920s, have been frequently identified in popular motoring histories as a golden age. In many accounts of the inter-war period, the sense of loss felt for this motoring epoch seems also to be tinged with a tangible feeling of a lost era of middle-class privilege, when car ownership conferred the opportunity to leave the 'smoky cities' and their working-class inhabitants behind. This mood was also evident in comments made by our sample of pre-1939 motorists. Tony Craven, a motorist since the early 1930s, offered the following observation:

> I don't want to sound in any way snobbish about this but when you got motor cars in the hands of the sort of chap who would go down to the seaside in his braces with mum and the kids in the back and so on, I think the standard of road behaviour probably dropped a bit, if you see what I mean. Well, in exactly the same way the regard for the British overseas sort of diminished when the package tour became popular.[27]

Contemporary commentators frequently remarked upon the 'herd instinct' of the touring motorist. Though the motor car was enmeshed in ideas of individual freedom and was said to give the motoring family the opportunity to explore Britain independently, it seems that all too often they chose to travel the same, all too popular, roads. Reports of congestion emerged in the early 1920s, with both cars and other forms of motorised transport contributing to the problem. John Rogers remembered the heavy holiday traffic that struggled across a bridge over the river Stour, *en route* to Bournemouth, during his childhood in the 1920s. The bridge had only one-way capacity and the RAC supervised crossing traffic, which often tailed back as far as half a mile.[28] Marjorie Sculthorpe recalled how, in 1937, her fiancé's second-hand car broke down after being caught in a traffic jam in the popular Southwest of England.[29] In 1925 the motoring writer John Prioleau described a recent summer trip on the London to Brighton road:

> One day last summer, it was my extraordinary ill-luck to drive up from Brighton to London in the evening between 6 o'clock and 9 o'clock, and as a result of those three appalling hours, I decided that nothing but 'life and death' shall drag me, either in my own or someone else's car, to Brighton during the summer. From the Brighton Aquarium to St James's Street I was not for one moment out of what can only be described as a queue of private cars, and motor bikes of every sort and size, and more chars-a-bancs than I believed existed. Quite apart from the dust, the crowd, and above all the intolerable noise, the danger to everyone concerned was considerable.[30]

This example is of interest in two respects. First, it tempers the golden-age imagery to some extent. Not only were roads narrower and of poorer quality than those of today, but if a motorist was unfortunate enough to end up in a traffic jam, the noise of dozens of inter-war motor engines would have been most unpleasant. Second, it is indicative of the skewed impact that the car had in the Southeast of England, where the affluent middle classes were to be found in the largest numbers. In 1938 just under 20 per cent of all households in this area owned a car compared with under 12 per cent in the North of England.[31]

For many motorists the new spatial freedom brought by car ownership was achieved by cost-cutting elsewhere in the family budget, and thus the car was not entirely appreciated by the traditional commercial outlets which had catered for the middle-class holidaymaker. This was certainly the case by the 1920s and 1930s as the reduction in car prices extended ownership amongst less affluent middle-income groups. The car offered owners the ability to travel quickly to a resort and back home again on the same day, thereby eliminating the need for accommodation. Motorists often carried their own food and drink, much to the chagrin of the service sector in coastal towns. Whilst letters in the motoring press complained of the excessive charges for parking made by the councils of seaside resorts, the business communities of those towns cursed the picnicking tourists and their cars. In 1933, for example, both Blackpool and Fleetwood corporations experimented by providing free car-parking on their respective sea-front promenades. Both trials were brought to an end by local critics. The chairman of the Fleetwood Ratepayers' Association said that he did not think 'motorists brought anything to the town in the way of renumeration' because most of them 'carried baskets containing refreshments, and littered the Promenade with their refuse'.[32]

A further cause for concern to the resorts that had been the traditional destinations of middle-class holiday-makers was the opportunity the private car gave for exploration of new destinations, whether smaller coastal towns or the historic highways and byways of rural Britain. The railways had concentrated provision for holidays in a comparatively small number of large resorts, each with its own place in the social spectrum: Bournemouth, Torquay, Scarborough and Southport were amongst those popular with the middle classes. Rising car ownership exacerbated the social segregation of seaside resorts. It also generated increased interest in resorts off the beaten track, such as Newquay and St Ives.[33] Increasing working-class utilisation of the charabanc and cheap excursion trains further exacerbated this tendency. As Alan Jackson has noted, it caused the 'beleaguered middle classes to range still further afield' to Devon and Cornwall, West and Northwest Wales and the Highlands and Islands of Scotland, or 'to strengthen their hold on existing bastions' such as Frinton, Southwold, Aldeburgh, Sheringham, Seaview, Sidmouth, Deal and Rye.[34] The testimony of Joan Russell, the daughter of a successful Liverpudlian chartered accountant, provides further evidence of this trend. She recalled the family holidaying in Blackpool in the 1920s with an aunt who resided there. However, by 1930 her father 'had forsaken Blackpool as a holiday resort' because 'in school holidays more and more people were taking their children to the beautiful sandy beaches, but my parents had a dislike of lots of noisy people.' The Russells 'tried Bispham and Cleveleys for a while before settling on Deganwy'. However, the increasing popularity of North Wales amongst motorists meant that their journey was frequently prolonged by road congestion.[35]

As has been seen, for many car ownership was only possible by combining incomes or making savings elsewhere in family spending. One result of this was an increasing incidence of day trips at the expense of more extended holidays by the sea or elsewhere. As has been indicated already, the picnicking motorist was perhaps the most commonly appreciated aspect of this phenomenon. Indeed, for many families there was something ritualistic about this aspect of motoring. Rod Hendrie, whose family lived in rural Sutherlandshire, recalled family picnics on the shores of Loch Ness in the 1920s and 1930s: 'outings seemed to be a ritual, if the weather was nice then every Sunday we'd be away in that car. Saturday night the ritual of the big roast joint, which would be got ready for Sunday. We always had a picnic, and the mainstay of the picnic would still be the roast joint, which eventually would be sliced up and served to us on bread.'[36]

It seems likely that by the 1930s the Sunday drive was just as popular as more deeply rooted rituals such as church-going. A Gallop Poll, taken in 1949, when motoring was still seriously hampered by post-war austerity, revealed that one in seven people went motoring on Sunday, the same number as attended a church service.[37] Certainly, throughout the 1920s and 1930s, church leaders expressed concern about the impact of private motoring on church attendance. In 1923 a Church of England conference was informed that the factors increasing 'paganism' amongst the young included 'cheap cars'.[38] By 1936 the Secretary of the National Sunday School Union was blaming the car for diminishing attendance at Sunday school, as parents took families on day trips instead.[39] Two years later Sir Sydney Jones told the General Assembly of Unitarian and Free Christian Churches that society was 'too immersed in the idea of speed' and had 'set up a golden calf' with 'four wheels' and 'fed on petrol'.[40] Of course, this particular strand of criticism of motoring should be seen in the context of long-term decline in church attendance. Car-owning families with strong religious beliefs could use their mobility to attend a church service during the course of their Sunday outing. By the late 1920s churches in popular motoring areas, such as Callow-with-Dewsall near Hereford and Cirencester, were encouraging motorists to attend their evening services before commencing the journey home.[41]

Other families, such as those of Mary Stanley and Gordon Cox, who held strong religious beliefs, did not motor on Sundays at all.[42]

Another group aggrieved by the growing impact of the car on middle-class leisure patterns was hoteliers. Having previously relied on the comparative lack of mobility among holiday-makers, hoteliers and others resented both the flexibility offered by the car and its drain upon family budgets. The trade magazine *British Boarding House Proprietor and Private Hotelier* returned to the subject of the car regularly throughout the 1930s.[43] One of its anxieties was over the increase of the 'touring habit' among car owners, motor-cyclists and cyclists and the concomitant tendency for such travellers to stay for one night only, causing greater uncertainty for hotel owners. The motoring organisations responded to this trend, producing a growing range of touring itineraries which catered for the differing budgets among their membership. The standard AA itinerary simply followed the most direct route available, but for holiday purposes a series of options were offered. Some itineraries tendered a fairly direct route from *A* to *B* whilst attempting to provide views of as much attractive scenery as possible. Alternatively, members could request an itinerary covering a predetermined number of days, with the distances to be undertaken also subject to the individual's discretion. A further possibility were *Day Drive Booklets* which offered recommended routes from a large number of towns that were used as touring centres. Examples cited in 1935 included Brighton, Oban, Monmouth, Scarborough, Torquay and the Lake District. The final alternative was the 'Tourlet', a series of short drives suitable for half-day or afternoon trips from a wide range of starting points. During the summer months of 1934, 700,000 itineraries were issued. No distinction was made between itineraries that might have been issued to cover business trips and those intended as holiday excursions, but this fragmentary information may offer one way of estimating the frequency of motor touring.[44] In 1934 the AA claimed a membership of 500,000, which suggests that there were 1.4 itinerary requests for every member in the summer of that year. Of course, it must also be assumed that for every expedition undertaken with the aid of an itinerary dozens more would have been undertaken without them.

From the hotelier's perspective this new flexibility gave rise to increasing and cheaper competition, and it seemed to *British Boarding House Proprietor and Private Hotelier* 'as if everybody with a spare room is advertising for bed and breakfast or offering teas'.[45] The family of Jean Rosolen were amongst those to whom car ownership was hard won, but one of its rewards was more control and flexibility over holiday accommodation and spending. Mr Rosolen ran a shop and lending library in Ward End, a working-class district of Birmingham, with his wife working as a hairdresser in the shop's rear. They and their two daughters lived in fairly modest accommodation, without an indoor toilet, above the shop. Jean recalled the excitement caused by the arrival of the family's first car: 'The front room we had as a sitting room and this overlooked the main road … Mother took us up there and said "Look through the window" – and we saw this little car – and she said "That's ours!" It was such a thrill!' She also remembered a holiday, undertaken in 1935, in the Minehead area, during which the family rented a room from a local woman who cooked meals based on food bought locally by the Rosolens, who spent their days touring Somerset.[46]

The increasing popularity of camping and caravanning also caused concern amongst hoteliers. In 1935 *Hotel and Boarding House* described the increase in camping holidays as 'prodigious'. It believed that 'the increasing popularity of the motor-car has done much to bring this about' because 'owners of cars can easily get about the country with a tent and folding beds packed with the luggage on the back. They can camp wherever they wish for as little as 1/–, and at the most 1/6 per night!'[47] A survey carried out by the magazine revealed that campers included 'many good class people who previously stayed in hotels'. Some had chosen this new form of holiday 'because they like the open-air life, others … because it saves money'.[48] However, the writer did not attempt to estimate the numbers involved in either category. It can be assumed that the majority of these campers were likely to be amongst the less-well-off motorists, making a virtue out of a necessity, such as Mollie Farrell and her husband. Both were teachers, working for the London County Council, but Mollie was forced by the marriage bar to give up work after their wedding in 1928. Family holidays, along with their two children, involved camping either at her father's farm in Berkshire or at the seaside.[49]

Caravanning, however, was a more expensive pursuit. Its popularity began to rise in the 1920s.[50] The costs of caravan ownership were prohibitive for many families. The cheapest models built by Raven, Cheltenham, Carlight or Airlight retailed at between £50 and 100.[51]

5   The domestic gender division of labour was replicated when Norman Owen's parents went caravanning in Barmouth in 1937.

Even these economy models represented a sizeable sum to the average middle-class salary-earner and by 1933 only 3,500 private caravans were in use.[52] An alternative was to rent a caravan; firms such as the Nomad Caravan Company, on the newly built Kingston by-pass, charged from five guineas per week in 1932.[53] This method offered far more motorists the chance to engage in caravanning holidays, and 150,000 families were estimated to have hired a caravan in 1935.[54] By this time, motoring magazines were making their readers aware of camping and caravan sites set aside for their use in Cornwall, Dorset, Hampshire, Kent, Somerset and numerous other counties and seaside resorts. From 1933 the AA annually published *Caravan and Camp Sites in England, Scotland and Wales*. Despite hoteliers' concerns about the twin threat of caravanning and camping motorists, it seems highly likely that both practices were confined largely to younger car owners who were more likely to have financial reasons to holiday in this manner and were also more willing to forgo the comforts of the conventional hotel or boarding-house holiday. In 1931, John Sailor, a farmer's son who had recently acquired his driving licence, drove from his home in Essex to a hotel in Porlock, Somerset where he deposited his mother for her week's holiday. John and a friend spent the week touring the surrounding countryside and camping out on Exmoor, where washing in the cold streams 'proved a memorable experience'.[55]

Just as the appearance of large numbers of working-class patrons at seaside resorts would ensure a migration of their middle-class contemporaries, so the arrival of large numbers of touring middle-class motorists on the highway encouraged more of the very wealthiest motorists to make for Continental roads. The inter-war years saw a significant rise in the numbers heading to Europe, creating a further distinction amongst the motoring classes that again centred on financial resources. Aldous Huxley's report of his own foreign motor touring indicates that, just as in earlier centuries, one of the attractions of the European tour in the 1920s involved the acquisition of cultural capital, with those engaging in this activity gaining 'merit and superiority over the stay-at-homes':

> The fact is that very few travellers like travelling. If they go to the trouble and expense of travelling, it is not so much from curiosity, for fun, or because they like to see things beautiful and strange, as out of a kind of snobbery. People travel for the same reason as they collect works of art: because the best people do it. To have been to certain spots on the earth's surface is socially correct; and having been there, one is superior to those who have not. Moreover, travelling gives one something to talk about when one gets home. The subjects of conversation are not so numerous that one can neglect an opportunity of adding to one's store.[56]

Continental motoring was obviously the exclusive pursuit of the very wealthiest in the years before the 1914–18 war, but its popularity had increased markedly by the end of the 1930s, as had the facilities on offer for the Europe-bound motorist. Immediately after the war the costs of Continental motoring were prohibitive. The greatest deterrent was the deposits that were demanded from motorists before they were granted entrance to their Continental destination. France, for example, demanded a deposit of £700 for a car valued at £1,000 in the early 1920s. This levy had been introduced to prevent British owners selling their cars in France. In 1922 the AA and the RAC announced that they were prepared to act as guarantors of the genuine touring nature of a motoring trip, but the traveller still had to stump up a £100 deposit, together with an approved banker's indemnity for the balance of the duty on the car.[57] There are no figures available for the number of motorised tourists leaving the UK before 1924, but with such obstacles in the way it is highly likely that very few of the 550,000 who left Britain to tour Europe in 1921 took a motor car with them.[58] However, the numbers of cars being taken on foreign touring trips rose steadily in the 1920s and 1930s, from an estimated 7,026 in 1924 to 17,784 in 1931.[59] These figures, calculated in 1933, suggest that between 50,000 and 60,000 holiday-makers were motoring abroad in 1930, if we adopt the original calculation of an average three travellers per vehicle. This figure would mean that approximately every twentieth British tourist visiting the Continent did so by car. With the total number of private cars in use in Britain in that year standing at 1,056,000 it is apparent that only a tiny minority, less than 2 per cent, of motorists were taking their cars abroad.

The records of the motoring organisations indicate that, following a blip during the economic crisis of the early 1930s, foreign touring continued to increase in popularity as the decade progressed. In 1934 the RAC and AA provided the paperwork for more than 22,000 Europe-bound cars; by 1938 this figure had risen by 72 per cent to 38,000.[60] There were a number of explanations for this growth, but the main one was that touring became less expensive as a result of competition between France and Germany to attract foreign currency. Bureaucratic procedures were also lifted as a result of this rivalry.[61] Most significantly the requirements for customs deposits on entering France and Germany were abolished.[62] Touring was also simplified in 1932 by the introduction of the Autocheque, a voucher which was handed in at Continental hotels in lieu of cash.[63] The *Autocheque Handbook* of 1936 described how the Autocheque covered dinner, room, Continental breakfast, gratuities and garage. Thousands of hotels were involved in the scheme, which encompassed Austria, Belgium, Czechoslovakia, France, Germany, Great Britain, Holland, Ireland, Portugal, Norway, Sweden, Denmark, Spain, Switzerland, Luxembourg and Italy.[64]

However, even after the reductions of the mid-1930s, the costs of travelling overseas with a car were still appreciable. In the immediate post-war years the Southern Railway Company had a monopoly on carrying cars to France, as they controlled all the steamers and charges were high. By 1930, the former shipping-insurance brokers Townsend Brothers Limited had a specially adapted cargo boat operating on the Dover–Calais route.[65] By 1935 fares on the Southern Railways operated

Autocarrier were from £2 5s 6d to £7 15s 8d, depending on the length of car and whether shipment was at the owner's or company's risk. Passengers travelled for 12s 6d: these were single fares only.[66] To these costs must be added the £3 charged by the RAC and AA for all necessary documentation and the actual costs of the holiday.

The majority of motorists, who could not afford Continental jaunts, nonetheless had a mobility that could be exploited in a variety of ways. Car ownership allowed them to transfer social space into geographical space, whether through family drives into the countryside or through visits to assorted commercial outlets, which were themselves arranged in a hierarchical fashion. An example were the out-of-town facilities that began catering for motorists, ranging from roadhouses, which sprang up largely in the Southeast, to private golf clubs and right up to the grandest country clubs.[67] In 1931 the *Autocar* offered its interpretation of the social function of such establishments, focusing on the Roadhouse:

> The working classes have their hops in the assembly rooms two or three times a week … but the time will come when more people, classified by their ownership of a car, will find suitable rendezvous of their own. One of the kind I have in mind already exists in The Bell House at Beaconsfield, a comfortable evening's run from Oxford, Maidenhead, Windsor, Staines and London. Here one can have a meal at very reasonable cost, or just a coffee, and there is a ballroom and a swimming-pool. A gay little place for motorists who want to shake themselves out of the rut occasionally in the company of people of their own kind.[68]

A similar sense of the car providing membership of a club emerged when interviewees spoke about its role in middle-class courtship. Several respondents claimed that, far from seeing a suitor's car as the site of potential moral danger, parents welcomed the spectacle of a young man come-a-courting their daughter in a smart-looking vehicle because it provided a clear indication that he was getting on in life. William McAvoy was one interviewee who felt this was the case. He said: 'I think it was more or less a sort of promise that the boy was going to get on, if he could afford a car he was going to get on. Because getting on was terribly important.'[69] Marjorie Sculthorpe, the daughter of an industrial chemist, had a similar impression, narrating how she and her fiancé had gone off on a motoring holiday in 1937 with her parents' approval. By the same token she was allowed to go to office dances that went on until two in the morning, but not 'Saturday night six-penny hops' in St Helens. She had met her fiancé through friends at work, two young women from Rainhill, whose social life she was drawn into. She described this as a 'different world' for her. Several of the young people in the 'Rainhill set' had cars, including her future husband. He taught in Liverpool and would alternate driving to work with one or two car-owning colleagues in order to save on running costs. Although his place in the motoring community was precarious, he maintained it for long enough to solidify his relationship with Marjorie, who subsequently viewed the role of the car in her life as a 'great liberator': 'The car made all the difference … We may not even have stayed together, or what shall I say, it may not even have got that far without a car because it would have been not impossible but a bit difficult.'[70] For them, the car was all-important. When the old Austin Seven finally gave up on them, on the way back from a holiday in the West Country in 1937, they were forced to sell it to a nearby garage for the knock-down price of 30 shillings. They did not replace it, saving instead to pay for their wedding. Bicycles replaced the car, for a number of years, as their mode of individual transport, although they did hire cars and holiday with friends in Anglesey in 1938 and Cornwall in 1939.

This example brings together the three threads of the argument that have been put forward here. First, it demonstrates that the car did have utility value in getting a young professional from *A* to *B*. It also had utility value in allowing a young middle-class couple to continue a courtship that would otherwise have been difficult. Second, it offers further evidence of the possible symbolic value of car ownership. In this case the car provided Marjorie's parents with evidence of a young suitor's social standing and credibility. Third, it serves as a further example of the need to examine the consumption of the car in its entirety, for the car was often central to people's images of each other as well as their dreams about themselves. Thus, car ownership had an emblematic status from its inception. The meanings of particular models, destinations and even of ownership itself changed as new social groups became motorists, but the car retained a clear role as marker of group and individual identity and status. In his autobiography, *Bright Morning*, Don Haworth tells the story of his Burnley childhood, offering a description of the Sunday-motoring rituals of his neighbours, the

Ryders, whose father was a senior bank clerk: "'Do you go to Black-pool?" my brother asked. "Better places than Blackpool", Harry [Ryder] said. My brother asked my grandfather where could be better than Blackpool. My grandfather couldn't think. "We want to get a car", my brother said, "then we'd find out".'[71]

Not very far away, in Southport, lived a young girl, Antoinette Duncan, who could have offered Harry an answer: 'We used to motor down to Juan Les Pins, through France. Roads were long and empty. We stopped for meals which I adored; long sticks of bread I loved and they smelt of sour dough. The waiters wearing aprons, and the red wine in bottles which I was not allowed to drink, so after the meal I stole the black cherries put on the table with fruit and I went up to the bedroom and squeezed them! It looked like red wine.'[72]

From motor clubs to joyriding: a range of motoring rituals explored

In the years before 1939 motoring was often described as a 'hobby'. However, as this study has shown, car owners were far from a homo-geneous group despite their shared interest in this burgeoning tech-nology. Within the ranks of motorists there were many groups, replete with their own elaborate rites, jargon and technical knowledge. Some of the more interesting of these circles will be reviewed in the remainder of this chapter. It will be shown that the practice of many of these motoring rituals reinforced the relationship between masculinity and the car. Nowhere was this truer than in the case of motor sport where, as Bert Moorehouse has indicated in his study of America's hot-rod culture, notions of masculinity have often been associated with danger and bravery. As a result, 'Men can gain pride, respect, assert and confirm identity by pitting themselves against fear.'[73]

As was seen in the preceding chapter, motor sport had a small number of women participants almost from its inception. However, it appears that as the sport developed and a supervisory structure evolved, the obstacles placed in the way of female competitors were multiplied. If women motorists were symbolic of shifting gender relations, then the women who took part in motor sport struck right at the heart of attempts to identify motoring with masculinity. Women drivers faced problems from the administrators at the premier British race track,

Brooklands, where they were not allowed to compete in ordinary meetings until 1931.[74] Even then their success or failure on the track depended not only on their skill at the wheel but also on the whims of the male committee. In 1931 the Brooklands' authorities banned Elsie Wisdom's 130 m.p.h. car, arguing that 'no woman could drive it.'[75] The following year Wisdom and her partner Joan Richmond became the first female winners of the British 1,000-mile race, beating sixty men. Their winning margin was five miles and their victory was the first-ever international class win for women on the track.[76] However, the following year the Junior Car Club considered banning women from the competition because it was, in their opinion, too dangerous.[77] Only in 1936 was equality allowed in all meetings by the British Automobile Racing Club, who were responsible for Brooklands.

Elsie Wisdom took the opportunity her high profile offered to castigate the racing establishment, who, in her words, had 'earned the unenviable distinction of being an anti-feminine organisation.'[78] This provoked a fierce response from readers of *Autocar*, one of whom offered this advice: 'to put it bluntly they [women] are not wanted in what are purely masculine events'. He believed that 'famous lady motorists' had achieved their status through 'the persistence of their press agents' rather than by actual performance. However, he was unable to articulate what he felt were 'the other purely masculine reasons why women are not wanted in what are regarded as exclusively male events'.[79] It is likely that attempts to exclude women from motor racing represented an attempt to define and defend the function of the sport as a bastion of manliness: a space where, in the absence of women, a rugged brand of masculinity could be celebrated. To enter this male world it was also necessary to learn the technical language spoken by its adherents. In R. Denne Waterhouse's novel *Week-End Ticket* (1934) Lois gains an insight into the motor-racing fan's idiosyncratic idiom: 'She learnt, for example, that a "blown bug" is not an exhausted woodlouse but a supercharged Buggatti, and that keeping up the revs. is not supporting the clergy but maintaining engine speed.'[80]

Reports on motor sport were one of the essential draws for regular readers of motoring magazines such as *Autocar* and *Motor*, as well as specialist magazines such as *Speed*. Coverage of motor sport was evocatively illustrated by artists such as F. Gordon Crosby, who was employed by *Autocar* from 1907.[81] Another cohort of motoring magazines were

The car seems rather inconsequential amongst the male camaraderie of the   **6**
1930s' University of Liverpool Motor Club.

produced by motor manufacturers, keen to establish marque loyalty amongst the owners of their cars. One or two such magazines were produced before 1914, but it was in the 1920s and 1930s that their numbers multiplied and each large manufacturer felt the need to produce one. By 1939 *Austin Magazine* claimed 35,000 readers; *Vauxhall Motorist* had an audited circulation of 43,000; *Modern Motoring*, published by the Rootes group, claimed a 23,500 circulation; and *Morris Owner* estimated its circulation at 43,000. Others included the *Standard Car Review* and the Singer Motor Club's *Popular Motoring*.[82] The publication of these magazines was part of a concerted effort by manufacturers to establish product loyalty amongst the motorists who drove their vehicles. Another feature of this approach was the encouragement and financial support offered by manufacturers to motorists who set up clubs based around the ownership of particular marques.

The earliest car clubs, such as the Essex Motor Club, which was created in 1904, were based around towns or counties.[83] They were reformed, and others formed, in the immediate post-war years. The committees of these clubs invariably contained members of the local elite, with members of both houses of Parliament often to be found on the membership roles, as were many Justices of the Peace. Membership levels varied in size. One of the largest, the Lancashire Automobile Club, had over 800 members in 1927 and over 1,000 by 1932.[84] By 1926 Blackpool and Fylde Motor Club boasted a membership of 500, whilst the Oxford Motor Club had 179 car owners and 40 motor-cycle owners on their register.[85] Many car clubs emulated the activities of those who sped around motor-racing circuits like Brooklands. Clubs such as those in Leeds and Stalybridge had their own private race-tracks and attracted large crowds; 5,000 attended speed trials at the Stalybridge track in June 1927.[86] Clubs which did not possess their own private facilities made alternative arrangements. In June 1928, for example, the Newcastle and District Car Club arranged a day's racing on the beach at Seaton Carew in County Durham. They were rewarded with a massive crowd, estimated at 80,000.[87] Other sand races were regularly held at Pendine, Porthcawl, Skegness, Southport and Weston-super-Mare, their popularity boosted by a ban imposed on speed events on public roads in 1925.[88]

Manufacturers appreciated the positive publicity offered by car clubs based on their marques. In a highly stratified society, such as early-twentieth-century Britain, the consumption of goods made firm and visible a particular set of judgements which enabled the categorisation of both people and commodities. This process was strengthened when consumption took place within the context of ritualised group behaviour which publicly defined status, power and meaning. Car clubs were there-fore a phenomenon that elicited a very evocative symbolism, and manufacturers were keen to harness their emblematic traits in order to emphasise the increased social status that could be gleaned by owner-ship of their products. Manufacturers who actively encouraged clubs to form around their cars included Arrol-Johnston, Aston-Martin, Austin, Jowett, Riley, Singer and Morris (including the separate MG Car Club). By the end of the 1930s events arranged by the clubs of the most popular cars attracted very large attendances. In June 1939, 2,500 Morris cars assembled at Donnington for a meeting organised by the magazine *Morris Owner*. Events held included a gymkhana competition, a coach-work competition and various tests of driving ability.[89] Two weeks later

Ford held their own gymkhana at Brooklands and attracted a reported congregation of 25,000.[90]

That such large crowds were drawn to these events in the summer of 1939 is in many ways at odds with the common perception of the car as the great vehicle of individualism.[91] The popularity of car clubs is explainable in two ways. First, it needs to be recognised in terms of consumption as a ritual activity, shared by members of a social group seeking to express their common values and status whilst simultaneously stressing their difference from other groups in society. This point was well illustrated by one speaker at the 1935 annual dinner of the Riley Car Club at London's Grovesnor House Hotel, when he described the club as the most exclusive in the world because the entrance fee was £298.[92] Second, the car clubs provided those who joined them with a sense of community and camaraderie within an environment which also enhanced individual identity because it was based on the ownership of an expensive commodity. In this respect they must have functioned as useful information exchanges for both technical and social knowledge. The early motor clubs were clearly socially exclusive, but many of those operating in the 1930s, particularly those for owners with popular models, offered a more democratic atmosphere. In 1934 the Worcester branch of the Austin Owner's Club described its purpose as 'being social and recreative for the owners of Austin cars and their families'. It met regularly all year, for Sunday runs and competitions, driving trials, treasure hunts, and map-reading contests, all of which could be undertaken with 'a minimum of personal expense'. Membership was 10s 6d with a further 7s 6d for the club car-badge, which was *de rigueur* for the members of all car clubs.[93]

Other practices that grew up around the car were of a far more informal, even illicit nature. In fact, the most common of these – speeding – was illegal for the majority of the period but became central to the car culture, whether in motor sport, car club trials or on the open road. The Motor Car Act of 1903 had installed a speed limit of 20 m.p.h., but most cars of that time were already capable of double that speed. What *The Times*, in 1907, called 'the intoxicating influence of speed' became one of the essential joys of motoring, and motorists' organisations fought vigorous and lengthy campaigns against the 20 m.p.h. speed limit.[94] Four years later, the same newspaper explained the attraction of speed to the motorist:

Speed in itself is nothing apart from a world in three dimensions, ruled despotically by the conditions of space and time. But this world is so constituted as the scene of human activity that, though it be the most costly of achievements, speed has proved itself in one phase or another to be perhaps the most vital element in human welfare. Its command invests individuals with such a large measure of what seems to be power that, when it is compassed in a fresh and unexpected manner, as it has been by help of the motor-car, men are liable to the illusion that there is a singular bliss in mere speed by itself.[95]

By the time of the 1930 Road Traffic Act, magistrates and police were dealing with hundreds of thousands of speeding cases each year, as the limit was being almost universally ignored. The 1930 Act abolished the speed limit, but it was reimposed at 30 m.p.h. by the 1934 Road Traffic Act. By that time psychologists were offering explanations of why the speed offered by the car had become part of the fabric of society. It was argued that, by the 1930s, a generation had grown up that 'unquestioningly accepted speed ... as part of its normal environment', so much so in fact that 'the desirability of the speed, even at the cost of a few thousand lives per annum', had become 'part of our cultural mosaic'.[96]

As was noted in the previous chapter, insurance companies noted the particular attraction of speed to young male drivers. For many of the young men who took the wheel, driving skill and prowess were equated with speed, an association promoted by the role models available in the motor-racing world. Manufacturers capitalised upon this facet of the car culture, highlighting speed in advertisements and through the marketing of sports cars. In fact, the journal *Advertiser's Weekly* was frequently critical of the emphasis upon speed in motoring advertisements in the light of the lengthening list of road casualties. One such advertisement was for a 1933 Delage. Described as the 'safest car on the road' because of its ability to take 'the average bend ... at 60mph in absolute comfort and safety', *Advertiser's Weekly* asked poignantly 'how average is the bend' and whether the pedestrian's comfort was relative or absolute.[97]

From the 1920s, manufacturers began to offer sports models to an eager public. Among the most sought-after British models were those by Alvis, Aston Martin, Bentley, Frazer-Nash, MG and Triumph. By the late 1920s, even the more commonplace touring cars had racing-car features, such as supercharging, adapted to them. A plethora of cheap 'would-be sports cars' such as the Wolseley Hornet also appeared on the market, although they were greatly deprecated by the owners of more expensive and 'legitimate' sports models. The Hornet was labelled the 'Wooly Whore's Nest' within motoring circles.[98] By the mid-1930s, British car designers were echoing American developments in stream-lining, aware, like Harley Earl of General Motors, that the purchase of a car was as much an emotional choice as a rational one.

Tinkering with the car was also a predominantly male pastime. *Practical Motorist* was launched in 1935 to cater for the growing number of car owners who undertook their own maintenance as a hobby. This, of course, was another aspect of 'leisure' which might well have been motivated by budgetary necessity. Phil Peacock proudly reported that only once in sixty years of motoring had he had to take his car to a garage to be repaired. In the early 1990s, when his memories of motoring were recorded, he still took great satisfaction from working on a 1930s' Riley that sat in his garage.[99] William McAvoy also enjoyed conducting repairs and maintenance on the cars that he owned from the 1920s onwards. As a Post Office Inspector he received travelling and maintenance expenses on his vehicles. By doing his own maintenance he made a profit on the running of the car.[100]

Other motorists strove to embellish their cars in order to add an air of individuality. It would probably be inaccurate to label this behaviour as customising, in the modern sense of the word, but many owners changed the appearance of their car quite markedly. Of course, many of the wealthiest early motorists had a hand in the design of the car bodies that were placed on to the standard manufacturer's chassis. Others who were less affluent were nonetheless quick to seek marks of distinction for their cars. Around 1910 motorists began placing their own mascots on the radiators of their cars. This development persuaded Rolls-Royce to commission what they felt was a more becoming mascot – the famous Spirit of Ecstasy – to be fitted as standard on all their models.[101] Individualised mascots were not always popular with motoring commentators such as the *Autocar*'s Owen John. In 1920, John blamed young women, or, as he put it, the 'new edition of flappers', for the continuing popularity of mascots in the form of teddy bears, bunny rabbits, 'effigies of Mr Charles Chaplin' and even some that courted trouble by making fun of the police.[102] By 1930 it was estimated that one car in five featured a mascot. One London firm offered a choice of over two hundred, including various animals, signs of the zodiac and classical figures.[103] The 1934 Hillman Melody Minx even included a harp mascot on the radiator cap.[104] The following year, *Practical Motorist* offered an explanation for the growing popularity of the solid bronze Lejeune mascots, available in over a hundred variations at 18 shillings each: 'In these days of mass-produced cars mascots are more popular than ever as a means of distinguishing one particular car of a series', and they did 'much to enhance the appearance of a car and to add a new note'.[105] However, many mascots proved dangerous in the event of collision, particularly for pedestrians or cyclists, and in 1937 the government placed restrictions on their design and location.[106]

Other motorists made greater aesthetic changes to their cars. In 1939 Reg Critchley had his second-hand Standard Big Nine embellished by a respray at the car factory where he was employed. The process cost only 30 shillings and Reg had gold stripes added along the sides of the car for good measure. Reg admired the custom-built bodies offered by Mulliners of Northampton and Carbodies of Coventry, particularly those with aluminium panels which were polished but not painted, but these were beyond his budget.[107] The motoring writer George Bishop believed that most motoring accessories were designed to mimic racing cars; 'We saw little sports cars which could hardly drag themselves along festooned with twin spare wheels, Le Mans slab tanks, stoneguards, giant spot lights and all sorts of fripperies. It did brighten the scene to gaze upon such a variety of body styles and added decoration, but how much the extra equipment had any real function is another matter.'[108] It should also be added that these particular 'fripperies' and patently non-utilitarian additions to cars were obviously more in keeping with male desires, fantasies and ideologies of the car than feminine ones.

One further motoring phenomenon – joyriding – is worthy of discussion, although its emergence did not meet with the approval of motorists or manufacturers. The term 'joyrider' is of pre-1914 origin. It was initially applied to all those who took their cars out for recreational drives. But even at this point, it was often employed in a negative manner by critics of the 'selfishness' and 'arrogance' of early motorists. It was in the inter-war years that the term took on its modern connotations. With knowledge about car mechanics beginning to spread more widely, joyriding – or taking a car for temporary use without the owner's consent – became a serious problem. Joyriding was another area of the car culture that related directly to notions of masculinity. While the male middle-class professional could signify his masculinity through ownership of the latest attractive motor car, joyriding offered his young working-class counterpart an opportunity to express, albeit fleetingly, his own manliness.

All the indications, from contemporary press reports and oral history interviews, confirm that the rituals of the pre-1939 joyrider differed, to some extent, from those of their late-twentieth-century counterparts. Once selected by the joyrider, cars were 'borrowed' and used, as they are today, to gain kudos amongst friends or to impress women. However, the pre-1939 joyrider's chosen vehicles do not appear to have been systematically damaged by excessive speeding or dangerous driving as is frequently the case today. A problem for the police and courts was that joyriders were not technically guilty of a criminal offence. The legal definition of larceny did not cover the 'borrowing' of vehicles without the owner's permission. Although the courts fulminated over the possibility of laying charges covering the theft of petrol from the 'borrowed' cars, the only recourse open to motorists who fell victim to joyriders was to launch a civil action. Because the defence of 'joyriding' may well have been submitted by professional car thieves, it is not possible to offer exact figures for the frequency of joyriding. However, the great majority of cars that were stolen were recovered swiftly, having been abandoned by the roadside. In the twelve months up to September 1929, for instance, 2,939 cars were stolen in the London area, with 2,316 recovered within a matter of hours.[109] Following the introduction of a private member's bill aimed at dealing with what was seen as an escalating problem, the 1930 Road Traffic Act introduced the offence of taking and driving away a motor vehicle without lawful authority.[110] Despite this, joyriding continued to be a problem in the capital. In 1931, 5,086 cars were stolen in London and 4,869 recovered.[111] Joyriding was also a problem in other major towns and cities. In 1936 the *Birmingham Post* reported on what was a growing problem in the city. Birmingham CID had dealt with 259 joyriding cases in 1934, 317 in 1935 and 153 in the first two months of 1936. They claimed that this crime was usually the work of 'irresponsible youths'. In addition Birmingham police were constantly receiving particulars of cars having been taken away in the surrounding counties, and officers were kept

7   Joyrider Larry Rankin poses with an unsuspecting motorist's car in the early 1930s.

working all day long on this offence.[112] During 1936 Manchester police dealt with 471 cars that were taken by joyriders, up from the 307 taken in 1935.[113] Also in 1936 Glasgow police bemoaned the increasing incidence of joyriding, which had become a 'perfect pest'. It had become necessary to establish a special detachment of officers to investigate the problem. The cars taken were invariably the latest and most expensive models.[114]

In the 1930s, Larry Rankin was involved with Glasgow's criminal fraternity and was a regular joyrider. In a subsequent interview he revealed many of the factors that motivated the joyrider. Once he had been taught to drive, by a local milkman, Larry found it 'was an easy thing for me to pick up cars'. Larry explained that there was a knack to selecting the right car for a joyride: 'We'd pick up a decent car to go around in because we found that we got more respect that way. If you go about with an old car the police was liable to pull you up, with a good car they just nodded their head and helped you on yer way.' Once he had taken a car, Larry made the most of the prestige it brought him: 'I could go about then, go out with girls, go to dancing … live like the people upstairs.'[115]

Contemporary commentators expressed concern with what they believed to be the car's role in the growing incidence of illicit sexual activity. For example, in a 1930 series on vice in Scottish cities, the *Weekly Record* painted a lurid picture of behaviour amongst young people in Dundee's dance halls and on the weekly 'monkey parades' in which young people promenaded the city's main thoroughfares in single-sex groups in the hope of pairing off with a member of the opposite sex.[116] As the *Weekly Record* noted with considerable alarm, young men had taken to using cars in order to lure prospective sexual partners away from the public arena of the parades. These 'car-ghouls' drove 'about the thoroughfares ogling and smiling at young girls parading the pavements'. The result of this 'gutter-crawling', which was especially pronounced in the summer months, was 'too often' the acceptance by young women of a run out to secluded country spots, to the inevitable detriment of 'the morals of Dundee'.[117]

It is clear that car ownership increased the potential attraction of many men. It is also apparent that recognition of this aspect of the car's appeal motivated many joyriders. In August 1930, Middlesex County Sessions heard the case of Richard Perry, a ship's cook, and Tom Fedyke, a chauffeur, who were accused of stealing a car from Golders Green. After taking the car, Perry and Fedyke met two young women who were employed as hospital maids. The foursome then proceeded to Spaniards Road, adjacent to Hampstead Heath, where one couple remained in the car whilst the other twosome disappeared onto the Heath. However, their amorous escapade was interrupted by two policemen whose approach caused Fedyke and Parry to flee the scene. Their departure, on foot, was rather less glamorous than their arrival. The deputy chairman of the bench remarked that this was not an isolated incident: 'Some of us have a very difficult passage along Spaniards Road, Hampstead, on account of young gentlemen such as these leaving their cars and indulging in caresses on the seats. I am in communication with the police constantly to try to keep this road clear.'[118] The two men pleaded the defence of joyriding, which was accepted by the judge, who directed the jury not to convict because although their action 'might be wicked and shameful' as the law stood, 'it was not an offence'.

Although this case ended in embarrassment for the four young people concerned, it is clear that joyriding was an alluring proposition to many young men. It offered them a chance to 'swank' in front of their contemporaries and a means by which to aspire, for an hour or two, to a lifestyle that was normally beyond them. For this reason it is interesting to note that Blackpool was known as a 'happy hunting ground' for joyriders. In 1932 nearly a thousand cars and motorcycles were 'borrowed' in the resort for less than two hours.[119] Mass Observation's investigations into the behaviour of working-class visitors to Blackpool indicated the extent to which, away from the watchful and censuring eyes of their own neighbourhoods, many holiday-makers indulged in actions that they would never have contemplated in their home lives. In the light of Blackpool's role as the site of what some historians have seen as working-class carnivalesque, Mass Observation registered surprise at the low incidence of sexual activity they discovered there in 1938. The observers had enthusiastically combed the resort's beaches at night in search of evidence of illicit sexual activity.[120] It is tempting to suggest that an investigation of a few parked cars might have produced more raw data for their study. Blackpool's association with joyriding suggests that the behaviour of those who took part in this practice can be partly explained in terms of the release and excess of the carnivalesque. This assessment is supported by joyriding's popularity amongst sailors of the Home Fleet. In 1938 the Commander in Chief of the Fleet was forced to threaten drastic action against any naval men found guilty of joyriding. The numbers of sailors indulging in the pastime had become so large that the Dorset Police Courts dealt with it more frequently than with drunkenness.[121]

Conclusion

To conclude a discussion of the car's uses with an analysis of the prevalence of joyriding may seem a little odd. In fact joyriding is very much central to the argument being made throughout this account of motoring between 1896 and 1939. The American historian Peter Stearns has recently noted that 'all major stages in the development of modern consumerism have produced new forms of theft', which can be identified as 'a deviant measure of yearning' for commodities. Offences catalogued by Stearns, in this context, include clothing thefts in the eighteenth century and kleptomania in the nineteenth century.[122] The twentieth-century phenomenon of joyriding must be added to Stearn's list. The diffusion of car ownership and the popularity of motoring can only be fully explained by acknowledging and exploring the extent to which the car offered owners symbolic value. Desire was as much a part of car ownership as the calculation of the pounds, shilling and pence needed to buy one. Of course, the car offered owners a convenience and mobility that other forms of transport could only partly equal, and this was essential in the course of its diffusion among almost two million households by 1939. Its utility added to the role it quickly assumed in communicating messages about status, taste, individuality and gender, making car ownership a virtual necessity for those with the appropriate incomes. Over the years between 1896 and 1939, ownership extended among a variety of social groups, from the most affluent to the professional and commercial middle classes, through to a small, but significant, group of working-class owners of second-hand cars by the late 1930s. For each group in turn the car was a powerful agent through which to mediate a plethora of potential meanings.

Notes

1 *Economist*, 7 December 1935; Political and Economic Planning, *Motor Vehicles* (London, 1950), pp. 58–9; J. Foreman-Peck, S. Bowden and A. McKinlay, *The British Motor Industry* (Manchester, Manchester University Press, 1995), p. 68.
2 J. Urry, *The Tourist Gaze* (London, Sage, 1990), p. 66.
3 *Ibid.*, introduction.
4 *Ibid.*, p. 66.
5 *Autocar*, 1 March 1929.

6 J. Ruskin, *The Complete Works*, Volume 8, cited in W. Schivelbusch, *The Railway Journey: The Industrialization of Time and Space in the Nineteenth Century* (Oxford, Berg Publishers, 1986), p. 54.

7 *The Times*, 2 September 1905; emphasis added.

8 *The Times*, 2 September 1905.

9 T. R. Nicholson, *Wheels on the Road: Road Maps of Britain 1870–1940* (Norwich, Geo Books, 1983), p. 50.

10 Respondent 33, Ronald Gene: born Great Sutton 1921.

11 G. Long, *English Inns and Road Houses* (Newcastle-upon-Tyne, W. Laurie, 1937), p. 168.

12 S. Cooke, *This Motoring* (London, Automobile Association, 1931), pp. 4ff.

13 *Automobile Association Annual Report* (London, Automobile Association, 1910 and 1914).

14 J. A. R. Pimlott, *The Englishman's Holiday* (London, Faber & Faber 1947), pp. 166–7.

15 *Automobile Association Annual Report 1910* (London, Automobile Association).

16 W. Plowden, *The Motor Car and Politics* (Harmondsworth, Pelican, 1973), pp. 81–100.

17 Cited in S. Kemp' review of T. Pinney (ed.), *The Letters of Rudyard Kipling: Volume Three, 1900–1910*, in *Times Higher Education Review*, 22 August 1997.

18 D. Levitt, *Woman and Her Car: A Chatty Little Handbook for All Women who Motor or Want to Motor* (London, Lane 1909), p. 52.

19 *Automobile Association Annual Report 1914* (London, Automobile Association).

20 Royal Automobile Club, *Report of the Annual General Meeting* (annual).

21 W. Plowden, *The Motor Car and Politics* (Harmondsworth, Pelican Books, 1973), p. 99; H. Bart-King, *A History of the Automobile Association 1905–1980* (Basingstoke, Automobile Association, 1980), p. 174.

22 Respondent 54, Mary Tye: born Preston 1917.

23 T. R. Nicholson, *The Vintage Car 1919–1930* (London, Batsford, 1966), p. 252.

24 Respondent 72, Betti Mansson: born Bebbington (date unknown).

25 Society of Motor Manufacturers and Traders, *The Motor Industry of Great Britain* (London, SMMT, 1932).

26 Respondent 35, Jean Rosolen: born Leamington Spa 1924.

27 Respondent 23, Tony Craven: born London 1913.

28 Respondent 16, John Rogers: born Christchurch 1919.

29 Respondent 21, Marjorie Sculthorpe: born Warrington 1915.

30 J. Prioleau, *Motoring for Women* (London, Geoffrey Bles, 1925), p. 77.

31 S. Bowden, 'The New Consumerism', in P. Johnson (ed.) *Twentieth Century Britain* (London, Longman, 1994), p. 248.

32 *Blackpool Gazette and Herald*, 29 April 1933.
33 H. Perkin, *The Age of the Automobile* (London, Quartet Books, 1976), pp. 155–8.
34 A. A. Jackson, *The Middle Classes 1900–1950* (Nairn, David St John Thomas, 1991), p. 299.
35 Respondent 52, Joan Russell: born Wallasey 1922.
36 Respondent 40, Rod Hendrie: born Sutherlandshire 1926.
37 Mass Observation, *Meet Yourself on Sunday* (London, Falcon Press, 1949), p. 6.
38 *Garage and Motor Agent*, 6 October 1923.
39 *Autocar*, 7 August 1936.
40 *Autocar*, 15 April 1938.
41 *Autocar* 8 June 1928 and 14 August 1931.
42 Respondent 37, Mary Stanley: born Liverpool 1916. Respondent 36, Gordon Cox: born Widnes 1914.
43 This magazine was published monthly from 1932 as *British Boarding House Proprietor and Private Hotelier*. In 1933 it became *Hotel and Boarding House* and in 1937 it was renamed *Hotel*.
44 Automobile Association, *Automobile Association Handbook 1935–6* (London, Automobile Association, 1935), pp. 565–9.
45 *Hotel*, July 1932.
46 Respondent 35, Jean Rosolen: born Leamington Spa 1924.
47 *Hotel and Boarding House*, September, 1935.
48 *Ibid.*
49 Respondent 27, Mollie Farrell: born Berkshire (date unknown).
50 W. M. Whiteman, *The History of the Caravan* (London, Blandford Press, 1973).
51 *Ibid.*, p. 92.
52 *Practical Motorist*, 27 July 1935; *Caravan and Trailer*, May 1933; C. W. Wilman, *Camping by Caravan* (London, Cassell, 1929), p. 13; cited in D. L. North, 'Middle Class Suburban Lifestyles and Culture in England, 1919–1939' (D.Phil. thesis, University of Oxford, 1988), p. 340.
53 *Autocar*, 27 August 1932.
54 *Advertiser's Weekly*, 5 March 1936.
55 Respondent 43, John Sailor: born Wimbish (Essex) 1914.
56 A. Huxley, *Along the Road* (London, Chatto & Windus, 1925), pp. 3–4.
57 *Autocar*, 25 March 1922.
58 A. Howkins and J. Lowerson, *Trends in Leisure, 1919–1939* (University of Sussex, Social Science Research Council, 1979).
59 F. W. Ogilvie, *The Tourist Movement: An Economic Study* (London, P. S. King, 1933).
60 *Autocar*, 25 January 1935 and 25 June 1937; C. Buchanan, *Mixed Blessings: The Motor Car in Britain* (London, Leonard Hill, 1958), p. 76.

61 R. G. Pinney, *Britain – Destination of Tourists?* (1944).

62 *Autocar*, 12 January 1934, 22 June 1934, 20 July 1934, 28 June 1935 and 1 May 1936.

63 *Autocar*, 20 May 1932.

64 Autocheques Limited, *Autocheques Handbook* (London, 1936).

65 *Autocar*, 18 April 1930.

66 *Autocar*, 25 January 1935.

67 I. Brown, *The Heart of England* (London, British Heritage Series, 1935), p.78. *Autocar*, 18 August 1933, listed thirty-three Roadhouses, the majority of which were in the Southeast.

68 *Autocar*, 4 December 1931. Although the Roadhouse phenomenon was comparatively short-lived, a variety of different facilities were given the name and the buildings had various architectural styles and offered a varied range of services. See Long, *English Inns and Road Houses*, p. 177.

69 Respondent 17, William McAvoy: born London 1901.

70 Respondent 21, Marjorie Sculthorpe: born Warrington 1915.

71 D. Haworth, *Bright Morning: Images of a Lancashire Boyhood* (London, Methuen, 1990), p. 101.

72 Respondent 76, Antoinette Duncan: born Southport (date unknown).

73 H. F. Moorehouse, *Driving Ambitions: An analysis of the American Hot Rod Enthusiasm* (Manchester, Manchester University Press, 1991), p. 151.

74 *News Chronicle*, 9 October 1931.

75 *Daily Herald*, 17 October 1931.

76 *Daily Telegraph*, 6 June 1932.

77 *Daily Herald*, 12 December 1932.

78 *Autocar*, 20 January 1933.

79 *Autocar*, 3 February 1933.

80 R. Denne Waterhouse, *Week-End Ticket* (Bristol, Arrowsmith, 1934), p. 89.

81 P. Garnier, *The Art of Gordon Crosby* (London, Hamlyn, 1978).

82 *Advertiser's Weekly*, 1 June 1939.

83 *Autocar*, 26 December 1925, reported the club's twenty-first anniversary.

84 *Autocar*, 14 January 1927 and 8 January 1932.

85 *Autocar*, 8 January 1926.

86 *Autocar*, 3 June 1927 and 2 July 1927.

87 *Autocar*, 17 June 1928.

88 A. B. Demaus, *Motor Sport in the 20s* (Gloucester, Alan Sutton Publishing, 1989), pp. 54–5.

89 *Autocar*, 9 June 1939.

90 *Autocar*, 23 June 1939.

91 E. H. Reeves, *The Riley Romance* (Coventry, Riley Motor Company, 1930).

92 *Ibid.*
93 British Motor Industry Heritage Trust Archives.
94 *The Times*, 11 July 1907.
95 *The Times*, 17 October 1911.
96 M. Culpin, 'The psychology of motoring', in *Practitioner*, 831 (September 1937) 213.
97 *Advertiser's Weekly*, 19 October 1933.
98 G. Bishop, *The Age of the Automobile* (London, Hamlyn, 1977), p. 81.
99 Respondent 15, Phil Peacock: born Birmingham 1919.
100 Respondent 17, William McAvoy: born London 1901.
101 Lord Montagu of Beaulieu, *The British Motorist: A Celebration in Pictures* (Bristol, Queen Anne Press, 1987), p. 36.
102 *Autocar*, 12 June 1920.
103 *Autocar*, 7 March 1930.
104 *Autocar*, 29 June 1934.
105 *Practical Motorist* 8 September 1935.
106 *Autocar*, 16 April 1937.
107 Respondent 14, Reg Critchley: born Nottingham 1912.
108 Bishop, *The Age of the Automobile*, p. 35.
109 *Autocar*, 8 November 1929.
110 Road Traffic Act (1930), clause 28.
111 *Autocar*, 1 April 1932.
112 *Birmingham Post*, 6 March 1936.
113 City of Manchester Watch Committee, *Statistical Returns of the Police, Fire Brigade and Weights and Measures Department 1936* (Manchester, 1936).
114 *Sunday Mail*, 9 February 1936.
115 S. Humphries and P. Gordon, *Forbidden Britain: Our Secret Past 1900–1960* (London, BBC Books, 1994), pp. 26–7.
116 For a full discussion of this practice, see A. Davies, *Leisure, Gender and Poverty: Working-class Culture in Salford and Manchester, 1900–1939* (Buckingham, Open University Press, 1992), pp. 102–8.
117 *Weekly Record*, 6 September 1930. See also S. Humphries, *A Secret World of Sex* (London, Sidgwick & Jackson, 1988), p. 104.
118 *News of the World*, 3 August 1930.
119 *Autocar*, 5 May 1933.
120 G. Cross, *Worktowners at Blackpool: Mass-Observation and Popular Leisure in the 1930s* (London, Routledge, 1990), pp. 187–91.
121 *Daily Telegraph*, 4 March 1938.
122 P. N. Stearns, 'Stages of consumerism: recent work on the issues of periodization', *Journal of Modern History*, 69 (1997) 105.

4

'These things will right themselves': road safety and the car

It has been argued in the previous chapters that social, cultural and economic determinants affected the design, marketing and uses of cars. In return, the car came to have a significant role in ideologies of class and gender. These themes will continue in this chapter with two related but distinct points being made. First, it will be maintained that a technology, such as the car, is not only socially constructed; it is also society-shaping. There are always technological alternatives; any specific machine is invariably the result of cultural, economic, social and political considerations. In this case, an obvious alternative would have been for British governments to invest in a fully integrated public-transport system at the expense of private motoring. Second, it will be argued that the infrastructure surrounding a given technology also has a dialectical relationship with social, cultural, political and economic factors. The evolution of legislation designed to cope with the less attractive aspects of motoring requires analysis from this perspective. Initiatives designed to accommodate Britain's cities to motor traffic will be assessed in this context.

Anyone driving along the parkways of Long Island, New York, might notice the unusually low clearance height of their underpasses, which in many cases are only 9 foot. Between the 1920s and the 1930s Robert Moses, the master builder of roads, parks and bridges for New York, deliberately designed these underpasses to prevent buses accessing many parkways. This enabled wealthy, automobile-owning whites to use these parkways for commuting and leisure, whilst limiting access to the less affluent. As a result of this class and racial bias, ethnic minorities and poorer social groups were excluded from the acclaimed Jones Beach State Park. Moses sealed this exclusivity by blocking the construction of a rail link to the beach.[1]

This is one example of what Langdon Winner has called 'technical arrangements as forms of order'.[2] American historians of the automobile have unearthed further examples of this transfer of social relations into geographical space.[3] British historians have been less productive in this respect, and the few studies of the social history of the car that exist have tended to envisage its development as technologically driven. According to this interpretation, cheaper cars must entail greater levels of ownership, more roads and greater accommodation of towns and cities to the car. This chapter will suggest that whilst it might be difficult to envisage a different set of developments, it is possible to understand that behind an apparently technologically inevitable process lay a great deal of contestation. Society's choices between possible technological developments are highly reflective of patterns of political, social and economic power. As middle-class car ownership grew, so powerful sections of opinion swung against significant restrictions on the car.

The chapter will begin by examining existing interpretations of the development of motoring legislation and road safety. These interpretations have largely been written from a perspective that views the process as simply one of trial and error. Such approaches are imbued with traditional notions of technology as neutral, driven largely by the logic of technical development. In fact, it is quite possible to identify a series of powerful class interests that moulded the way in which ideas about the car, road transport and road safety developed. Increasing numbers of middle-class car owners, and the various industrial and commercial groupings that benefited from the growth of motoring, were highly influential in these developments. Middle-class motorists appreciated the advantages the car brought to them and increasingly saw the casualties caused by motoring as the fault of a series of scapegoats – from foreign chauffeurs to careless pedestrians. Thus the concept of a new science of road safety, concentrating on the education of all road users rather than further restrictions on motorists, gained credence amongst influential sections of society. Commercial motoring interests pushed this line by financing the propaganda campaigns of the National

Safety First Association (NSFA). The middle sections of this chapter will describe this process, employing hitherto unused archival material to explain how government and society came to terms with a dangerous technology.

The final section will examine the impact these ideas had in terms of the control of traffic and planning in the urban environment. This will prove fruitful as a means of probing changing reactions to the car. It will also reveal that on occasion local authorities, with responsibility for their own transport systems and to their own citizens, had different priorities than those of national government. However, it will be seen that motoring interests were also influential in this sphere. Indeed, as the period drew to a close, motoring groups were confidently antici-pating that the urban environment and the way people lived would change to accommodate the car rather than the other way around.

The historiography of road safety

In 1993 the *Guardian*'s educational supplement featured a story on the history of road safety. Its opening sentence was striking: 'More than half a million people have been killed on Britain's roads this century, but that figure would be far worse were it not for the many road-safety measures that have accompanied the history of the motor car.'[4] It is difficult to imagine half a million deaths from any other cause being treated in such a casual manner. The car has become such a dominant artefact in everyday life that death and destruction, as by-products of mass car ownership, have been accepted as a natural and inevitable part of modern living. Robert Davis has made this point very forcefully in his book *Death on the Streets*. He outlines what he calls an ideology of road safety, identifying ideology as

> a body of ideas and attitudes, generally in a derogatory sense because the ideology mystifies or distorts reality. It works as part of a particu-lar power structure, in a set of social relations, and helps maintain that structure. Ideology sets hidden agendas of discussion, forms back-ground assumptions about the nature of those discussions and, above all, makes certain features of a society appear natural or necessary.[5]

In the case of the car, society has worked within the assumption that the high casualty figures that accompany mass motoring can gradually be eradicated by increasing safety measures, overseen by the various road-safety professionals – traffic police, road and vehicle engineers, road-safety officers and so on. Earlier anger about motoring accidents has become muted as concepts of road safety have taken on a neutral, more scientific image. In effect, the dangers brought by motor vehicles have been legitimated. According to Davis the process has been deeply influenced by a motoring lobby whose ideological and political interests have become dominant. He acknowledges that efforts by road-safety specialists can be effective, citing anti-drink-driving campaigns as an example. However, large numbers of casualties are inevitable in the use of a technology with such a high potential for causing harm.[6]

Historical writing has not investigated the hypothesis suggested by Davis. In fact there has been a tendency tacitly to accept the outlook he criticises. Accounts of road-safety legislation offered by Kenneth Richardson and Harold Perkin both fall into this category.[7] These studies are largely technologically orientated; Perkin, for example, wrote of the 'triumph of the internal combustion engine', which lends an air of scientific inevitability to the development of motoring.[8] Richardson's work also transmitted a sense that the car had an inevitable developmental trajectory which was largely determined by technological progress. Thus, of the 20 m.p.h. speed limit in force between 1903 and 1930, he wrote: 'the speed limit of 20 miles an hour laid down in the 1903 [Motor Car] Act was being universally disregarded and rightly held to be far too low for the engines of the time.'[9] There is, therefore, much that can be added to our knowledge by adopting a conceptual framework which offers insights into the fact that technological developments can embody specific forms of power and authority.

The major work in this area is William Plowden's *The Motor Car and Politics*, which provides an informed interpretation of the competing claims of various interest groups that influenced government motor-transport policy.[10] His account provides a useful antidote to those studies which fail to report this process. Plowden identified the central role of the private car in debates about the 'motor problem'. As the number of motor vehicles rose, particularly in the 1920s and 1930s, contemporaries fretted about the spiralling number of road casualties. During those two decades, analogies were frequently drawn between the number of road fatalities since 1918 and the Boer War casualty list. In 1909 recorded road-transport fatalities stood at 1,070 and injuries at

26,091. By the 1920s the average number of annual road fatalities had risen by over 400 per cent to 4,121, whilst the average number of injured stood at 87,255, an increase of equal magnitude. The rising number of vehicles on the highways ensured that road-casualty figures rose again in the 1930s, the average number of those killed on the roads reaching 6,640 whilst average annual injuries climbed to 182,834.[11]

The involvement of the car in large numbers of road deaths guaranteed its unpopularity in some circles, as did the disproportionate ratio of casualties between motorists and non-motorists. From the first year of detailed statistical collection, in 1926, to the outbreak of war in 1939, the proportion of pedestrian fatalities did not fall below 45 per cent of all road deaths. If cyclists are included in the non-motorist category, then the figure never fell below 63 per cent and in 1936 was as high as 70 per cent of all fatalities.[12] In contrast the number of drivers of motor vehicles killed was a minor proportion of the total, being only 4.7 per cent in 1937, with passengers in motor vehicles providing another 8.1 per cent of road fatalities in that year.[13]

It was also, as we have seen, a period when many cars were used solely for leisure, giving accidents involving the car a different complexion to those involving goods or public-service vehicles. For the victim of a road accident it may have been easier to see the necessity of a bus full of passengers driving into town than that of the car owner out for a spin. This combination of factors guaranteed that the car's role in road casualties received frequent coverage. However, as Plowden noted, the vociferous defence of the private motorist by the Automobile Association (AA) was in some ways counterproductive, ensuring that the car never left the public's mind when the issue of road casualties was raised. The AA was formed in 1905 with the primary aim of frustrating police speed traps and was by 1939 the biggest motoring club in the world. Its original function was widely resented, with the Permanent Secretary at the Home Office, Sir Edward Troup, likening the AA to an 'association of burglars'.[14] Victims of motoring accidents were equally unhappy about the role of AA road scouts. In 1911 angry residents of Dunston Green, a village on the road between Tonbridge and the Kent Coast, met to protest at a series of fatal road accidents. Addressing the assembly, T. A. Green expressed amazement that the purpose of the AA road scouts was 'not to warn mad and wreckless drivers to drive carefully, but to warn them to keep out of trouble.'[15]

In fact, the AA's defence of the rights of the motorist became, at times, extremely polemical. Several campaigns went far beyond those of a consumer organisation and at times the AA's actions clearly did not represent the views, or interests, of the majority of its members. For example, in 1927 a survey of 100,000 AA members revealed that 92 per cent favoured the abolition of the 20 m.p.h. speed limit.[16] The AA had long campaigned for this and the 1930 Road Traffic Act removed it. However, as road casualties increased in the aftermath of the 1930 Act, the majority of opinion came to favour the reintroduction of a speed limit. In 1934 another survey of AA members revealed that a majority favoured a speed limit and the implementation of a driving test. Despite this, the AA opposed both these aspects of the 1934 Road Traffic Act. They funded the campaign against the new 30 m.p.h. limit and, along with the RAC, refused to provide staff to act as driving-test examiners.[17]

Plowden also catalogued the ebb and flow of events and factors which dictated changing perceptions of road safety. Amongst these were the technical arguments put forward by various parties, the status of each generation of ministers involved in the process and their individual determination to find solutions, the relative importance of road safety as an issue at any given time and the subsequent allocation of parliamentary time.[18] His work exhaustively explored the long-winded process of negotiation between governments and the motoring lobby, which began in the twilight years of the nineteenth century, about how law affecting the car could be brought in line with 'technical developments'.[19] Plowden described the manner in which the motoring lobby was provided with drafts of bills for its perusal throughout the 1896–1939 period, a procedure which he called a 'strange act of abdication'.[20] This illustrates the emerging motoring lobby's leverage in debates concerning motoring legislation. They were consulted at every stage of each government initiative and although government policy did not always meet with their approval, they were often successful in limiting the extent of motoring legislation.

However, Plowden did not attempt to explain the extent to which the motoring lobby was able to employ the politics and language of *laissez-faire* to influence national policy. Nor did he investigate the role of the NSFA in the development of road-safety policy. The NSFA was nominally an independent organisation, which came to be recognised by the government as the official body for the propagation of road-safety propaganda. However, its agenda was barely distinguishable from that of the motoring lobby, who provided the NSFA with much of its finance and many of its officers.

More recently, Clive Emsley's account of the development of road-traffic legislation was a welcome addition to this largely uninvestigated area of twentieth century history. However, his interpretation was heavily reliant on Plowden and exhibited an even greater misconception about the NSFA.[21] Emsley employed V. A. C. Gatrell's concept of the 'policeman state' to explain the development of motoring legislation.[22] This model envisages the criminal justice system as having 'generated its own momentum', as experts and bureaucrats set about solving the perceived problems of the day. Consequently, Emsley rejected the idea that motoring legislation was in any way inspired by class interest. In this respect, he paid less regard to Gatrell's conclusion that historians 'might profitably remind themselves that the history of crime is a grim subject, not because it is about crime, but because it is about power'.[23] Gatrell's advice will be accepted here; and the role of capital and class in the evolution of road traffic legislation, road-safety policy and ultimately in the remoulding of the urban landscape will be acknowledged.

It will be argued that the failure of previous researchers to investigate the role of the NSFA was an important omission. A brief analysis of differing national responses to road accidents will illustrate this point. According to James Foreman-Peck, legislative responses to the negative social consequences of motor vehicles arrived earliest in countries with no indigenous motor-manufacturing industry, which together with the wider motoring lobby would protest about the suppression of an emerging industry. Thus, it was the Scandinavian nations, with few motor vehicles in use by international standards, who were amongst the earliest and most stringent legislators. From 1903 these nations began imposing accident liability on the car owner. Such laws could only be generally effective if compulsory insurance was in force and if road-accident victims were to be compensated. The Scandinavians led the field here too, introducing legislation in 1918.[24]

The cost of British road accidents in 1938 was estimated at a massive 1.3 per cent of gross national product, a figure which Foreman-Peck believed to have been 'deliberately downward-biased'.[25] Yet, the policy reaction was strangely muted, a function of what he believed to be 'distribution of the costs and benefits of motor vehicles among the affected population. Those affected by accidents were generally not in a position to influence policy and those at risk … were easy to ignore.'[26] In particular, Foreman-Peck emphasised the role of the 'powerful pro-motoring pressure groups which had an interest in avoiding constraints on motor vehicles'.[27] In Britain the Society of Motor Manufacturers and Traders (SMMT) made no secret of its intent to answer any press article of 'an anti-motoring nature'.[28]

It is clear, therefore, that the role of the motoring lobby requires serious attention. It is essential to describe how society arrived at a concordance with the car and how an ideology of road safety played a part in the process. However, it will prove useful to begin by out-lining the process by which the responsibility for road accidents shifted from the technology – the car – to various types of motorist who could be offered up as scapegoats for the negative consequences of increased motoring. Once the notion arose that it was individual drivers who were the fundamental cause of increasing danger on the roads, not the mode of individual transport being used, it became possible for the motoring lobby to promote the idea that planning and education could eventually provide a policy solution.

'Outside the brotherhood of the road': the construction of motoring scapegoats

On its arrival, in the years around the turn of the twentieth century, the motor car was met with a great deal of criticism. The representatives of motoring groups often found themselves on a defensive footing. A particular problem for them was the widely propagated image of motorists as rich, arrogant joy-riders, out to have fun at everyone else's expense. One of the earliest critics of the car was the *Daily Telegraph*, which ran a campaign against this 'social juggernaut' in 1903.[29] *The Economist* was another of early motoring's antagonists. *The Economist* was critical in 1913, remarking that the 'vehicles of the rich kill and maim far more people than the vehicles of the poor'.[30] In June 1914, an editorial in the *Daily News and Leader* discussed the increasing inci-dence of motorists fleeing the scene of fatal or serious accidents. Six such episodes had been reported in the previous month. The editorial argued that it was 'horrible enough that any man should employ a powerful and dangerous instrument so recklessly in the pursuit of his amusement as to kill his fellows; but that having killed he should leave his victim lying on the road and himself take flight from all responsibility is a degree of baseness almost too horrible even for fiction.' But it was the car which had 'evolved this form of offence'; it 'alone enables men to kill and offers them the prospect of escaping detection.'[31]

What is important about these examples is that the critique offered was concentrated on the car itself. But it is also apparent that deaths and injuries involving the car had the potential to bring the wealthiest sections of society into conflict with the majority who were not car owners. For example, in July 1914 the *Daily Citizen* offered a harsher tone on the subject of drivers who fled accident scenes. Labelling these drivers 'kill-and-scuttle' motorists, the article asked who was most likely to be imprisoned: the unemployed worker, forced to steal bread to offset starvation, or the reckless motorist. It concluded that, 'The truth of the saying that there is one law for the rich and another for the poor was never better exemplified.'[32]

One outcome of the threat of class friction over the private car was the creation, within the motoring community, of a series of scapegoats. These groups were often held responsible for the bad driving that provoked antagonism towards the car. Thus in 1919 the motoring correspondent of *The Times* wrote that, 'The speed fiend is no motorist, nor is the man who regards a car merely as a sort of animated armchair … but they may be safely ignored as outside the brotherhood of the road.'[33] Evidence already considered in the chapter on gender suggests that the woman driver represented a perennial scapegoat. Indeed the use of the term 'brotherhood of the road' in the last example is revealing. However, some scapegoats were more transient than others, reflecting contemporary issues and prejudices, and over the years a plethora of alternatives were offered. In the earliest days of motoring easy scapegoats for bad driving were the servants who found themselves in the privileged position at the wheel – chauffeurs. For example, in 1903 *Justice of the Peace* singled out foreign chauffeurs as a problem. This group were doubly attractive as scapegoats, being both servants and non-British.[34] In 1906 the Royal Commission on the Motor Car listened to several claims that 'gentlemen' were not at fault for poor driving. The vice-president of the National Cyclists' Union, E. B. Turner, told the Royal Commission he did not believe the 'owners of cars' were guilty of poor driving; rather, it was 'the drivers' of their vehicles.[35] Sir Horace Curzon Plunkett, vice-president of the Irish Department of Agriculture and president of the Irish Automobile Club reported that there was little poor driving in Ireland. In his opinion foreign chauffeurs were the only noteworthy exception to the rule.[36] The chief constable of Hertfordshire, commenting on speeding in his district, claimed that it was a crime that could be laid at the door of 'jockeys and other people of that kind' who were making their way to Newmarket races.[37]

The assumption that good breeding and manners would be inherently transferred to good and courteous driving was also revealed in *The Times*. Discussing the bad driver, or 'road hog', in 1903 it maintained that these motorists emanated

> from a class which possesses money in excess of brains or culture, and which has not had an opportunity of learning insensibly, in the course of generations, the consideration for the rights of others which is part of the natural heritage of gentlefolk. For people of his order the law is an educational influence of the highest value; and when he has once received the ineffaceable stamp of the gaolbird society may be expected, before long, to range itself on the side of the law, and to complete the reformation which it will be the work of the magistracy to begin.[38]

Such preconceptions continued to frame the debate about road safety for the next three decades. As motoring became more widespread and new social groups bought cars, they were met with caustic comments about their social origins and the potential effects of any lack of gentility upon their driving. For example, in the years immediately following the 1914–18 war a very frequent whipping boy in the letters pages of the motoring press was the *nouveau riche* war-profiteer. An editorial in *Autocar* in May 1919 expressed concern about the spread of car ownership and a problem this could engender:

> the present scramble for cars does not necessarily seem to be entirely one amongst pre-war motorists. Rather, it would seem that it originates mostly from a certain class of individual who have grown rich out of the war, and now must motor at all costs. Such individuals are apt to prove, perhaps, a danger, and certainly a nuisance, to other road users, and to adopt a somewhat overbearing attitude towards all who do not get out of their way.[39]

In 1920, Alderman Ashton told a Manchester council meeting of his concern over the 'number of reckless and impudent drivers in Manchester', particularly those 'who had recently become rich and had bought motor-cars', because they did not have 'the consideration for other people that gentlemen would have'.[40] The advent of cheaper baby cars in the 1920s presented an obvious target for those who subscribed to this doctrine. In 1926 one *Autocar* correspondent offered the following critique of drivers of popular small cars:

> I am on the road a good deal, and in my opinion the driving of the public gets worse and worse, not so much from incompetence as through absolutely wilful caddishness and bad manners. I presume that the class of person who nowadays go about in motor cars and who, ten years ago, were riding in buses like to think themselves gentlemen. I submit that it would be greatly to the public benefit if they went a little further and behaved as such![41]

Others offered further categories of driver that were held to be damaging motoring's reputation. Owners of American cars were often characterised as unpatriotic, as well as being described as the most 'inconsiderate on the road', by several correspondents in *Autocar*.[42] One reader denounced fat people for their selfishness and inconsiderate attitude at the wheel, whilst a further debate emerged around the possible merits and demerits of young and old drivers.[43]

After 1926 letters about upwardly mobile motorists virtually disappeared from *Autocar*. It was at this time that Churchill, then the Chancellor of the Exchequer, was making the first raid on the road fund in order to provide finances for non-motor-related areas of government expenditure. The fund was established in 1909 with what motoring groups thought was a sacred promise that the monies collected were to be used exclusively for road building and maintenance. Churchill's *modus operandi* was to portray motoring as a luxury hobby.[44] As such, car owners were expected to contribute to the national coffers when times were difficult. In response, the motoring organisations and magazines naturally sought to emphasise the increasingly diverse social groups who were using motor vehicles for everyday business purposes. Perhaps Churchill's raid, and the fear of further taxation on motoring, because of its perceived luxury status, persuaded motorists that the spread of car ownership was a blessing rather than a curse. Or, more probably, the editors of motoring journals took a decision not to publish letters attacking members of social groups new to the motoring community. As was seen in the last chapter, the editor of *Autocar* did at one point announce his decision to publish no more letters on the divisive subject of the woman driver. The arbiters of motoring opinion were wary that legislation relating to the car was still a matter for debate and they clearly perceived the need to nurture a strong sense of common interest amongst motorists. Motoring magazines were also a commercial enterprise and therefore bound to seek to appeal to as large a number of readers as possible. It is possible, therefore, that the number of published letters from drivers maligning their contemporaries, from a gendered or class perspective, represented the tip of an un-published iceberg.

The National Safety First Association

The almost caste-like preconceptions revealed above were to prove influential in the framing of motoring legislation. Debates surrounding various categories of problem drivers began a process through which the car and other motor vehicles, the fundamental cause of rising road casualties, were removed from centre stage in discussions of road safety. By the 1920s the car offered personal mobility, convenience and freedom for a significant and increasing minority of the population: this minority was significant because of its relative wealth and position in the professional and commercial middle classes. National interests were also tied up with the economic success of the motor industry. In 1939 the SMMT estimated that 1,385,000 jobs were directly or in-directly dependent on the industry.[45] By 1936 Britain exported 65,000 cars, only marginally below the combined French, German and Italian exports.[46] During the late 1930s it also became increasingly apparent that the motor industry would be called upon to make a vital military contribution to the nation. Thus the motoring lobby was very powerful and British governments were unlikely to introduce radical measures to curb car use, notwithstanding the high economic cost of motor accidents.

In contrast to many of the quotations cited above, discussion of road-safety issues from the mid-1920s was increasingly sprinkled with appeals to English common sense. In 1929, for example, *The Times* castigated Labour MP Dr Alfred Salter for describing road casualties as a 'calamitous holocaust of pedestrian life', admonishing such language as an attempt 'to divide mankind into two irreconcilable classes'.[47] In 1931 it was calling for co-operation between motorists and pedestrians against the common enemy – selfishness; an enemy that was not likely to be defeated 'so long as selfish men and women are able to salve their consciences by enroling themselves in rival organisations and exhibiting a partisan spirit wholly foreign to the traditions of the English highway.'[48] This call for a vision of a united body politic failed to take account of the reality of the skewed balance of power in this debate. On one side were marshalled the large motoring organisations with their influential membership from the professional and business middle classes, the commercial motor interests and motor manufacturers, as well as the road-building lobby as represented by the British Roads Federation and the Roads Improvement Association. Dwarfed by these groups, on the other side of the argument, was the Pedestrians' Association.

The apparently neutral rhetoric of road safety was, in fact, heavily influenced by the motoring lobby. At the heart of this process was the NSFA, which was funded by successive governments as a recognised agency for road safety. The NSFA had enormous influence in formulating conceptions of road safety. The organisation's archives reveal the regularity with which its observations appeared in the press. For example, between 23 July and 11 November 1930 newspapers carried 821 mentions of their campaigns.[49] Regular road-safety warnings on the BBC were also based on advice from the NSFA.[50] The organisation also sowed its perspective on road safety amongst official opinion by distributing free copies of its journal *Safety First* to chief constables, borough surveyors and others involved in traffic administration.[51] The true nature of the NSFA's role has not been recognised in the existing historiography. Emsley described the NSFA as a neutral body when explaining its presence in the lobby for the abolition of the speed limit in 1930.[52] Foreman-Peck described it as a pressure group, which opposed the motoring lobby from the 1920s onwards.[53] Given the organisation's name, it is easy to make this assumption. Even Plowden's exhaustive enquiry failed to examine the NSFA's history, membership and funding, although he did indicate that the Pedestrians' Association was suspicious of its close links with the motoring lobby.[54] A brief survey of the NSFA will suggest that it was far from being a neutral agency.

The NSFA grew out of the London Safety First Association, which was formed in 1916.[55] Its industrial wing was doctrinally *laissez-faire*, favouring voluntary measures and worker education within factories rather than safety legislation. This approach was replicated in its road-safety propaganda, which continually stressed the responsibility of the pedestrian in accident prevention. Such a philosophy attracted the motoring lobby, which became the NSFA's chief source of private-sector finance. During the early years of its existence the NSFA claimed its financial liquidity was due to 'the exceptional – and solitary – generosity of Mr. Gordon Stewart [who] has kept the road safety campaign alive'.[56] Stewart funded its campaigns with donations total-ling £4,425 between 1931 and 1934.[57] He was the managing director of Stewart and Arden Ltd, the main London dealers for Morris Motors, and obviously would not have provided such sums had the NSFA been likely to call for greater restrictions on motoring. An NSFA letter to *The Times* in 1933 demonstrated that the organisation did exactly the opposite: 'The concluding words of your leading article to-day exactly define what has always been the contention of the National "Safety First" Association – namely, that "safety appears to be much more a matter of education and of administration than of altering the law".'[58]

At that point the NSFA was campaigning against the reintroduction of the speed limit for private motor vehicles. This campaign was fought despite widespread public concern over the increase in road casualties following the abolition of the 20 m.p.h. limit in 1930. The NSFA stance was backed by funding of £1,000 provided by the AA and SMMT under the cover of the Motor Legislation Committee (MLC).[59] The NSFA was also funded by very healthy advertising receipts from its safe-driving publications, over £19,000 being received between 1929 and 1932.[60] Many of the advertisements were placed by motor manu-facturers, motor dealers, component manufacturers, the AA and RAC. This financial backing was matched by an eagerness to direct NSFA policy by serving within its organisation. The NSFA's list of leading officers in 1932, for example, read like a Who's Who of motoring interests. The chairmen of the AA, the Omnibus Owners Association and the RAC acted as vice-presidents, as did the presidents of the Commercial Motor Users' Association, and the Society of Motor

Manufacturers and Traders. This group was reinforced by the presence of Herbert Austin of Austin Motors, who took his place as the representative of the National Union of Manufacturers.[61]

As an alternative to legislation, the NSFA consistently led campaigns to 'educate' the non-motoring public, particularly children. The NSFA also called for increasing segregation of different types of road user, in future highway design, and the scientific analysis of road accidents. These policies had a wide appeal, although as will be seen their claims to offer a neutral scientific approach should be treated sceptically. The NSFA's strategies for improving road safety proved attractive for a number of reasons. In one way or another they appealed to the interests of a variety of groups. First, they proved highly convenient for motoring interests, whose sponsorship of the NSFA was motivated by a desire to ensure legislation did not affect them commercially. Second, they appealed because they offered a largely *laissez-faire* approach to a political establishment still fundamentally inclined to such a philosophy. Third, education and propaganda were attractive to the police forces and courts that had to prosecute ever-greater numbers of motorists. For example, the total number of motoring offences dealt with by police in England and Wales during the second six months of 1928 was a massive 114,541.[62] Fourth, the road-safety policies of the NSFA had an unconscious appeal to legislators, law enforcers and opinion formers, such as journalists, as they became car owners themselves. They no doubt began to realise that one day their ownership of that technology could result in their being labelled as selfish road hogs. The reliance which each of these groups came to place on what Davis calls the ideology of road safety will now be examined. Their motivations will be investigated and it will be suggested that efforts to place road-safety policy on a scientific footing were doomed from the start. Too many of the issues they sought to evaluate were not conducive to objective analysis.

Road-casualty figures, and the publicity that accompanied them, were not good news for motor manufacturers. Many first-time car buyers were middle-aged, having been prevented from becoming motorists earlier due to factors such as steady career progression, mortgage repayments and childrens' school fees.[63] Such buyers were likely to be apprehensive about the thought of purchasing a machine which might lead them into physical danger, as well as possible litigation.

Manufacturers were understandably keen to minimise talk about the danger of the car at every possible occasion.[64] Whereas the individual motorist might apportion blame for motoring accidents to some form of motoring 'other', such an approach was problematic for any manufacturer seeking maximum sales.

A more appealing option was offered by what was, on the face of it, a more logical, scientific, assessment of the road-accident problem. A feature of the response to escalating road casualties was an increasing emphasis, promoted from the mid-1920s by the NSFA, on the analysis of road-accident data. Once again, the spotlight was removed from the motor vehicle, as various groups sought to make use of statistics to support their own theories and interests. The motoring organisations, in particular, made the most of any figures purporting to show that pedestrians were often responsible for accidents. Thus, pedestrians were condemned for their negligence, becoming regular scapegoats in the motoring press, which combed police reports to glean statements about pedestrian carelessness. In 1929, for example, the Chief Constable of Liverpool was reported to have described that city's pedestrians as the worst in the world, blaming them for 75 per cent of traffic accidents.[65]

The scientific presentation of the road-accident statistical findings also allowed for a move away from the actuality of dead and injured citizens, and any concomitant emotive discussion, towards the self-professed science of traffic control of Alker Tripp, the assistant commissioner of police at Scotland Yard, who wrote coldly of the need for cyclists to become an 'efficient traffic unit'.[66] The collection of road-accident data was subject to innumerable flaws, not least of these being the deaths of many potential witnesses, particularly pedestrian ones. The proceedings of an inquest investigating the death of what appears to have been the first person to have been killed by a car, in 1896, followed a pattern that became all too familiar. Accounts of the events leading up to the death of forty-six-year-old Bridget Driscoll varied. One of the car's occupants maintained that it was travelling at no more than 4.5 m.p.h.; another that 8 m.p.h. was its maximum speed. Yet other witnesses claimed that the vehicle was travelling faster than any coach and horses that they had ever seen. Whatever the exact truth of the matter, Bridget Driscoll was killed immediately by the impact, having received massive head injuries that left her brain protruding from the skull.[67] When the collection of road-accident statistics became systematic, in the 1930s, they consistently placed a higher degree of responsibility for accidents on pedestrians in the case of fatal accidents than non-fatal ones. For example, the Ministry of Transport calculated that 36.5 per cent of fatal road accidents in 1936 could be attributed to pedestrians, whereas the figure for non-fatal accidents was only 27.9 per cent. It would appear that some motorists took advantage of the unavailability of pedestrian witnesses to escape possible liability for their actions.[68]

Compiling the details of accidents was often the responsibility of a single police officer, who, for a variety of reasons, could not always be relied upon to produce accurate data. The first potential problem was that of assessing competing interpretations of the events leading up to an accident. Furthermore, constables often displayed 'considerable laxity' and 'gross carelessness' in recording the circumstances of street accidents with, for example, vehicle registration numbers often recorded inaccurately.[69] However, the officer's verdict was the one which went towards the compilation of the official statistics. Accident reports, such as that presented by the House of Lords Select Committee on the Prevention of Road Accidents, which analysed 100,000 road accidents that took place in 1937, were also based on several categories tending to attribute blame, for a significant number of the accidents, to pedestrians. For example, 64.7 per cent of all fatal, and 57.4 per cent of all non-fatal, accidents were assigned to pedestrians, who were described as 'heedless of traffic', or as 'walking or running out in front of or behind a vehicle or object which masked his or her movement'. These categories were not interrogated in any way. If visibility was obscured should not motor vehicles have been travelling at a speed which took account of that factor? In effect, society sought solace for growing road casualties in the belief that the study of road-accident causes would lead to the design of new roads and propaganda campaigns that would all but eliminate road casualties.[70]

The neutral, scientific, language of road-accident reports was paralleled by the discourse within which much of the discussion on road safety took place. The debate was conducted in what were seen as the best British traditions of moderation, with the accent on 'reasonableness', 'the avoidance of panic and extreme measures', and 'seeing the other fellow's point of view'.[71] The 1930 Road Traffic Act removed the speed limit on the grounds that the great majority of motorists could be entrusted to drive with due care and attention. The few bad apples, or 'road hogs', would be dealt with by tougher maximum penalties for dangerous or reckless driving. Meanwhile, the introduction of compulsory third-party insurance would cover the financial consequences of any accident. At the same time, it was argued that *The Highway Code*, rather than legislative restrictions, would have the best results with the free-born British motorist. The Minister of Transport, Herbert Morrison, and various motoring interests were quick to seize on any evidence that *The Highway Code* had improved driving behaviour. Describing the principles behind it in 1931, Morrison said that it 'goes upon the basis that this is what the decent drivers will do, and that it is just as ungentlemanly to be discourteous or to play the fool on the King's highway as it would be for a man to push his wife off her chair at the Sunday tea table and grab two pieces of cake'.[72] Commenting, in the same year, on a 10 per cent fall in London's accident figures, Morrison argued that, 'The moral is plain. Tell the motorist, in parliamentary language, that he is a gentleman and should drive like one, remove the element of compulsion inherent in a speed limit, substitute a "highway code" of a purely persuasive character, and the motorist will rise to the occasion and agreeably surprise the pedestrian.'[73]

This emphasis on compromise was a feature of every aspect of the blossoming ideology of road safety. NSFA road-safety propaganda films had titles steeped in a discourse of 'Englishness', employing classless sporting references, such as *Sportsmanship on Wheels* and *Playing the Game*.[74] The veneer of consensus with which discussions of road safety were frequently covered was not, however, all encompassing. Teachers' organisations were not entirely happy with the nature of the road-safety propaganda directed at children in the 1930s. The 1935 conference of the National Association of Head Teachers rejected a government scheme to teach children to walk on the left hand side of pavements. One delegate said: 'You cannot Hitlerise the British public in this way.'[75]

Road-safety discussion on the BBC also had its critics. The corporation's approach to the question mirrored the tone of the debate elsewhere by stressing the need for national consensus and the avoidance of class friction. Thus, in the early 1930s, the Pedestrians' Association was refused air time on the BBC on the grounds that 'it was undesirable to excite controversy'.[76] Instead, the BBC chose motorists, particularly racing drivers, to give a series of talks. In April 1934, one of these contributors, Lord Cottenham, argued that the two worst driving faults were sticking to the crown of the road and driving too slowly.[77] In 1934 the Pedestrians' Association wrote to Sir John Reith to protest that an unbalanced perspective was being offered, arguing that

> Nothing has, in our opinion, done more to make the roads what they are to-day than this delegation to motorists of the task of saying what constitutes safety. It is surely wrong that after sixteen years of continually rising casualties, little or nothing should have been heard over the wireless on behalf of pedestrians, whose point of view is necessarily different from that of other road users.[78]

They received no reply from Reith. A letter from a 'minor official' informed them that all road-safety issues were dealt with in consultation with the Ministry of Transport. In fact several of the racing drivers whose advice was broadcast during the series on 'road sense' had been involved in serious motoring accidents on and off the race track. The most serious of these involved Kaye Don, who was imprisoned in 1934 for manslaughter, following the death of a mechanic on the Isle of Man.[79]

The press, like the BBC, followed the lead set by government and entrusted much of its coverage of road-safety issues to 'Our Motoring Correspondent'. Alternatively, the opinion of the motoring associations was sought, and their influence should not be underestimated. The AA and RAC were massive commercial concerns with a great deal to gain from the continued expansion of motoring, but the *Manchester Guardian*, for example, described them as an 'unimpeachable authority'.[80] Equally important was the increasing number of motoring readers, as well as the resulting advertising revenue newspapers and magazines received from motoring interests. In December 1934, Tom Foley, the president of the Pedestrians' Association, corresponded with the editor of the *Daily Herald* and its TUC backers about its coverage of road safety. He believed that

> The *Herald* has made no effective protest against this disgraceful state of affairs. Why has it not supported measures to regulate the use of the dangerous machine so that this danger was reduced to a minimum? … Instead, when individuals or organisations like the Pedestrians' Association have attempted to take these matters up they have been subject to cheap sneers, notably from the motoring correspondent, and pious humbug deprecating 'squabbling about rights'.[81]

Foley accused the paper of being pro-motorist and anti-pedestrian in its attitudes towards the driving test and speed limit. He felt its motoring correspondent, racing driver Tommy Wisdom, had written 'a continual stream of anti-pedestrian propaganda'.[82] Foley said he understood the Herald's desire not to offend the commercial interests who advertised cars, oil and petrol, but suggested they consider their non-motorist readers.

Certainly, the press took a more temperate line when discussing the enormous road casualties that occurred year after year than might have been the case if they were the result of some working-class pastime. Indeed, some coverage was extremely pro-motorist. In October 1933 the motoring correspondent of the *Daily Express* offered a less than consensual perspective when analysing the failures of the 1930 Road Traffic Act. He noted that it had rightly removed the old 20 m.p.h. speed limit, which in his opinion had been a farce. However, accidents had risen in the years since it was passed. What was to be done now? he asked. His answer was to compel 'jaywalkers' to take proper care. Many accidents, he believed, could not reasonably be called 'motoring accidents' at all and should be termed 'walking accidents'. This line of thought was perhaps most crassly articulated in the *Morris Owner*, in 1932, which argued that 'Legislation has dealt only with the motorist, whereas the foolish pedestrian is almost exclusively to blame, the mental deficient who will not look where he is going when he steps in the road.'[83]

At the same time a tendency emerged to perceive the majority of motoring offences as inconsequential. In December 1933, an editorial in the *Manchester Evening News* entitled 'Be Fair to the Motorist' labelled the majority of the 330,000 motoring offences that year as trivial. In the previous year, the *Daily Express* had made what it saw as unnecessary motoring cases part of its general campaign against financial waste. It believed that only 5 per cent of cases could be described as serious.[84] In 1937, *Autocar* commented on changing press attitudes towards the motorist and wondered whether these newspapers had realised that their readers now owned cars themselves. Formerly headlines had spoken of 'Hoot and Kill' motorists: by 1937 they talked instead of 'Fair Play for the Motorist' or 'Suicidal Pedestrians'.[85]

In fact, by the late 1930s, the ideas pushed by the NSFA and for many years reiterated by the media seem to have been commonly held.

A Gallup poll conducted in 1939 suggested that only 5 per cent of people believed that reducing the number of cars would also reduce road accidents. The same proportion felt that harsher penalties for offending motorists was the answer, whilst 8 per cent felt that lowering the speed limit would be most effective. The biggest proportion, 28 per cent, felt that the solution could be found through greater caution and common sense.[86]

The increasing resources expended on prosecuting motorists and the middle-class character of the defendants were a further factor that made the policies offered by the NSFA attractive to many in authority. Motoring misdemeanours brought large numbers of middle-class individuals into conflict with the police for the first time. Rising car ownership led to a greater and greater number of motorists coming before the courts. Between 1900 and 1909 only 6.3 per cent of all persons tried for indictable and non-indictable offences faced charges relating to motoring violations. However, in the years from 1930 to 1933 this figure had soared to a massive 43.2 per cent.[87] This development clearly caused a degree of embarrassment to police, courts and motorists. Enforcement of the speed limit, set at 20 m.p.h. in 1903, potentially criminalised all motorists whose vehicles were well capable of speeds in excess of a limit which was routinely flouted. Motorists were not averse to using their individual or collective class positions to dissuade the police from employing speed traps. In 1909, when the Surrey police launched a campaign against the AA's use of scouts to warn motorists of speed traps ahead of them, the latter replied by urging its members to launch an economic boycott of the area during the summer months.[88] On other occasions, some motorists attempted to intimidate individual police officers, or offered bribes to escape prosecution.[89] This was the case at Esher in November 1907 when PC Miles stopped a car for speeding, only to be offered a sovereign to overlook the offence. The motorist, William Darnborough, was doubly unsuccessful, being committed for trial for attempted bribery.[90]

Another common response was for motorists to accuse the police of infringement of their liberties. For instance, police speed traps were attacked as un-English and lacking sportsmanship by one MP in 1924.[91] The police were also consistently subjected to the claim that they should be protecting property rather than bothering law-abiding motorists. In 1937 one motorist vented his criticism of the police for their failure to solve a number of burglaries in his East Acton street: 'Are they short of men? Of course there is a shortage of men, when luxurious mobile police limousines are touring London streets with 3 or sometimes 4 passengers, who might profitably be employed in their proper duty, which I maintain is to protect property.'[92] One result of concerns about the antagonism between motorists and police was the emergence, in the late 1930s, of 'courtesy cops' whose role was to aid and advise motorists rather than censure them. In 1935 the Church Assembly urged more courtesy on the roads, a sentiment supported by the AA, and in 1937 the first 'courtesy cops' appeared in government-financed pilot schemes in Lancashire, Cheshire, Liverpool, Manchester and Salford. Officers received special training at Hendon police college, which prepared them to be the educators of motorists rather than prosecutors.[93]

Motorists were also receiving increasingly sympathetic treatment in the courts. In his 1935 annual report, the commissioner of the Metropolitan Police noted that 'efforts to enforce the speed limit had not been supported by some of the Courts as well as might have been expected.'[94] Growing car ownership amongst magistrates gave them a different perspective on motoring offences. On one occasion, in 1925, Coventry magistrates dismissed cases of motorists caught in a speed trap, their chairman, Major Woollcome-Adams, explaining that the bench disliked this method. He had himself been apprehended by a speed trap.[95]

Despite the evidence of such cases, motorists felt victimised by both the police and the courts. For some this sense of victimisation was stretched as far as a willingness to defend hit-and-run drivers:

> Such reprehensible and cowardly conduct is not characteristic of an Englishman and has forced me to endeavour to find a cause for it … our sense of injustice is very developed, and it is inborn in us to revolt at injustice … motorists run away after causing accidents because they know their case will not be tried free of prejudice and they feel they will not obtain justice.[96]

As William Plowden demonstrated motorists were, if anything, securing more lenient treatment from magistrates in the 1920s and 1930s than they had done in the early days of motoring. Average fines for all motoring offenses were 71 per cent lower in real terms in 1938 than in 1904/5. Average fines for speeding on the two dates reveal that the real value of fines was 81 per cent lower in 1938 than in 1904/5. Average fines for dangerous driving fluctuated; being 69 per cent below the 1904/5 level in 1929, but only 11 per cent below the early figure in 1935, before the gap widened again to 27 per cent in 1938.[97] There was also an increasing tendency for courts to see even serious motoring offences as technical ones, a proclivity which must have been enhanced by the fact that motoring offenders took up a position in the well of the court not the dock.[98] This was an extremely important symbolic concession to motorists.

Uncomfortably located between magistrates, who were often ambivalent in their prosecution of motoring offenses, and antagonised middle-class motorists, the police began to see the decriminalisation of speeding as one means of reducing the problems they faced. The chief constable of Kent, Major Henry Chapman, told the Royal Commission on Transport, which sat between 1928 and 1930, that 37 of 55 chief constables favoured ending the speed limit. Appropriately enough, he had himself been prosecuted for a speeding offence, in his chauffeur-driven car.[99] Almost from the minute the 1903 Motor Car Act introduced a 20 m.p.h. speed limit, the motoring lobby began a long campaign to have it increased or removed altogether. It was argued that it was archaic, given the technical capabilities of motor vehicles. They also maintained that speed was not a significant factor in road accidents, or in the severity of injuries. In 1902 the legislators had absolutely no data upon which to base their decision to set the limit at 20 m.p.h. However, today we know that accidents that occur at 20 m.p.h. or less produce far fewer casualties than those that occur at greater speeds. Pedestrians, of course, are particularly vulnerable once impact speeds pass 20 m.p.h. Whereas only 5 per cent of pedestrians are killed when struck by a vehicle travelling at 19 m.p.h., the figure rises to 37 per cent at 31 m.p.h. and soars to 83 per cent at 43.5 m.p.h.[100]

Explaining the rationale behind the abolition of the speed limit in the 1930 Road Traffic Act, Herbert Morrison, the Minister of Transport, placed great importance on the police's view:

[The] police … are in an impossible position. Nominally they have to enforce the law. In fact they know that *the law is not supported by the general body of public opinion, and they tolerate the breaches of the law which now exists*. That is not a fair position in which to place the police. If the law is there, the police should be expected to enforce it, and the

police should be given every support and every encouragement. If the
public do not expect it enforced, if the general level of opinion is
against it being enforced, well the British police have enough common sense not to be too meticulous in enforcing laws which are not
in accordance with the general body of public opinion.[101]

The 'general body of public opinion', referred to by Morrison, was
made up of the motorists themselves, their representative bodies, motor
manufacturers, magistrates and the overworked police who increasingly
saw virtually all motoring offences as technical in nature and impossible to enforce. It did not, presumably, include the victims of road
accidents or their relatives.

The determination to decriminalise speeding in 1930 can be usefully
juxtaposed with the decision not to repeal the Street Betting Act of
1906. This Act was also widely flouted and magistrates often failed to
take tough action against offenders when police brought them to court.
Emsley points out that in 1923 a parliamentary committee considered
the arguments in favour of its repeal.[102] He also correctly suggests that
it has not traditionally been popular with legislators to rescind a law
because people break it. However, rather than legalise an essentially
harmless and massively popular aspect of working-class culture, it was
the dangerous practice of speeding that was de-criminalised.[103] Predict-
ably, this experiment in *laissez-faire* on the road proved unsuccessful as
casualty figures continued to rise. The 1934 Road Traffic Act reimposed
a limit, set at 30 m.p.h. in built-up areas, and introduced the driving
test, in spite of the opposition of the AA, RAC and NSFA. It also
included innovations in the regulation of pedestrian movement by
introducing pedestrian crossings. Regulations introduced in London
soon after made it possible for pedestrians to be fined for not crossing
the road at recognised points.[104]

The 1934 Act was the final piece of traffic legislation with regard to
private motoring in this period. From this point, increasing emphasis
was placed on propaganda and the education of all road users. By the
late 1930s, the government, the police and the media seemed to have
accepted that all that could be accomplished in terms of legislation had
been realised. Hundreds of thousands of motorists continued to be
prosecuted for a variety of offences but casualty figures remained
depressingly high. So more and more hopes were pinned on the efforts
of teachers, the BBC, the press, and the police in their new guise of

'courtesy cops' to educate all road users. Education, safer vehicles, new road design, and greater segregation of road users were expected to reduce road casualties.

By the end of the 1930s, what Davis identifies as the ideology of road safety had been widely taken up. Where once the press had called for extreme restrictions to be implemented to control the motorist, each new set of frighteningly high accident statistics was met by much hand-wringing and calls for more education and propaganda on road safety. In terms of central government and the national press the road-safety lobby had, by the 1930s, largely won the day. The last official words on road safety in this period were issued by the Alness Committee, established in 1937 to consider means of reducing road casualties. Its report was criticised by the Pedestrians' Association as 'openly and unreservedly pro-motorist', an assessment recognised by Plowden when citing a key passage from the committee's report:

> Propaganda should be employed for the purpose of making those who do not own motor-cars realize how much they owe to motor transport for the supply of their food, for passenger services and so on. There still remains in the public mind a prejudice against motor-cars, born no doubt in the old days when few people owned them, and when they were considered as luxuries rather than part of an essential national service, as they are today.[105]

The body the committee proposed to carry out this propaganda was, aptly enough, the NSFA.

'The majority is not master of its own house': road safety in the urban environment

This final section examines the impact of the increasing use of motor transport in the urban context. As society came to a concordance with the private car in particular, a process began of shaping the urban landscape to suit motor vehicles rather than the reverse. It is worth examining developments at the local level because, unlike central government, provincial authorities ran their own public-transport systems, which gave them different priorities than national government and could, at times, prompt attempts to develop local responses to increasing motor traffic.

Furthermore, the potential for opposition to the car was more apparent at the local level. This was probably for very practical human reasons. Six or seven thousand road deaths nationally, when experienced year after year, may have become a meaningless figure, whereas a hundred or more road deaths in an individual town inevitably carry more resonance. In smaller areas still there may be a tendency for a greater and greater intensity of feeling. However, it will be seen that on many occasions, when such incidents arose, the arguments of the road lobby held more sway at the Ministry of Transport than those of concerned local residents. Whenever local authorities sought to depart from the general dictates of national policy they faced two problems. First, individual initiatives were generally thwarted by a combination of motoring and commercial interests. A second obstacle was government unwillingness to sanction any action on road-safety policy that was not agreed by all parties and implemented nationally.

By 1905 what was to become a familiar pattern had been set in motion. By May of that year, the authorities in the City of London, Beverley, Bury, Dover, Kingston-on-Thames, Leeds, Leigh, Newport, Todmorden, Winchester and Whitehaven had all applied to the government for permission to impose 10 m.p.h. limits on the roads under their jurisdiction. Each of these requests had been rejected amid accusations that the AA, Motor Union and other motoring organisations were wielding a powerful influence with the national government.[106] At this point, such accusations were premature: the government had priorities other than road traffic, which it hoped had been dealt with by the 1903 Motor Car Act. Moreover the AA, given its unpopularity amongst several police forces, had some way to go before it established itself as a respectable organisation in government eyes. However, together with commercial motoring groups it was to form a powerful lobby group. In 1919 a group of ten separate organisations, the most significant being the AA and the SMMT, crystallised into the Motor Legislation Committee (MLC).[107] In the words of the AA's Stenson Cooke, the MLC's brief was to combat 'any Corporation, Municipality, Urban or Rural council in the House of Lords or Commons or in the press'.[108] Offering an example of the local authority proposals the MLC had fought, Cooke cited the case of measures which several local authorities attempted to introduce in relation to motor vehicles and the safety of tram passengers. A discussion of this example will illustrate the differences of interest that often arose between local communities and motoring representatives.

In 1914, Glasgow Corporation responded to growing concerns about the rising toll of fatalities and injuries occurring at tram stops. Passengers alighting from trams were frequently endangered by passing motor vehicles. A new by-law was introduced which forced all vehicles to pull up if a tram in front of them was dropping off passengers. In 1915 the by-law was confirmed by the Secretary of State for Scotland.[109] Glasgow's measures were noted south of the border, where there were calls for their implementation in English and Welsh cities. The *Manchester Courier*, for example, suggested the adoption of the tram-stop by-law in its home city.[110] However, the onset of war seems to have focused minds on other issues. Immediately following the war, much popular opinion in Manchester was antagonistic to the car. In September 1919 the Manchester-based *Daily Dispatch* published an editorial entitled 'The Holocaust' which said: 'Daily we read of people being run over and smashed ... There is no rule of the road. The motor car, the taxi car, takes care there shall not be.'[111] The editorial called for stricter supervision of drivers, a Manchester speed limit and the implementation of a tram-stop by-law. This final suggestion caused a great deal of controversy in Manchester in the 1920s. On three separate occasions, between 1921 and 1930, Manchester Corporation bills included clauses that would force all motorists to pull up behind trams that were dropping off passengers. However, Manchester's bid to introduce such a scheme was resisted at every stage by motoring and commercial interests. In January 1921 a ratepayers' meeting, attracting only a few hundred citizens, convened to discuss a Corporation Bill and vote on the various clauses.[112]

The tram-stop clause proved to be a casualty of organised opposition from motorists, the Chamber of Commerce and the Manchester Taxi Cab Owners' Association. The following month, the corporation organised a plebiscite of its voters, in a bid to rescue the clause and several others. On the eve of the vote, the *Daily News* told its readers that a 'vote for the interests of safety tomorrow is one of the first duties of citizenship'.[113] Of the 17,000 citizens that took part in the plebiscite just over 80 per cent voted for the clause, with less than 10 per cent voting against.[114] In March the MLC issued its response to the council's proposal. It asked the city to drop the clause, as Liverpool

Corporation had been persuaded to do, because it threatened to create a dangerous lack of uniformity in road-safety law. It also urged the corporation not to imperil their whole bill 'by persisting in a clause strongly opposed by a large and influential section of their constituents'.[115] The corporation's parliamentary committee followed this advice and dropped the clause, claiming that they had received evidence, which could not be made public, that made it necessary to abandon the tram-stop clause.[116] This was greeted with indignation in the city, with the *Daily News* accusing the corporation of having 'simply yielded to the representatives of the big motor interests of the country'.[117] A full council meeting responded by reinstating the measure following a close vote (39 to 36).[118] The next, and final, hurdle proved to be the House of Lords, where a Committee of the House, chaired by Lord Wemyss, finally rejected the clause in May.[119]

In 1924 a similar process came to an end, at the hands of a committee headed by the Earl of Clarendon. The committee heard petitions against the tram-stop clause from the AA, the RAC, the Commercial Motor Users' Association and a group calling itself the Manchester Committee of Road Users. The evidence of Manchester's chief constable in favour of the proposal was rejected, as Clarendon's committee followed the Ministry of Transport line that legislation should be of a national, not a local nature. The Manchester press was highly critical of this second rejection of the wishes of the Manchester electorate, who had again shown their support for the measure in a plebiscite.[120] The *Manchester Guardian* recalled that much used to be heard of allowing colonial administrations to get on with handling their own problems, but in contemporary Manchester 'the majority is not master of its own house, and our overlord seems singularly studious of the minority's interests'.[121] The *City News* went further, describing, in an article entitled 'Who governs Manchester?', the victory of sectional interests: 'In other words the minority has the right to rule and not the majority of citizens. Perhaps no other decision could be looked for from a body which represents nobody but itself. The traditional upholders of privilege have once more demonstrated their faith in themselves.'[122] The council planned another attempt to implement their safety proposal in 1930 but withdrew it following the publication of the government's Road Traffic Bill. The bill included provision for *The Highway Code*, which was to include a suggestion that drivers halt when trams were dropping off passengers. When the local branch of the Pedestrians' Association asked to see the Lord Mayor to protest about the decision, they were told that there would be no point in having the meeting.

In Manchester, as nationally, a tendency emerged during the late 1920s to focus on pedestrian responsibility for road accidents. In October 1929, Chief Constable Godfrey of Manchester's neighbour, Salford, spoke on radio to state his opinion that in some motor-vehicle-related fatalities the inquest should return a verdict of suicide by the pedestrian.[123] By November 1933 he was describing the pedestrian as the most unrestricted individual in the country.[124] The following month he was championing his force's use of road-safety lectures in schools, describing how children were 'taught how their careless actions reflect on the characters of the schools, of their homes, on their city and country: that they are not justified in causing so much mental anguish to others by being careless on the streets.'[125] An uncharitable critic might conclude that Godfrey maintained a high profile for his force in road-safety matters because it had been tarnished with serious allegations of corruption involving illegal gambling.[126]

Also in 1933, Manchester's chief constable, Maxwell, attributed almost 58 per cent of fatal accidents in the city to pedestrian carelessness.[127] A year earlier Manchester's city coroner, Mr Surridge, had attributed most of the road fatalities in the city to the same cause.[128] Manchester was by this time fully in step with national policy. Thousands of children went annually to see road-safety films and the city had an annual safety week. Meanwhile Manchester police's motorised section insisted that they be seen as friends and advisers of the motorist, rather than as a primarily punitive body.

However, in the wake of the 1934 Road Traffic Act a number of local authorities became involved in a dispute with national government once again. The Act introduced a speed limit of 30 m.p.h. in built-up areas, but it was possible to appeal to have the limit removed from individual roads. The limit was resented by some motorists, particularly it seems younger ones, and there were many incidents of the new speed limit signs being torn down or defaced. University of Birmingham students were amongst those making boisterous protests against the 30 m.p.h. limit.[129] Throughout 1935 and 1936 motoring groups petitioned for the removal of the limit from major roads in several towns and cities, becoming embroiled in disputes with authorities in Birkhenhead, Birmingham, Cardiff, Coventry, Edinburgh, Glasgow, Gillingham, Liverpool, Manchester, Plymouth, Reading, Southampton, Stoke, Swindon, Wallsey and Worthing.[130] The Ministry of Transport arranged enquiries into each disputed request for de-restriction. J. S. Dean of the Pedestrians' Association, who monitored this process, claimed that the motoring lobby's request for de-restriction won the day in 75 per cent of cases.[131] Such decisions were met with by regret amongst many in the authorities concerned. A member of Birmingham's Watch Committee greeted the decision to remove the speed limit from the busy Bristol Road by saying it would 'revert to what it was before – a racing track'.[132] When a speaker at a Southampton Motor Agents Association Dinner hailed de-restriction of several roads in that city as 'a victory' for the motor industry over Southampton Corporation, the Mayor reminded him that their victory was won 'against the wish of the people living in these streets, as the petitions from these people show.'[133]

It seems likely that the financial costs, as much as the possible human consequences, of de-restricting several city roads were uppermost in the thinking of many of the councils who fought moves to de-restrict roads under their jurisdiction. De-restricting several roads necessitated the erection of speed-limit signs at points where motorists returned to restricted sections of the highway. Manchester, and other councils, complained to central government about the extra costs this would entail. Manchester claimed that if all its roads were subject to the limit, road signs would cost only £1,500, but if several arterial roads were to be exempted costs could rise to £30,000. The city, along with several others, defied Ministry of Transport instructions to de-restrict the roads in question. A public inquiry was held in October, with the council, the Pedestrians' Association and the Manchester and Salford Trades Council opposing the de-restriction orders. Supporting the Ministry's decision were the AA, RAC and a group calling itself the Society of United Motorists. The latter groups won the day: twenty-four of the twenty-eight roads were de-restricted by the Ministry. Mr A. A. Purcell, the secretary of the Manchester and Salford Trades Council, was highly critical of the process: 'Of all the travesties and mockeries of an en-quiry I never saw one to equal that, Manchester Corporation is the governing body in the city, and yet the AA and the RAC put Manches-ter Corporation in the box and then examined it.'[134]

In other parts of Britain local residents' groups took part in spontaneous de-restriction revolts which were the result of passionate views about the dangers of traffic, the car in particular. Such was the case in four areas of London in the late 1930s. Residents near Falloden Way (Hampstead), Westway (Shepherds Bush), The North Circular Road (Willesden) and Western Avenue (East Acton) found themselves living alongside roads that had been de-restricted. They responded by organising demonstrations that halted traffic, much to the fury of passing motorists. The first two of these protests were successful in their aim of re-imposing the 30 m.p.h. limit. Also in 1937, mothers living near the Kingstanding Road, in Birmingham's Perry Bar area, protested about the dangers their children faced from speeding motor traffic. The following year, mothers living near the Kingston by-pass at Tolworth in Surrey, engaged in protests which held up traffic. Fifty police were needed to clear them away.[135] Elsewhere, parents protested against the dangers of road traffic by keeping their children away from school.[136]

One demonstration, in 1937, by residents living in a Hammersmith council estate alongside Westway, culminated in violent clashes with the police.[137] Locals complained that cars travelled at very high speeds along the road and failed to stop at pedestrian crossings. The *Acton Gazette and Express* supported their case: 'On Tuesday evening the cars were flashing along Westway at very high speeds, and groups of children stood at the pedestrian crossings waiting for a chance to dart across the road. A "Gazette" reporter who spent about an hour walking up and down Westway did not see one car stop at any of the crossings.'[138]

Many motorists resented the reimposition of the 30 m.p.h. limit on new arterial roads. They felt that since their motoring taxes had paid for the roads, subsequent ribbon development should not entail an end to their freedom to travel at speed along the new highways. As *Autocar* put it: 'Every time it is the motorist who pays out vast sums to find a way of avoiding all danger to children and pedestrians, and every time these pedestrians settle down like a swarm of bees around the amenities which he, the motorist has provided – and then complain of the danger!'[139] *Autocar* called for commercial boycotts of shops and businesses in areas that refused to de-restrict the roads in question.[140] It felt that the speed limit had an irrational 'magic power … in the minds of local authorities'. In the case of Westway, *Autocar* noted that the Ministry of Transport had offered Hammersmith Borough Council grants towards the cost of guard rails, subways and overhead bridges for pedestrians.[141] Clearly, so far as the motoring community was concerned, the following years would see the car altering the urban landscape and the movements of other transport users rather than the other way around. For them speed had won the day.

Conclusion

In his 1942 book, *Town Planning and Road Traffic*, H. Alker Tripp argued that 'any town so planned that its citizens are killed and injured in vast numbers is obviously an ill-planned town'.[142] This statement brings us to the crux of the matter, for it asked questions of how cities were planned, but said nothing about the form of transport which brought the 'vast numbers' of deaths and injuries to those cities. There is no single British example as striking as that of Robert Moses' planning in New York to demonstrate what the infrastructure around a technology can reveal about the embodiment of specific forms of power and authority – although the abolition of the speed limit in 1930 comes close. However, an embodiment of class interest was a very significant feature in the emergence of motoring legislation, road-safety policies and eventually the design of Britain's towns and cities. It has been demonstrated that attempts to restrict the growing hegemony of motor transport were blocked by an influential ideology and powerful interests. Once car ownership began diffusing amongst the influential professional and commercial middle classes there was little chance that an effective opposition to private motoring might arise. The newspapers that these groups read also began changing their attitudes towards the car. These developments made it possible for motoring interests to employ a language of *laissez-faire* and 'Englishness' in urging minimal government interference with the motorist. With motoring offering new freedoms to many in the middle classes, large numbers of jobs for working people and increasing financial revenue for the government, it became convenient for all concerned to place their hope in the claims being made by the emerging 'science' of road safety. So, a belief that education and propaganda, better roads and safer technology were better alternatives than legislation made mass car ownership a palatable option, salving anxieties about the deaths and injuries that continued unabated on the roads. In the process, many of the assumptions made and decisions taken reflected the realities of the distribution of power in a class society. Speaking against the reimposition of the speed limit, in 1934, Lieutenant-Colonel Moore Brabazon MP, later to become Minister of Transport, unconsciously revealed the chilling class assumptions that lay at the root of the ideology of road safety:

> It is true that 7,000 people are killed in motor accidents, but it is not always going on like that. People are getting used to the new conditions … No doubt many of the old Members of the House will recollect the number of chickens we killed in the old days. We used to come back with the radiator stuffed with feathers. It was the same with dogs. Dogs get out of the way of motor cars nowadays and you never kill one. There is education even in the lower animals. These things will right themselves.[143]

Notes

1 L. Winner, 'Do artifacts have politics?', *Daedalus*, 109 (1980) 121–36.
2 *Ibid.*, 123.
3 For example, H. L. Preston, *Automobile Age Atlanta* (Athens, GA, 1979) reveals the impact of growing car ownership on the population of Atlanta's black ghetto. Their geographical and social isolation was increased by the construction of new highways that facilitated an early example of 'white flight'.
4 *Guardian*, 7 December 1993.
5 R. Davis, *Death on the Streets: Cars and the Mythology of Road Safety* (Hawes, Leading Edge Press and Publishing Company, 1993), p. 37.
6 *Ibid.*, pp. 9–10.
7 K. Richardson, *The British Motor Industry 1896–1939* (London, Macmillan, 1977); H. Perkin, *The Age of the Automobile* (London, Quartet Books, 1976).
8 Perkin, *The Age of the Automobile*, p. 135.
9 Richardson, *The British Motor Industry*, p. 177.
10 W. Plowden, *The Motor Car and Politics in Britain* (Harmondsworth, Pelican Books, 1973).
11 Royal Society for the Prevention of Accidents, *Road Accident Statistics 1938–1951* (London, ROSPA, 1951). The average for the 1930s is estimated on the years 1930–1938. The wartime blackout contributed to even greater casualty figures in 1939.
12 Department of Transport, *Road Accidents, Great Britain* (London, HMSO, 1991).
13 H. Alker Tripp, *Town Planning and Road Traffic* (London, Arnold, 1942), p. 325.

14 Plowden, *the Motor Car and Politics*, p. 90.

15 *The Economist*, 11 October 1913.

16 H. Barty-King, *The AA: A History of the Automobile Association, 1905–1980* (Basingstoke, Automobile Association, 1980), p. 162.

17 *Ibid.*, pp. 168–9.

18 Plowden, *The Motor Car and Politics*, pp. 117–20.

19 *Ibid.*, pp. 117ff.

20 *Ibid.*, p. 405.

21 C. Emsley, '"Mother, what did policemen do when there weren't any motors?" The law, the police and the regulation of motor traffic in England, 1900–1939', *Historical Journal*, 36 (1993), 357–81.

22 V. A. C. Gatrell, 'Crime, authority and the policeman state', in F. M. L. Thompson (ed.), *The Cambridge Social History of Britain, 1750–1950*, 3 vols (Cambridge, Cambridge University Press, 1990), vol. 3, pp. 243–310.

23 *Ibid.*, p. 246.

24 J. Foreman-Peck, 'Death on the roads: changing national responses to motor accidents', in T. Barker (ed.), *The Economic and Social Effects of the Spread of Motor Vehicles* (London, Macmillan, 1987), p. 270.

25 *Ibid.*, p. 269.

26 Foreman-Peck, 'Death on the Roads', p. 269.

27 *Ibid.*, p. 270.

28 *Ibid.*, p. 270.

29 Plowden, *The Motor Car and Politics*, p. 32.

30 *The Economist*, 23 August 1913; Plowden, *The Motor Car and Politics*, p. 86.

31 *Daily News and Leader*, 14 June 1914.

32 *Daily Citizen*, 2 July 1914.

33 *The Times*, 18 January 1919.

34 Plowden, *The Motor Car and Politics*, p. 28.

35 *Report of the Royal Commission on the Motor Car: Volume II Minutes of Evidence* [Cmnd 3081], paragraph 1647.

36 *Ibid.*, paragraph 1844.

37 *Ibid.*, paragraph 802.

38 *The Times*, 1 August 1903; Plowden, *The Motor Car and Politics*, pp. 27–8.

39 *Autocar*, 21 June 1919.

40 *Manchester Guardian*, 19 February 1920.

41 *Autocar*, 17 September 1926.

42 *Autocar*, 22 August 1930.

43 *Autocar*, 1 August 1924 and 29 September 1933.

44 Plowden, *The Motor Car and Politics*, pp. 208–9.

45 Society of Motor Manufacturers and Traders, *The Motor Industry of Great Britain 1939* (London, SMMT, 1939).

46 S. M. Bowden, 'Demand and supply constraints in the inter-war UK car industry: did the manufacturers get it right?', *Business History*, 33 (1991), Table 2.

47 *The Times*, 6 and 9 November 1929.

48 *The Times*, 4 April 1931.

49 University of Liverpool, Records of the Royal Society for the Prevention of Accidents, D266/2/11.

50 *Ibid.*, D/266/2/29.

51 *Ibid.*, D266/2/11.

52 Emsley, 'Mother, what did policemen do', 376.

53 Foreman-Peck, 'Death on the roads', pp. 269–70.

54 Plowden, *The Motor Car and Politics*, p. 288.

55 In 1941 it was granted the royal charter and became part of the Royal Society for the Prevention of Accidents.

56 Public Records Office, MT 34/142, Accidents: Contribution from the road fund towards a campaign for the reduction of accidents, 1933–35.

57 *Ibid.* The sums involved were £1,025 in 1931, £1,000 in 1932 and 1933 and £1,400 in 1934.

58 University of Liverpool, Records of the Royal Society for the Prevention of Accidents, D266/2/11.

59 Pedestrians' Association, *Occasional Newsletter*, October 1934; Plowden, *The Motor Car and Politics*, p. 288. The Motor Legislation Committee was a national pressure group set up in 1919 by the AA and the Society of Motor Manufacturers and Traders.

60 PRO, MT 34/142. The annual sums were £5,478 in 1929, £5,458 in 1930, £5,202 in 1931 and £3,086 in 1932.

61 *Ibid.*

62 Home Office, *Return showing by Police District, the Number of Persons dealt with for Motoring Offences during the Period July to December 1928* (London, Home Office, 1929).

63 Richardson's *The British Motor Industry* contended that many new motorists in the 1930s were middle-aged. This would have been a consequence of the pattern of rising real incomes, identified in Chapter 1, as well as the painfully slow career progress of many middle-class men, as discussed in R. Samuel, 'Middle class between the wars', *New Society*, January-June 1981.

64 *Advertiser's Weekly*, for example, reported that they were particularly sensitive about the portrayal of motoring as dangerous in advertising by manufacturers of other products.

65 *Autocar*, 19 April 1929.

66 Alker Tripp, *Town Planning and Road Traffic*, pp. 28–9.

67 *The Times*, 21 August and 26 August 1896.

68 *The Times*, 1 April 1937.

69 J. Klein, 'A new breed of law breaker: how traffic law influenced class relations between the police and the public in the interwar period', paper delivered at the *Social History Society Annual Conference* 1994, p. 3.

70 House of Lords select committee on prevention of road accidents, *Report and Evidence*, HL 35, 192 (1937–8); *Report and Evidence*, HL2, (1938–9). For a critique of these reports, see J. S. Dean, *Murder Most Foul* (London, Allen & Unwin, 1947), pp. 12ff.

71 Dean, *Murder Most Foul*, p. 47.

72 *News Chronicle*, 17 July 1931.

73 *Manchester Guardian*, 24 July 1931.

74 PRO, MT 34/142.

75 *Autocar*, 28 June 1935.

76 Pedestrians' Association, *Quarterly Newsletter*, January 1935.

77 *Listener*, 10 April 1934.

78 Pedestrians' Association, *Quarterly Newsletter*, January 1935.

79 *Autocar*, 20 July 1934; Dean, *Murder Most Foul*, p. 89.

80 *Manchester Guardian*, 24 July 1931.

81 Modern Records Centre, University of Warwick: mss. 292/790.3/2.

82 *Ibid.*

83 *Morris Owner*, October 1932.

84 *Manchester Evening News*, 7 December 1933; *Daily Express*, 13 December 1932.

85 *Autocar*, 5 February 1937.

86 Gallup Poll on Road Safety (1939). Many thanks to Peter Thompson for this reference.

87 Emsley, 'Mother, what did policemen do', Table 3.

88 *Ibid.*, 370. Economic boycotts were a tactic favoured by the motoring press, not only in attempts to end 'trapping' but also against towns whose police were felt to be overzealous in summoning motorists for obstruction, or where high charges were made for parking. See below for a description of their proposed use in the de-restriction controversy of the 1930s.

89 Emsley, 'Mother, what did policemen do', 372–3; Klein, 'A new breed of law breaker', 7–8.

90 *The Times*, 15 November 1907.

91 *Autocar*, 5 June 1924.

92 *Autocar*, 16 April 1937.

93 Plowden, *The Motor Car and Politics*, p. 289; *Autocar*, 29 October 1937.

94 Cited in Plowden, *The Motor Car and Politics*, p. 289.

95 *Autocar*, 3 April 1925.

96 *Autocar*, 17 December 1926.

97 Plowden, *The Motor Car and Politics*, Appendix B. Figures are available for 1906–28.

98 *Autocar*, 14 May 1937; S. Cooke, *This Motoring* (London, Automobile

Association, n.d.), p. 4.
99 *Minutes of Evidence taken before the Royal Commission on Transport: Volume One*, 18 April 1928.
100 Davies, *Death on the Streets*, p. 56.
101 *Hansard*, Sixth Series, vol. 235, col. 1207–8, 10 February 1930 (emphasis added).
102 D. Dixon, *From Prohibition to Regulation: Bookmaking, Anti-gambling and the Law* (Oxford, Clarendon Press, 1991), p. 258; cited in Emsley, 'Mother, what did policemen do', 377.
103 For example, it is estimated that up to 70 per cent of men and 50 per cent of women in some working-class districts of Liverpool gambled regularly. A. Davies, 'The police and the people: gambling in Salford, 1900–1939', *Historical Journal*, 34 (1991) 87–115.
104 *Autocar*, 15 June 1934.
105 HL 2, 52 (March 1939) para. 31; cited in Plowden, *The Motor Car and Politics*, p. 290.
106 *The Times*, 17 May 1905.
107 Plowden, *The Motor Car and Politics*, p. 109.
108 Cooke, *This Motoring*, p. 241.
109 *Manchester Evening News*, 25 January 1921.
110 *Manchester Courier* 20 May 1914.
111 *Daily Dispatch*, 6 September 1919.
112 *Manchester Guardian*, 20 January 1921.
113 *Daily News*, 31 January 1921.
114 *Manchester Guardian*, 2 February 1921.
115 *Manchester Guardian*, 10 March 1921.
116 *Manchester Evening News*, 23 March 1921.
117 *Daily News*, 21 March 1921.
118 *Manchester Evening News*, 23 March 1921.
119 *Manchester Evening News*, 3 May 1921.
120 *Manchester Guardian*, 21 May 1924.
121 *Ibid.*
122 *City News*, 22 May 1924.
123 *Manchester Guardian*, 16 October 1929.
124 *Manchester Guardian*, 16 October 1929; *City News*, 25 November 1933.
125 *Autocar*, 8 December 1933.
126 Davies, 'The police and the people', 95, for discussion of scandals in 1932 and 1936.
127 *Manchester Guardian*, 31 March 1933.
128 *Evening Chronicle*, 2 January 1932.
129 *Autocar*, 22 March 1935.
130 Dean, *Murder Most Foul*, p. 84.
131 *Ibid.*, p. 83.
132 *Autocar*, 21 August 1936.

133 Dean, *Murder Most Foul*, p. 86.
134 *Daily Dispatch*, 19 December 1935.
135 *The Times*, 29 August 1938.
136 Dean, *Murder Most Foul*, p. 89.
137 *Autocar*, 5 February 1937.
138 *Acton Gazette and Express*, 15 January 1937.
139 *Autocar*, 22 January 1937.
140 *Autocar*, 29 March 1937.
141 *Autocar*, 5 February 1937.
142 Alker Tripp, *Town Planning and Road Traffic*, p. 16.
143 *Hansard*, Fifth Series, vol. 288, 10 April 1934. Moore-Brabazon was Minister of Transport in 1940–41 and had been parliamentary secretary at the Ministry of Transport in 1923–24 and 1924–27.

5

Dealing with a contradiction: the car in the countryside

Although much of the criticism levelled at the car was a result of its threat to human life, there was also controversy over its impact on the countryside. This chapter examines the factors behind this development. At its heart is the conflict between images of the countryside held by middle-class urbanites and suburbanites and the economic realities faced by those who lived there. Car ownership allowed many to indulge their fantasies about rural life, whether by visiting the countryside regularly or by establishing a new home there. There was, though, a contradiction inherent in this development; for although the car enabled them to enjoy rest and solitude in rural surrounds, it was also increasingly identified as a major factor in the despoliation of the countryside. However, the negative portrayal of the car's role in the countryside did not acknowledge the full complexity of the impact of increasing motor traffic. Rising car ownership had a positive side for many in the countryside. The second half of the chapter will examine the economic opportunities middle-class motorists could offer rural entrepreneurs, whilst also advancing an assessment of the changes cars brought to rural owners.

The chapter begins with an examination of the interest in rural life that was a significant feature of British society at the turn of the twentieth century. The role that the car came to have in this process is then explained, as are reactions to these developments from motorists and anti-motorists. Reactions to the car from within rural communities will then be delineated. It will become apparent that the anti-car feelings of rural preservationists were not always mirrored by those who worked and lived in rural Britain. At times the intrusion of motorists and other urbanites caused annoyance; this was particularly true in the earliest part of the century. However, attitudes towards the car in rural Britain seem to have softened as greater use was made of cars by members of rural communities and as increasing motor traffic offered financial opportunities to rural entrepreneurs. As part of this investigation it will prove valuable to analyse each of the areas in which the car came under attack by preservationists.

Rural England: image and reality

Several historians have identified the growth in interest in the rural traditions and landscape of Britain that emerged from at least the mid-nineteenth century.[1] Although the nation had become predominantly industrial, the ideology of 'Englishness' remained suffused with ruralism to a remarkable degree. Rural life fascinated writers, artists, politicians and the public.[2] This interest reached its zenith in the inter-war years in the movement to the great outdoors.[3]

The idealisation of rural society has several important implications for this study. First, the image of country life most commonly portrayed was a romantic and conservative one. It was frequently represented as the quintessential form of English society, whose hallmarks were simple living, common-sense values, tradition; and was seen as a realm where status was 'prescribed by a well defined hierarchy'.[4] It was a perspective on rural society that was class-specific, offering a vision of an ordered society which managed to be reassuringly hierarchical and yet almost classless.[5] Second, the defining and valued qualities of the English landscape were predominantly identified with the southern counties of England, the so-called 'south country'. Features judged to be attractive included half-timbering, village greens and hedgerows, which were characteristic attributes of 'the country south of the Thames and Severn and East of Exmoor … the counties of Kent, Sussex, Surrey, Hampshire, Berkshire, Wiltshire, Dorset and part of Somerset'.[6] A third feature of the interest in rural England followed the second. The interest taken in certain physical architectural and topographical features resulted in their being aestheticised. Increasingly it was the landscape and scenery

of the English countryside which was held to be the repository of
essential national values. The countryside was depicted as an object of
consumption and new forms of transport made it possible for ever
greater numbers of people to take part in this commodification.

A growing literature catered for these tastes. *Country Life*, for example,
which first appeared in 1887, became an immediate success, and by
1904 newspapers such as the *Manchester Guardian*, with its essentially
liberal and urban readership, were including a 'Country Diary' in their
contents.[7] Works like Ford Madox Ford's *The Heart of the Country* (1906),
Edward Thomas's prose collection *The South Country* (1908) and Hilaire
Belloc's *The Heart of England* (1913) all promulgated the romantic notion
that the old order of the countryside was at the heart of 'Englishness'.
These literary, artistic and journalistic images of the countryside often
omitted any trace of the real economic and social life of country people.
They addressed a desire for an intensely personal 'away from it all'
immersion in the beauties of an unspoiled scenic landscape.

Prompted by the success of H. V. Morton's *In Search of England*
(1927), which had gone through twelve editions by 1936, a number of
publishers introduced series designed to exploit the interest in tradition
and scenery.[8] The dominant sentiment and theme in this genre can be
illustrated by the example of Hutchinson's 1939 pocket guide to *Kent,
Surrey and Sussex*. Readers were informed that it was in the 'splendour
of our old domestic architecture' and 'country gardens' that the 'charm
of England' was to be found. In 'renewing contact with the countryside' the townsman was only two generations from 'the completely
rural life of his forbears'.[9] Thus, the enthusiasm for and content of
country magazines, guide books and rural novels ensured that their
largely middle-class readership was well informed of only selected
aspects of country life. It was relatively simple to become an expert in
the aesthetic qualities of the English landscape and vernacular architecture, or about the history and traditions of rural life, but the economic
situation of British agriculture and its employees was a much less familiar topic.

From the late nineteenth century preservationists were motivated by
similar preoccupations. Their interests lay predominantly in preserving
buildings, scenery and landscape rather than in investigating or inter-
vening in the economic and social issues central to the lives of rural
inhabitants. The first of these was The Commons, Open Spaces and

Footpaths Preservation Society formed by William Morris in the 1860s. It was followed by The Society for the Protection of Ancient Buildings (1877), SCAPA or The Society for Checking the Abuses of Advertising (1893) and the National Trust (1894). Pressure groups grew in number throughout the inter-war years as the countryside was encroached upon either for leisure or for new suburban or rural housing. In 1926 the Campaign for the Preservation of Rural England (CPRE) was founded with broad-based support. It was to be the most active conservationist grouping in this period, its archives attesting to its involvement in a variety of issues, from the aesthetics of country garages to the problems of litter. Other societies campaigned on single issues. For example, the Roads Beautifying Association, formed in 1928, published guidelines on planting trees along arterial and trunk roads in country areas. The lobbying efforts of the CPRE and others ensured that central government was also increasingly involved, legislating on numerous occasions in the interests of rural preservation. Legislation containing measures to protect the countryside included the National Trust Act (1907), the Roads Improvement Act (1925), the Petroleum (Consolidation) Act (1928), the Town and Country Planning Act (1932), and the Restriction of Ribbon Development Act (1935). However, as was the case with the growing literature on life in the countryside, these initiatives did little to address the problems of those who depended on the rural economy for their livelihood. A brief review of the economic situation in rural Britain reveals that developments there ensured that the interests of many in the countryside were often at odds with the more romantic notions of urban Britain.

One of the most significant trends in rural Britain in the early decades of this century was the continuing break-up of landed estates due, most frequently, to the growing burden of death duties. The reverse side of this process saw the proportion of owner-occupied farmland rise from 11 per cent in 1913 to 20 per cent in 1921 and 36 per cent by 1927, representing the largest change in land ownership since the sixteenth century sale of monastic lands.[10] Between 1918 and 1922, 25 per cent of the land surface of Britain changed hands.[11] Many great estates were broken up, engendering a significant shift in the class structure of rural society. The old landed elites left the scene to be replaced by a new breed of owner-occupying commercial farmers. The transfer of ownership left the new commercial farmers heavily mortgaged and vulnerable to the fall in agricultural prices that occurred in the 1920s and 1930s. At the same time the decline of craft industries increased to a dangerous extent the rural populations' reliance on agriculture. The inter-war rural economy has been likened to that of a one-industry town, and certainly economic and social decline were continual features of the scene at that time.[12] The comparatively lower living standards in the countryside encouraged rural–urban migration, particularly amongst young adults. This trend was reflected in a fall of 27 per cent in numbers employed in agricultural production between 1921–24 and 1938.[13]

As we shall see, in these circumstances there were many in the countryside who had reason to welcome aspects of urban encroachment. The interest shown in the countryside by the increasingly mobile, comparatively wealthy urban middle classes combined with the depressed state of the rural economy to produce a plethora of developments that were to leave the preservationist movement constantly agitated. As Denis Cosgrove has observed, an uneasy tension prevailed between scenic values and unrestricted production for exchange within the rural sphere.[14] The high cultural value placed on the consumption of an almost imaginary traditional rural world encouraged the continual encroachment of modernity into that environment. The car's role in this process was central, both symbolically and materially. Its position as transport for the individual family made it the perfect facilitator of the intensely personal 'away from it all' immersion in the beauties of the countryside. Yet, at the same time, the arrival of large numbers of motorists in rural Britain threatened to destroy traditional life there.

The car and the countryside: the motorist's perspective

The pages of motoring magazines, novels and guides were for the most part written in a Mortonian spirit.[15] *Country Life*, for instance, carried a regular motoring column which depicted rural Britain as a playground for the motorist. In 1914 it stated that the 'average reader' of the magazine found many uses for a car's running board, on which could be placed 'golf clubs, fishing rods, gun cases and other long luggage'.[16] Another issue, in the same year, suggested that local authorities should be made liable for damage done to 'smart vehicles' damaged when traversing rural roads that were being tarmacked.[17] Discussion of the car and the countryside in the pages of *Autocar, Motor*, numerous one-marque magazines and various guides was formulaic. Their pages were filled with reports of journeys through rural idylls, stories of the simplicity of country living, rural legends, and hurried visits to historic sights, churches and castles punctuated only by halts at quaint tea shops.[18] Once again, there was minimal discussion of the people of rural Britain. So, much of the motoring equivalent of the general countryside literature followed a familiar pattern, but the voyeur's mode of travel – the car – created a sense of irony in the relationship between motorist and countryside.

In 1929 John Prioleau produced the first edition of *Car and Country: Week-End Signposts to the Open Road*.[19] It offered a series of recommended drives around the scenic highways and byways of England and Wales. Its contents page revealed a series of familiar preoccupations. Selections on offer included details of 'hidden villages', Kiplingesque references to 'Puck and his rewards and fairies', romantic sorties into 'Robin Hood's country', and advice on 'the industrial patch and how to avoid it'.[20] As with other literature of its type, there was sparse reference to countryside inhabitants, although Prioleau reminded readers that Sunday was a bad day to get 'farm help to pull you out of [snow] drifts into which you may have incautiously sunk'.[21] This patronising attitude towards rural inhabitants resurfaced in a description of Wells in Norfolk; the bandstand on its village green being described as 'unassuming and rustic' where any tunes played would surely be 'gratifyingly unsophisticated'.[22] If what little of country life that appears is reassuring and obliging, so too is the landscape depicted, which is made the epitome of unassuming, yet majestic, 'Englishness'. Of Horsell Common in Surrey, Prioleau wrote: 'It is a tiny common, but like so many of its kind in England, manages to put on an air of immense size.'[23] The *Shell Guides*, which have come to hold a significant place in the heritage canon, also emanate from this period. The first, by John Betjeman on Cornwall, was published in 1934 and set the tone for what was to follow, which has been colourfully described as 'aggressively and squire-archically up-market and blood-sporting Anglican'.[24]

Although much of the motoring literature was structured along tried and tested lines, the modernity of the car created tensions which produced a number of interpretations of its role in the countryside. One way was to do what Prioleau, the Shell writers and many others did and simply ignore the issue. Many motoring writers evaded the question of the changes the car would inevitably bring to their image of stable, traditional, rural society. Another response was also one made by Shell in skilfully exploiting the tension between motoring and rural preservation. The company's advertising made use of pre-existing concepts of the countryside as a utopian world holding residues of history. Michael Bommes and Patrick Wright's discussion of this process is an interesting one, although they appear to overestimate the originality of Shell's strategy.[25] From 1923 Shell began removing its advertisements from rural locations, replacing them with a celebrated series of 'lorry bills' by artists such as McKnight Kauffer, Paul Nash, Graham Sutherland and Ben Nicholson.[26] Their work placed the car centrally in 'natural' or 'historic' scenes, which were depicted in a striking modernist style. The countryside was thus caught up in a tense movement between a traditionalist display of nature, conditioned by the cyclical time of the seasons, and a stylised celebration of the machine, with the car representing the irreversible progress of time.[27] The results of this work were often arrestingly attractive and reassuring. The large UK oil distributors all reacted simultaneously to animosity towards their rural advertising. Realising it was in their interests to depict themselves as defenders of the rural environment, they removed their advertising from the countryside.

As the 1930s drew on, the car lost its central position within Shell's advertising. The decade witnessed increasing car ownership and country motoring: consequently the concerns of preservationists grew. In this period a third response to the problem of reconciling car and countryside seems to have been the most commonly expressed. Mirroring the debate over road safety, it acknowledged the damage increased motoring could cause in the countryside, before closing the discussion with reassurances about the advantages of the car. In 1938 Rupert Croft Cooke's *How to Get More Out of Life* noted that motoring had been fun but it was becoming apparent that the fun had to be paid for 'by a blotched landscape and a beastly noise'.[28] However, motoring had 'changed England from a garden to a park', from the train it was only possible to gaze at the countryside, in the car the motoring family becomes part of it.[29] In 1937 *Autocar* reacted to claims that farm labourers were finding it difficult to find affordable accommodation because of the growing number of car-owning families buying up old cottages. In a less than sympathetic rejoinder, it suggested that the phenomenon had been exaggerated and that in any case it meant that old buildings were being renovated. Furthermore, it argued, people who normally lived in smoggy cities were benefiting from country air.[30]

W. R. Calvert's novel *Family Holiday* (1932) provides the best literary example of the motoring community reconciling itself to the contradiction between the modernity of their transport and their quest for a romantic old Britain. The novel described a motoring holiday through idyllic and historical England and Wales. The family's car facilitates travel from one historic church to another, from village to village, enabling them to travel off the beaten track to stay in an idealised farmhouse rather than a hotel. Their idyll is described in suitably flowery prose: 'In time they climbed again that winding, wooden stairway. They leant through wide-flung casements and listened to the tuneful silence of the night and breathed the mellow, scented garden breath. And so to sleep.'[31]

However, there was a price to be paid for the access to rural beauty offered by the car. Finding themselves overlooking a beauty spot, the protagonists of *Family Holiday* are jolted from their musings by evidence of the modern world. At first they enjoy 'a strange indefinable sensation engendered by the sea of greenery down below, steadfast yet ever moving, seeming solid yet known to be well-nigh as insubstantial as a dream'. But they are brought back down to earth by 'the inevitable orange peel, cigarette cartons and other litter always to be found in beauty spots'.[32] They are also disillusioned by the unsightly corrugated iron shacks selling sweets, postcards, pottery and illustrated books to motorists visiting Devil's Bridge in Wales. This is one example of a tourist industry that was already making itself felt in rural areas by catering for an increasingly mobile urban society. By the end of this particular novel the author/protagonist is beginning to come to terms with this commodification of the countryside. Thus, although the one person to be seen in Welsh national costume is dressed in that fashion only to facilitate the sale of postcards to motorised tourists, he welcomes this 'charming' sight:

> What matter that it was worn purely for a mercenary purpose – for the more certain sale of picture post cards? It was … a breath from the romantic past … Let the mercenary value of this costume-play be stressed … so that there be a renaissance in such matters. The kilt in

the Highlands, the red hood in Wales, yes and the shawl and clogs in Lancashire with the smock in Sussex. We should bring them back by every means in our power ... Why should uniformity spread its drab hand over every place and person so that we may no longer distinguish a Welsh maiden from a Tooting typist? ... Yes, let the Welsh girls wear their national costume again, if only for the sake of selling picture post cards, and cigarettes, and tickets of admission to Nature's beauty-spots. They little realise how travellers long to see it in its lovely setting.[33]

There is, of course, tremendous irony in this plea. Here was a motorised member of the modern world who wished to holiday in a rural Britain which existed more in folklore than reality. This was a rural Britain to be consumed by wealthier members of urban society, whose ideal inhabitants were picturesque remainders of a romantic and simple past. However, the car took middle-class motorists on a nostalgia trip during which they found their image of rural life jarred by the realities of the modern world. For modernity meant that the car, and motor transport more generally, was followed into the country by garages, roadside advertising, ribbon development, and road-traffic accidents.

'Beauty sacrificed on the altar of the speeding motorist': rural preservationists and the car

Other voices, from outside the motoring world, also commented on the commercialisation of the rural environment that the car encouraged. They proved to be far more critical of that encroachment than the narrative voice of Calvert's *Family Holiday*. One of the earliest of these critics was C. F. G. Masterman, whose influential book *The Condition of England* (1909) described cars as 'wandering machines, travelling with an incredible rate of speed ... along all the rural ways'. He described how they could be seen 'on a Sunday afternoon, piled 20 or 30 deep outside the new popular inns, while their occupants regale themselves within'. Masterman claimed their impact was also in evidence along 'the dust-laden hedges of the south country roads, a grey mud colour, with no evidence of green' and 'in the ruined cottage gardens of the south country villages'.[34]

As ownership levels grew massively after the 1914–18 war, the car was subjected to a barrage of invective by a group of self-appointed defenders of the countryside. At one point the *Garage and Motor Agent* complained about anti-motorist 'highbrows' at the BBC continually attributing the despoliation of the countryside to cars and garages.[35] In this respect, the middle-brow ambitions and lifestyles of the average middle classes were often the subject of vitriolic attack by an unusual coalition of intellectual and social elites. Stephen Spender, for example, described the incursion into rural Britain as '*laissez faire* run mad, a huge inflation of Tudor villas on arterial roads, wireless sets, tin cars, golf clubs – the paradise of the bourgeoisie'.[36] However, it was the philosopher C. E. M. Joad who proved to be the most consistent campaigner against the car in the countryside.

Joad's most detailed assault appeared in *The Horrors of the Countryside* in 1931. In very colourful language he denigrated the activities of the motoring classes who had disrupted his relaxing country walks. He likened the irritable noise of cars on country roads to 'a regiment of soldiers' who 'had begun to suffer simultaneously from flatulence'. Joad depicted the motorists within their machines as being 'strained and angry' and in 'no frame of mind for aesthetic enjoyment'. They were only interested in passing each other and were completely cut off from the country and its sounds, smells and silence. Indeed their horn-blowing, which Joad likened to a 'pack of fiends released from the nethermost pit', destroyed that silence.[37]

This Swiftian language was employed frequently in the literature of rural preservation. Those writers who appeared in Clough Williams-Ellis's *Britain and the Beast* (1937) certainly found no problem in conjuring up a plethora of pollution metaphors to press home their point about rural despoliation. Each contributor was commissioned to reveal the levels of damage to the countryside in a particular area of Britain. Sheila Kaye-Smith, herself the author of romantic novels of Sussex country life, believed that the car brought increased problems to the countryside of Kent and Sussex because it offered 'a coast within reach of a London car-ride, and the car, unlike the train, does not clot its horrors at the journey's end but smears them along the way'.[38]

Other contributors identified a recently departed halcyon age where the countryside was defended by paternalistic great landowners; an age when it was possible 'to impose the cultural views of a small minority on the great mass of the population'.[39] Geoffrey M. Boumphrey felt that the 'last hope of that goes with the slipping away of the land from the great owners, who are owed so much for their creation and preservation of the beauty of the past'.[40] He lamented the fact that power in the countryside was slipping into the hands of the local authorities, the majority of whom were described by another contributor, Howard Marshall, as 'uninformed and quite unfitted to deal with this particular duty of preserving our amenities. After all, what are most local authorities? The butcher, the baker, the candlestick maker – and frequently the local builder or contractor into the bargain.'[41] He urged that efforts be made to ensure that the 'right people are elected as local authorities – people capable of planning with integrity and intelligence'.[42] However, he was pessimistic and feared the continual decline of the rural landscape under the auspices of 'local tradesman': 'Advertisements and petrol stations and shanties ruin our villages … A gimcrack civilisation crawls like a gigantic slug over the country, leaving a foul trail of slime behind it.'[43]

The writers in this volume clearly saw themselves as guardians of the British countryside. Their most condescending assertion was offered by Joad. The people's claim on the land was paramount but they could not yet be trusted to take it up. The countryside should 'be kept inviolate as a trust until such time as they *are* ready' and it was the duty of Joad's readers, 'together with such others as can be brought to realize their responsibility in the matter', to act in the interim as the people's trustees'.[44] For Joad, motorists were the most hated intruder in the countryside because of the maelstroms of destruction they created. They were worse than the hiker because they devastated a wider area. Of course, as a hiker himself, Joad had more than a passing interest in defending the walker against the motorist.

In his 1988 doctoral thesis, on middle-class suburbanites in inter-war Britain, D. L. North argued that the establishment's distaste for suburban expansion was most clearly articulated by the preservationist movement, who were strongly propelled by 'a feeling that social inferiors were invading – with both cars and new houses – a hitherto exclusive social preserve'.[45] The scatological language used by Joad and others in the preservationist movement suggests that North had a strong case. Fred Hirsch has argued that it is possible to view the countryside as a 'positional good' whose consumption is dependent on one's social position. It follows that a relatively privileged elite, with access to it, may seek to preserve its amenity value by restricting the access of other social groups.[46] However, as was the case in the urban environment, motoring had a growing and fundamental economic importance in the countryside. The car was also being used by the influential professional and commercial middle classes, who might otherwise have been supportive of measures to reduce its part in the despoliation of rural Britain. Even the most outspoken of its opponents offered no firm solutions to the car's part in the erosion of the countryside.

Many of the contributors to *Britain and the Beast* were supporters of the CPRE; Williams-Ellis was the president of its Welsh equivalent. In many respects the CPRE sought an accommodation with the motorist, hoping to achieve progress by persuasion and self-regulation rather than coercion. The CPRE's archives suggest a similar pattern of events to those that surrounded the car and road safety. The CPRE was founded in 1926 and by 1927 had established a close relationship with the AA. The AA provided the CPRE with financial backing, eye-witness reports from its road scouts on developments in the countryside, and advice on issues which involved motoring. From 1927 the AA was a sponsor of the CPRE's efforts to the tune of fifty guineas a year, the latter viewing the former as invaluable in assisting in the organisation of its local committees.[47] The AA also expedited the distribution of CPRE pamphlets.[48]

It is clear that the CPRE felt indebted to the AA and was willing to return the favour by aiding its promotion when the opportunity arose. In September 1931, the AA's deputy secretary, E. H. Fryer, lunched with H. G. Griffin, the general secretary of the CPRE. They discussed *This Motoring*, the story of the AA, which had just been written by its secretary, Stenson Cooke. Griffin promised to help promote the book by sending it to journalists sympathetic to his organisation. He kept his promise, taking the opportunity to suggest to the reviewers that they urge the AA to take a stronger line on the issue of unsightly rural petrol pumps.[49] However, the AA was unwilling to take any significant action against the Motor Agents Association, whose members were responsible for many of the offending artefacts. Between late 1932 and early 1933 the CPRE's Reading branch suggested that the AA be encouraged to urge its members to boycott all country garages which affronted the country-lover's taste because of their garish multi-coloured petrol pumps, corrugated iron and asbestos construction or the advertisements with which they were regularly covered. The proposal foundered when it became clear that the AA would not co-operate.[50]

In 1933 the AA rejected calls for a conference of CPRE constituent bodies on the question of the unattractiveness of AA shelters and telephone boxes to be found on country roads.[51] The Earl of Crawford and Balcarres, the president of the CPRE, informed Griffin that it might be best to drop the issue; the AA were their 'constituents, and we ought to be on most friendly terms with them. Not only are they in themselves important, but as a source of intelligence they might really be invaluable.'[52] This intelligence often came through the observations of AA road scouts, who in 1938, for example, described the 79 car dumps they had discovered in town and country. The AA comments on a dump in Ryde on the Isle of Wight described it as situated 'in a poor part of town and not out of keeping with the neighbourhood'.[53] In such a case, the dumping of dilapidated motor vehicles was unlikely to raise the hackles of the AA's or CPRE's predominantly middle-class memberships. Clearly, as in the case of road safety, the AA managed to secure an influential role in the debate about motoring and the countryside. In its role as financier, constituent member, and adviser to the CPRE and voice and mentor of several hundred thousand motorists, it ensured that no initiatives arose in the inner councils of the CPRE that in any way limited the motorist's access to the countryside. The only move to limit the extent of car use in the countryside was one proposed by the Pedestrians' Association, which made its way into the 1930 Road Traffic Act. The clause stipulated that private motor vehicles were not to be driven more than fifteen yards from the road.[54]

Of course, many of the CPRE's membership were no doubt amongst those benefiting from the mobility the car offered, in terms of accessing the beauties of the countryside. In the case of the car and motoring generally, the CPRE and other preservationists proved more adept at identifying problems than in proposing solutions, largely because they wanted to have their cake and eat it. Their comments on the commercialisation of the countryside – and the car's role in that process – often displayed a contempt and ignorance for those who had to make a living there. The arrival of large numbers of motorists in rural Britain, at a time of agricultural depression, provided many country-based 'butchers, bakers and candlestick makers' with new money-making opportunities. On occasion they even ensured that motorists got their cake, served in one of the newly opened 'Olde English tea rooms'. The next sections of this chapter will offer an assessment of rural responses to the increasing number of cars on country roads. The extent to which cars were used by country-dwellers themselves will also be investigated.

'I am nobody's good man for a shilling a night': rural antagonism towards the motorist

It is a generally accepted belief that urban visitors, motorists particularly, have not always been welcomed in rural Britain. This was certainly true in the case of the earliest motorists. The Royal Commission on the Motor Car of 1906 found that the car was viewed disapprovingly by many rural dwellers. Rural roads were unsuitable for this new form of transport; large dust clouds were thrown up by speeding motor vehicles and crops were covered with the resulting debris.[55] A plethora of witnesses that appeared before the Royal Commission in 1906 reported their concern about this issue.[56] County councils were reluctant to have the rural rate-payer finance road improvements that they felt were the responsibility of wealthy motorists. One result of this animosity was the appearance of speed traps in many counties. Local authorities, magistrates and police felt that heavy fines for motorists who broke the law on their roads were a neat way of finding the funds required for road repairs and improvements. As has already been indicated, it was this initiative which led to the formation of the AA in 1905. The fines levied on speeding motorists continued to go straight into local authority coffers until 1920.[57] However, the Roads Board, set up in 1910, provided local authorities with large grants to improve roads. The project was financed by an increased taxation on the motorist introduced in the 1909 budget. Following the First World War, the Ministry of Transport continued these improvements, with the result that complaints about dust clouds were less common in the 1920s and 1930s. There were, though, a number of other issues which were not dealt with so straightforwardly.

Graves and Hodge's *The Long Week-end* provides evidence that country people's hostility towards the car could match in physical violence the verbal assaults of Joad and others. They reported that '[c]ountry people grew to hate cars for their noise, smell, danger and the unconcerned bearing of the drivers, and often encouraged children to pelt them with stones and line the road with glass and upturned tacks to cause punctures'.[58] It would appear that the *Autocar* was referring to such issues when it reported, in 1919, that it was common for children and others to throw stones or bottles at cars. In July of that year the AA offered a reward of one guinea for information about people who were placing broken bottles on roads.[59] What caused this hostility to the car in country districts? The motivations listed by Graves and Hodge would seem to be an appropriate starting point in seeking an answer to this question.

Whilst no reference to the smell given off by motor vehicles has become apparent, there were occasions when the noise of motorists' vehicles caused acrimony. This was true of the motor trials regularly organised in rural districts, with hilly areas proving particularly appealing to the sporty motorist. In 1923 *Autocar*, recognising the potential for damage to the motoring cause, urged the RAC, the official body for all motor-sports events, to limit the number of permits it granted to Sunday trials. The large number of cars attending such trials was causing noise and nuisance to church-goers.[60] By 1935 the problem had not abated; complaints about noise, as well as the damage caused by spectators and their parked cars, were still being made.[61] In 1938, the Ministry of Transport warned of a ban on such events if the situation was not brought under control. Rural authorities formed an association to lobby central government on the issue and a number of separate protests were made, the worst affected areas being the Home Counties, the Cotswolds, the West Country and the area around Buxton in Derbyshire.[62]

The danger caused by increased motoring was a further cause of friction between motorist and country-dweller. The treatment of road-accident victims caused a serious drain on the resources of many rural hospitals. Smaller cottage hospitals on popular motoring routes were most vulnerable, at times becoming 'weekend casualty stations'.[63] It appears that even cottages near danger spots could become unofficial dressing stations for 'dozens of cases in a single holiday season'.[64] Until 1930 there was no compulsory motor-car insurance and accident victims, hospitals and motorists were expected to come to some kind of semi-formal arrangements over fees for treatment and compensation. For example, in 1906 the Duchess of Connaught's car was involved in an accident that left a young boy called Coker dead. The Duchess made a donation to the Hounslow cottage hospital where he had been treated and bought a number of tickets for a charity performance that took place at Hounslow Hippodrome, the proceeds going to Coker's mother.[65] The 1930 Road Traffic Act attempted to address this issue, introducing a system of payments from insurance companies to hospitals. However, the measure does not appear to have worked well in practice. In the six months following the Act, expenses for the treatment of road accident victims in thirty-six Yorkshire hospitals amounted to £4,500, but only £123 was recovered from insurance companies, who were obviously disputing liability.[66] According to the British Medical Association the national figures for 1931 were: costs incurred £64,132; amount recovered £6,575.[67]

The safety problems that arrived with the motorist could also precipitate tensions that were not just confined to country-dwellers. Other urbanites seeking rest and relaxation in the countryside had reason to regret the arrival of the car. Many of the estimated 500,000 hikers who joined the motorist in the discovery of rural Britain did so off the roads which had served the Edwardian walker because they had become too dangerous.[68] Cyclists did not have that option. Addressing the Royal Commission on the Motor Car in 1906, Mr E. B. Turner of the National Cyclists' Union maintained that many cyclists, females in particular, had greatly reduced their cycling. This was most true of the London region and on the major roads, where the problem of dust was most acute.[69] James Boyce of the Scarborough Cyclists Touring Club also had his own concerns. He registered his disquiet at an advertisement in *Badmington Magazine* for 'The Motor Whistle'; it was described as the 'loudest alarm on the road', and 'indispensable for every car' as it 'saves the brakes considerably'.[70] By the 1930s, the numbers of cars and cycle owners had increased dramatically and the pages of their respective magazines bore witness to tension between the two groups, cyclists often accusing motorists of behaving as if they owned the roads because their road tax paid for their upkeep.[71]

The question of the motorist's speed on rural roads also aroused controversy. Samuel Kidner of the Central Chamber of Agriculture told the Royal Commission in 1906 of the change in attitudes towards the law that the car seemed to have created: 'before these motor cars came in it was looked on as a disgrace for a man to be had up and fined for furious driving, but all that seems to have gone now. A lot of wealthy men are being fined continually, and there seems no disgrace attached to it at all.'[72] As was the case with urban councils, the motoring lobby was always ready to object to the imposition of speed limits by rural councils. In 1933 West Riding Council sought Ministry of Transport approval for a 10 m.p.h. speed limit in the village of Addingham near Leeds. The limit had formerly been in force there because the narrow, winding main road offered poor visibility at several points along its 792 yards. The limit was calculated to add only thirty seconds to the journey time through the village. However, the AA opposed the application, their case being upheld by the Ministry, which ruled that the road did not differ from many other village roads.[73] The damage done by the car to rural roads that had been designed to take the strain of more traditional forms of transport was another source of annoyance to the rural community. A string of witnesses who appeared before the Royal Commission offered gripes about the dust clouds raised on rural roads by motorists. Farmers complained about dust spoiling crops; those living beside busy roads complained of it entering their homes; and a writer even complained that her typewriter was ruined. The appeal of speed traps to magistrates, police, rural councils and many of those who lived in the countryside was a large one. This was particularly the case until 1920, from which date the fines imposed on motorists found guilty of breaking the 20 m.p.h. limit no longer went to the local purse.[74]

The final cause of the country-person's ill-feeling towards the motorist was what Graves and Hodge described as their 'unconcerned bearing'. The privileged social position of early motorists, together with the facility the car offered for anonymity and a speedy get-away encouraged some appalling behaviour. John Drysdale, a tenant farmer from Stirlingshire who represented the Scottish Chambers of Agriculture at the Royal Commission in 1906, testified to that effect. His horse-drawn milk van had twice been crashed into and on both occasions the car had fled the scene of the accident. On other occasions Drysdale claimed to have seen motorists 'jeering and laughing' after having forced a horse into a roadside ditch.[75] Schooled on a literature which encouraged them to envisage the countryside as a playground in which they could indulge their interests, most motorists were not well-versed in knowledge of the real life of agricultural Britain. Ill-considered behaviour or comments about the 'simplicity' of country folk were guaranteed to raise the hackles of any harassed farmer or other rural residents. Many motoring families were also accustomed to having servants clear up after them, and expecting country dwellers to do likewise caused offence. The motoring press carried discussion on littering and admonished offenders. In 1923 one correspondent complained in *Autocar* about littering near Arundel and appealed to women to stop their menfolk and children from doing it. Being the best in the world, the English housewife would be able to do this, it was argued.[76] Despite claims, in the run-up to the 1930 Road Traffic Act, that the problem was largely solved, the issue continued surfacing throughout the 1930s.[77] During this period, the *Autocar* employed the tried and trusted method of social emulation, to encourage motorists to leave the countryside clean and tidy following visits there: 'Among campers and caravanners of the better class', it told readers in 1936, 'it is a matter of honour that they leave no litter; motorists are becoming as conscientious. It is up to everyone to set an example.'[78] The *Austin Magazine* struck a similar note in a 1930 editorial entitled 'On playing the game'. It stated that 'the motoring class has distinctive traditions which every member should uphold. So long as traditions are good there is nothing snobbish or anti-modern about respecting them.'[79]

Litter was also a concern of the CPRE, its files revealing that motorists were often guilty of this offence. In 1932 Flora Russell wrote to the CPRE to complain about motorists littering Newlands Corner in Surrey, suggesting that an AA scout be employed there to police picnickers.[80] Stung by criticism, some motorists took action to solve the problem. In September 1930 a New Forest Campaign group, which included Lady Montagu of Beaulieu from the well-known motoring family, organised 'motor litter parties'. Cars patrolled the forest collecting litter, which was ceremonially burned on Lyndhurst Common.[81] Anti-litter leagues were formed in several areas, including Surrey where, in 1929, pioneering legal action was taken against two offending motorists. One case was dismissed while the other resulted in a £1 fine for the car's owner.[82] Certain areas were more affected than others by this problem; those which had been idealised in literature or were closest to cities with high car ownership suffered most. In 1931 Mr Peek, a farmer and chairman of Ottery Urban Council, urged Devon County Council to introduce by-laws aimed at forcing motorists to remove their rubbish, which was an eyesore and a nuisance.[83] Bottles, left by picnickers, could also injure livestock.[84] As well as leaving refuse behind, some motorists took pieces of the countryside home with them, in effect committing theft on many occasions. For instance, in 1939 Ian Hannah MP told the Association for the Preservation of Rural Scotland about motorists who had taken stones from his walls, presumably for the adornment of their garden rockeries.[85]

In time, the farming community came to see these issues as an occupational problem. A. G. Street was a Wiltshire farmer whose writing and radio talks on country life were popular in the 1930s. His was one of the few voices offering a real insight into the working life of the countryside. He remarked upon the bad behaviour of many towns-people, motorists and others, who expected access to somebody else's business premises without permission. However, such intrusions were regarded by farmers as inevitable. Any damage caused was looked upon in the same fashion as that 'done by rats or rabbits – an unavoidable expense which their businesses must bear'.[86]

If such developments could be endured, it was more difficult to suffer the patronising tone and ignorant manner of many motorists. Motoring guides such as Prioleau's *Car and Country* did little to lessen the condescending images of country people with which many motorists entered rural Britain. Even *Autocar*'s attempt to limit the damage such attitudes incurred revealed a patronising perspective on country life. An article written by 'Yokel' in 1939, giving advice to motorists intending to tour the countryside, reminded readers that it was inhabited. The tendency to treat it like a playground had resulted in 'antagonism on the part of the country-dwellers'. The article concluded with advice that might be offered today to a tourist heading for a small Greek island. Readers were instructed to remember that the countryside contained many conservative, religious, even old-fashioned folk. Their ideas matched 'the tempo of their lives' and changed slowly. For them 'sex films, smart fashions and cocktails are things not real, as they are to town-dwellers, but just outside their world, savouring a little, still, "of the devil".'[87] As the Scott Committee on land utilisation in rural areas noted, it was just this sort of depiction, which was interpreted as 'amused contempt' by country-dwellers, that contributed to a feeling of discontent amongst them.[88]

A. G. Street was one who could stomach the ignorance and bad manners of many visitors to the countryside, but those who patronised him pushed his tolerance to breaking point. Like many other farmers, Street augmented his income by allowing caravanners and campers to holiday on his land, even though this often caused him inconvenience. He maintained that those who felt farmers were 'coining it' at a shilling a night per tent or caravan were mistaken, and he provided amusing examples of the harassment he suffered. On one occasion, he was summoned from his dinner at 8.00 p.m., after a long day hay-making, to meet a young married couple. He helped them secure their caravan and was then informed that they wanted milk and water brought out to them and a bit of sacking for their dog 'Binkie' to sleep in. Street's patience almost broke: 'It is too much. Milk and water, yes, but a bag for Binkie, no, definitely no. I am no servant of Binkies.' He beckoned the husband out of earshot of his wife, intending to inform him of how hard he had worked that day. The young motorist followed him pensively, 'looking a little frightened. He probably thinks that I am one of the many rural mental defectives, about which he has read so much', thought Street. But Street relented: '[m]ost of these campers are such charming helpless folk, that I shall drive meekly back to the farm, and get the milk, the water, and the little bit of bag for Binkie.' However, Street had his limits. One motorist, incorrectly reading his social status from a glance at his oil-stained work clothes, patronisingly addressed him as 'my good man'. Street's own social sensibilities were activated by this; the result being the exit of the motorist, having being told that Street was 'nobody's good man for a shilling a night'.[89]

The Scott committee identified further sources of animosity towards the car and the motoring classes. The committee viewed 'with profound disapproval' the growth of 'abuses' which came to be associated with the term 'roadhouse'. They called for greater strictness in managerial control and licensing, particularly where the roadhouse was situated in or near a village. They reported evidence of disturbance caused through the late hours kept by such establishments and of the ensuing resentment of rural communities.[90] It is difficult to quantify the actual extent of this problem but it seems clear that the roadhouse phenomenon was comparatively short-lived and largely confined to the Home Counties.

The Scott committee also mentioned the motorist in connection with the continuing shortage of housing for the rural working class. One factor increasingly associated with the shortfall was the 'growth of the week-end habit'. Wealthy townspeople were acquiring former agricultural cottages 'bought because of their picturesque character and brought up to date with all modern conveniences'.[91] Car ownership abetted this process, particularly in areas near the outskirts of cities, where to provide themselves with a weekend cottage middle-class motorists were able to pay three or four times the amount an agricultural labourer could manage. For example, Neil Blatch, the son of an architect, narrated how the family's new 1920 Humber 16 tourer would carry them all from their Liverpool home to their weekend cottage near Mold.[92] Weekenders' cars must have been a very obvious material object through which their privileged status could be identified by any disgruntled agricultural labourer, priced out of the housing market by the new arrivals. However, the farm worker was, at times, given as much reason to resent his employer's motor car. In 1923 *Reynolds News* reported the use Norfolk farmers were making of their cars in their efforts to defeat striking labourers.[93] Ironically, flying pickets were using bicycles in a bid to curb the use of non-union labour.[94]

This example brings us to the question of the uses to which the car was put in rural Britain. An evaluation of its uses by country-dwellers will permit a greater knowledge of the complexity of issues surrounding country motoring than was displayed by many rural preservationists in the period. The next section of this chapter will attempt to provide this evaluation.

Rural uses of the car

The car was used in the countryside by several social and occupational groups. As elsewhere in society the very wealthiest were the first car owners, but they were quickly followed into ownership by farmers, professionals and business groups. A final development saw many who worked in towns and cities using the new mobility that the car offered to relocate their family home in rural areas. On the basis of their econometric analysis, Bowden and Turner have concluded that the degree of rurality of the population, as well as professional occupation and income, was an important factor in the diffusion of cars in any given district. They suggest that in rural areas the utilitarian returns of car ownership were higher than in urban areas where distances to work were smaller and public transport better.[95]

The most commonly identified rural owners were farmers. They realised numerous advantages through car ownership, not all of which were welcomed by other social groups. By 1921 *Autocar* was reporting that the majority of rural owners were farmers. It also revealed that this had led to increasing problems between farmers and commercial groups within their local market towns. In Reading, for example, local innkeepers and others had complained about the parking of farmers' cars in the town and the police had taken action. Resentment had allegedly arisen because car ownership permitted farmers to return home more promptly than had previously been the case. Out-of-pocket publicans and others were not impressed with this development.[96] The Scott Committee believed that car ownership provided farming families with 'the advantages of the wider range of shopping facilities in larger centres', thereby making them less reliant on local traders. Alternatively, new forms of transport and commerce meant that purchases could be made 'through the mail-order system, or from commercial travellers of big firms'. However, the Committee concluded that in providing 'many of the varied services the countryman needs', whether for commercial, professional, educational or leisure requirements, 'the market town still plays an important role in the countryside'.[97]

Farmer's Weekly often reported the accusations of profiteering levelled at car-owning farmers.[98] In fact, many farmers entered the motoring community at the very lowest end of the scale, buying large but cheap second-hand cars. The first motoring farmers not surprisingly bought Fords, the car that had proved so popular with the American farming community.[99] By the 1930s regular articles in their weekly journal were advising farmers that they now needed two cars. In 1936 Malcolm Campbell told them that an older car could be used on the farm, but every farmer should also possess a good modern car for off-farm use.[100] However, Campbell's advice may not have been entirely based on a desire to encourage efficient agricultural practice; the Austin Motor Company board minutes reveal that he received payment from that firm in order to encourage motoring wherever and whenever he could.[101] In the same issue another freelance motoring writer, Harold Pemberton, argued that farmers should see their car as an investment. The ideal car should be dual-purpose, capable of absorbing the punishment entailed in taking a load to market, possibly with the assistance of a trailer, and of taking the family on their annual holiday. By this stage it would appear that cars popular with the farming community were in the ten horsepower category, with Morris and Austin cars as prevalent among farmers as other motorists.[102] Older more powerful cars, which could be picked up cheaply, were also sought after by farmers. As *Farmer's Weekly* put it: 'In the USA town motorists abandon their old cars in the countryside; English town motorists can sell their old cars to the countryside.'[103] By the late 1930s it was reporting the use of high-powered 'but antique' cars for hauling the mower, driving the hay sweep and other heavy jobs.[104] As A. G. Street acknowledged in the *Listener* during 1933, the farmer using the car for such purposes could also employ one worker to do the work of four, something which was 'unavoidable' given the 'economic squeeze' on farming.[105] The farmer's car could also transport several farm workers a mile, in a couple of minutes, to the site of another job; it could do the same in the case of materials or tools. Resourceful farmers even used exhaust fumes to gas rats.[106]

In the light of these considerations it is not surprising that farmers' representatives who gave evidence before the Royal Commission on Transport in 1929 were not drawn into criticism of the car. Their evidence suggests that, for them, the problems brought by increasing motor traffic were outweighed by the benefits accrued. Although traffic made it more difficult to drive livestock along the road than had been the case, that was simply 'a natural consequence with which we have got to put up'.[107] In return motor vehicles offered the farmer the convenience of door-to-door transport. The representatives largely confined their comments to road design, calling for wider roads to accommodate increasing agricultural traffic more safely. They also asked that grants be made available to fund the erection of fencing to protect livestock.[108] This evidence contrasted sharply with that offered by farming representatives to the Royal Commission of 1906.

Of course, farmers were not the sole rural car owners. The professional middle classes were also represented. If the car proved a utilitarian aid for the average farmer, it would have been equally so for the country doctor, solicitor or clergyman. Car ownership also made it possible for members of the professional middle classes who practised their calling in cities and towns to move from urban and suburban homes to more rural locations. After decades of depopulation, the 1930s witnessed an increase in the population in the rural districts of England and Wales.[109] Acknowledging this, A. G. Street attributed a good deal of it to increasing car ownership, which in his opinion was beginning to change the social composition of many villages. There had been a 'great alteration in the personnel of many villages' where car owners could now live whilst continuing 'their town employment'.[110]

Life in the countryside was also altered by the possibilities the car offered to the rural family. The car, and the bus, extended the connections of county towns with their hinterland, often at the expense of smaller market towns.[111] As the Scott Committee noted, car ownership increased the incidence of business, shopping and cultural visits to the larger county towns at the expense of local, but smaller, towns. For others, in more isolated areas, it allowed more frequent trips to the nearest town than had been possible previously. As was the case for the urban middle classes, car ownership could also boost the rural owner's social status. All of these factors are neatly summed up in the recollections of Eironwy Phillips, who was brought up in the 1930s on her grandmother's farm in the Neath Valley. The farm was five miles from the nearest town and her first memories are of all transport, both within the farm and outside, being by cart, trap or foot. Then car ownership changed her family's lifestyle. Eironwy fondly recalled 'BNY 750', 'a shimmering, black Ford 8', with its 'gleaming chrome handles and bumpers' and green leather upholstery. Her grandmother's life was 'revolutionised' and 'she could go to chapel in style, deliver milk and eggs … even carry the occasional calf or pig, hens and ducks, all in double-quick time and come rain or shine.' 'Not to be outdone', Eironwy's schoolteacher father bought his own Ford 8, 'CNY 616', which was replete with 'the most wonderful red leather upholstery'. Eironwy and the other children would 'stand on the running-boards, clinging on for dear life as we pretended to be gangsters, as per James Cagney films, seen at the Empire cinema in Neath'. Eironwy's closing remarks also serve to remind us once more of the irrational side of our relationship with the car. The Fords were 'magic machines' that 'seemed benevolent, giving, generous, reliable, protective, as though they loved life and had come into being to share the fun of life with us. Sounds potty I know but this is how I personally experienced the advent into my childhood of the motor vehicle.'[112]

Such perceptions were fundamentally different from those of Joad and his ilk, who did not experience what the car could offer to the previously isolated rural family. Ownership also furthered opportunities for the extension of one's circle of friends and social life. One way of measuring this development would be a project which studied the incidence of marriage between individuals from wider geographical areas. It must be assumed that rising car ownership ensured that this was an increasing trend. Farmer's daughter Patricia Channon recalled that car ownership meant that she could join the Young Farmers' club and have 'a bit of a social life'. It was there that she met her husband in 1935.[113] Christine Paul remembered that the car enabled her to travel further afield for dances, hockey, tennis, and more frequent visits to relatives.[114] Furthermore, it was not simply car-owning families who might experience the benefits of the car in the country areas; motoring farmers received requests for lifts from neighbours for trips to the doctor, for example.[115]

It is possible to see, therefore, that the impact of increasing motor traffic in the countryside was rather more complex than the preservationists often wanted to acknowledge. The car transported the urban middle classes to the countryside most frequently as day-trippers, but also increasingly as either weekenders or permanent residents. As the key determinant of the relocation of such people, the car was playing a central role in the changing economy of the countryside. Another of the preservationists, Sheila Kaye-Smith, noted this in her assessment of the failure of public opinion to prevent increasing construction work in the countryside. She believed that motorists, 'satisfied with speed and roadhouses', did not care about rural destruction. Moreover the people who sold the land and those who built on it were 'all making money and the people who live in the new houses probably spend more in the neighbourhood than the farmers and landowners they succeed'.[116]

For those who made a living from the land, its value lay not in its scenic qualities but in its commercial value. They viewed rural Britain as a business and they sold, bought and hired pieces of it to make the profits that assisted their survival in an era of falling agricultural prices. There was a clash of interests between the motorist and the pressure groups on the one hand and rural entrepreneurs on the other. One side wanted to perpetuate the countryside as a traditional rustic playground, whilst still having the convenience of travelling through at high speed in their cars. The other sought to profit from the new forms of transport and the opportunities offered in providing fuel, food and drink, accommodation, land for development, and advertising space. Each of the areas where debates emerged over the car's involvement in rural despoliation will now be detailed.

Rural entrepreneurship and the car

The most visible effect of increasing levels of motor traffic in the countryside were garages, petrol pumps and filling stations. Oil companies and small-scale entrepreneurs also saw opportunities to profit from increasing motor traffic. They provided a precious new source of income to a rural economy which had witnessed the death of virtually every industry but farming. The sale of land for garage sites must also have been welcomed by many farming families struggling to pay off mortgages. By 1929 there were an estimated 54,000 petrol stations, many of which had been established by ex-serviceman in the years after the 1914–18 war. Mervyn Gorman, vice-chairman of the RAC, told the Royal Commission on Transport in 1929 that the small sums such men had to invest in their new businesses provided the explanation for their often unsightly condition.[117] Specialised garage-building firms were appearing, but many were the work of local builders using cheap materials such as corrugated sheeting and asbestos slabs.[118] Criticism of unsightly garages was at its fiercest when they were to be found in a rural location. The CPRE argued that the problem stemmed from the fact that many garages had previously been cycle-repair shops and their owners had little capital to invest in aesthetically pleasing premises.[119] In 1928 the Petroleum (Consolidation) Act gave local authorities the power to prohibit the location of petrol stations in specified areas and to regulate their appearance in others. However, as was the case with other legislation of this nature, its implementation was at best irregular.[120]

Concerns about the appearance of these establishments were often driven by the urban outsider's image of how rural Britain should look rather than by practical considerations. In 1930 *Autocar* offered advice on the construction of new garages; advocating the principle of 'English architecture for English soil', they suggested Tudor and Queen Anne architectural designs.[121] Whilst claiming to be against 'exaggerated rusticity', the CPRE produced a booklet on approved garage designs, recommending building materials that included timber framing for walls and hardwood or thatch for roofing.[122] The journal *Architect* labelled such suggestions 'incomprehensible' and dangerous.[123] Not surprisingly, such inappropriate design suggestions went largely unheeded. Reporting in 1941, the Scott Committee identified the unsightly petrol station as an ongoing problem.[124] Many small-scale rural entrepreneurs established petrol pumps in unlikely spots. The first roadside pump in Britain appeared in Shrewsbury in 1914; following that, hand-cranked pumps appeared in village pubs, shops and other spots. By 1940 the small Warwickshire village of Arley, for example, had a bakery that doubled as a petrol-filling station.[125]

Motoring on rural roads provided advertising firms with a new arena for their campaigns. The holidaying or weekending motorist represented a lucrative consumer, and roadside advertising became a further area of controversy involving the car. The magazine *Autocar*, in its role as moral guardian of the motoring community, quickly became aware of the potential damage that roadside advertising could do to motoring's image. In 1922 it was arguing that motorists should support SCAPA. As was noted above, Shell gained much positive publicity by removing its road-side advertising, replacing it with a series of lorry posters. However, the issue of roadside advertising was still causing concern in the late 1930s. The Ministry of Health's planning advisory committee bemoaned unsightly advertising along 'many main roads', which had ruined the countryside's charm and disfigured villages.[126]

The Scott Committee also castigated rural advertising, arguing that it was 'aesthetically and morally an offence that relatively small sections of the community should be able to exploit this common possession'.[127] Roadside advertising was particularly prevalent in areas where the middle-class motoring family might be found. By 1938 an eighty-mile stretch of road, from Manchester to Newby Bridge at the foot of Lake Windermere, was bedecked with 755 large advertisements, including 103 displaying several advertisements.[128] As in the case of country petrol stations, legislation did exist to limit advertising but it was irregularly used and somewhat flawed. The Advertisement Regulation Acts of 1907 and 1925 gave county councils and rural district councils powers to introduce by-laws preventing disfigurement of the countryside by advertising. There were, though, several problems surrounding the enforcement of any such by-law. The greatest was an unwillingness to act on the part of local authorities, given the expense any such action might entail. Any danger of recourse to the courts may have dissuaded councils from taking action. For example, an advertisement might be placed in a position adjacent to a panoramic view rather than in the viewer's direct line of vision. If a dispute arose and a case went to court, the ultimate decision might be guided by the aesthetic opinion of an individual magistrate. At the end of the legal process there was nothing in law to prevent another advertisement being erected in the same spot. Moreover, local by-laws were only applicable in the case of notices of twelve foot in diameter and over.

However, once again preservationist thinking was at odds with the interests of sections of the rural community, who saw the countryside as their business world. There is a good deal of evidence to suggest that the appearance of advertising signs was testimony to the changing economy of the British countryside. It is clear that much of the advertising which came in for criticism was placed there by the local population. Many advertised a service of their own, bed and breakfast being one example, whilst some farmers took advantage of the convenient position of their land in relation to busy roads by renting out sites for advertising hoardings. For instance, in 1929 Merionethshire police followed up a number of successful prosecutions under local by-laws with visits to boarding-house keepers, café proprietors and farmers, the result being that a large number of advertising signs were removed.[129] Farmers not only erected signs on behalf of others; they also advertised their own goods and services, from farm-produced food, sold from farm shops, to teas or bed and breakfast for visitors to the countryside. John Moore remarked upon this development amongst smallholders in the Cotswolds, who were 'naturally eager to sell their produce at the highest possible price', and to do so would 'erect horrible little sheds and shelters at the side of the roads and stick up scrawled notice boards about the price of asparagus or plums'.[130] In 1930 the vice-chairman of the Design and Industries Association informed the CPRE of rising concern about the advertising for roadside tearooms, the untidiness of which was said to rival the 'average garage'. The proprietors of such establishments were patronisingly described as 'small men anxious to attract attention', but having 'neither means nor education to build anything very decent'. The letter concluded that they should be encouraged to do better in order that 'country motoring should remain popular'.[131]

In some areas earnings from these new sources of income were significant. In 1945 Elizabeth Brunner reported that 'many farmers in holiday areas, such as Devon and Cornwall, calculate on a substantial part of their livelihood being devised from the money they make taking in tourists in the summer.'[132] As well as noting the 'rash of petrol pumps and wayside cafes' that had been established, she commented on the particular appeal the farmhouse had for mobile travellers. J. A. R. Pimlott estimated that during the agricultural depression of the 1930s some Devonshire farmers derived between 50 and 75 per cent of their income from the tourist trade by the sale of teas, providing accommodation and by letting camp sites.[133] The trade press of the hotelier also consistently reported the new competition presented by rural entrepreneurs.[134] Hoteliers were particularly upset that the flexible holidaying opportunities offered by their semi-professional rivals deprived them of some of their wealthier, car-owning, customers. In some cases, of course, as a consequence of having bought a car, family finances were reduced enough to make staying in an idyllic rural farmhouse or cottage financially prudent as well as aesthetically attractive.

Conclusion

In his comments on dealing with the motorists who camped on his farm, A. G. Street pointed out that he did not much appreciate the advice the campers and caravanners received from their camping association on dealing with the countryside's 'inhabitants'. He objected to being called an inhabitant, as if he was from a different country. But in many ways he was. What a study of the car in the rural environment reveals is that it was used there by two very different groups with contrasting outlooks on the countryside. For the urban middle-class motoring family the car provided the means by which they could escape city life and immerse themselves in a rural world that was to a large extent an imaginary one. Despite the fact that a key symbol of modernity, the car, had brought them there, they were often disturbed to see the countryside of their dreams increasingly subjected to the modernity they thought they had left behind in the city. For country-dwellers the car could be a nuisance or a positive boon, the individual's perceptions being shaped by their own access, or lack of it, to a car. Even for those who had no car of their own, the car might be looked upon as the conveyor of wealthy customers, who were a source of welcome capital at a time of economic uncertainty. Thus, the countryside was not about to reject the car, and, though many middle-class Britons might have regretted the changes that increased motoring brought to rural Britain, they nonetheless wanted to motor there themselves. For them the countryside was a positional good; it was the access of others that they would have been happy to prevent, not their own.

Notes

1 Contemporaries used the phrase 'English landscape' most often, although this at times included Wales, Scotland and Ireland.

2 G. Stedman Jones, *Outcast London: A Study in the Relationship Between Classes in Victorian Society* (Oxford, Clarendon Press, 1971); A. Howkins, 'The discovery of rural England', in R. Colls and P. Dodd (eds), *Englishness: Politics and Culture 1880–1920* (London, Croom Helm, 1986), p. 63; M. Bunce, *The Countryside Ideal: Anglo-American Images of Landscape* (London, Routledge, 1994), p. 53; M. Weiner, *English Culture and the Decline of the Industrial Spirit 1850–1980* (Harmondsworth, Penguin, 1992); S. Miller, 'Land, landscape and the question of culture: English urban hegemony and research needs', *Journal of Historical Sociology*, 8 (1995) 94–107.

3 Howkins, 'The discovery of rural England', p. 63; A. Potts, '"Constable country" between the wars', in R. Samuel (ed.), *Patriotism: The Making and Unmaking of British National Identity*, Vol. III (London, Routledge, 1989), p. 165.

4 C. E. M. Joad, *The Horrors of the Countryside* (London, Hogarth Press, 1931), pp. 18–19.

5 Howkins, 'The discovery of rural England'; R. Williams, *The Country and the City* (London, Paladin 1973).

6 E. Thomas, *The South Country* (London, J. M. Dent, 1909), cited in Howkins, 'Rural England', p. 64.

7 Bunce, *The Countryside Ideal*, p. 82; Weiner, *English Culture*, ch. 4, n. 36, p. 61.

8 In 1929 Longman began its 'English Heritage' series, which included titles on folk song and dance, and the parish church. The following year Batsford began an 'English Life' series which featured illustrated volumes on villages and hamlets. Bunce, *The Countryside Ideal*, p. 53.

9 W. S. Shears (ed.), *Kent, Surrey and Sussex* (London, Hutchinson, 1939), pp. 9–11.

10 J. Sheail, *Rural Conservation in Interwar Britain* (Oxford, Clarendon Press, 1981), p. 21.

11 H. Newby, *Country Life: A Social History of Rural Britain* (London, Weidenfeld & Nicolson, 1987), p. 152.

12 Sheail, *Rural Conservation in Interwar Britain*, p. 22.

13 An average of 816,000 worked in agriculture in 1921–24, but only 593,000 were employed in 1938.

14 D. E. Cosgrove, *Social Formation and Symbolic Landscape* (London, Croom Helm, 1984), pp. 264–5.

15 V. Cunningham, *British Writers of the Thirties* (Oxford, Oxford University Press, 1988), p. 228. The phrase is borrowed from Cunningham's assessment of the impact of H. V. Morton's work.

16 *Country Life*, 14 February 1914.

17 *Ibid.*, 25 April 1914.

18 See, for example, *Austin Magazine*, *Modern Motoring* (published by the Rootes Group), *Morris Owner*, *Standard Car Review* and *Popular Motoring* (the official organ of the Singer Motor Car Club).

19 J. Prioleau, *Car and Country: Week-End Signposts to the Open Road* (1929). Prioleau had formerly been sales manager at Morris Motors. Many of the short pieces collected in this book had previously appeared in the *Observer*.

20 *Ibid.*, p. 155.

21 *Ibid.*, p. 40.

22 *Ibid.*, p. 189.

23 *Ibid.*, p. 9.

24 Cunningham, *British Writers of the Thirties*, p. 228.

25 M. Bommes and P. Wright, 'Charms of residence: the public and the past' in R. Johnson (ed.), *Making Histories* (London, Hutchinson, 1982).

26 *Ibid.*, p. 285.

27 *Ibid.*, p. 285.

28 R. Croft Cooke, *How to Get More Out of Life* (London, Bles, 1938), p. 153.

29 *Ibid.*, p. 155.

30 *Autocar*, 1 October 1937.

31 W. R. Calvert, *Family Holiday* (London, Putnam, 1932), p. 51.

32 *Ibid.*, p. 56.

33 *Ibid.*, p. 112.

34 C. F. G. Masterman, *The Condition of England* (London, Methuen, 1909), p. 72.

35 *Garage and Motor Agent*, 22 February 1936.

36 S. Spender, *Forward from Liberalism* (1937); cited in Cunningham, *British Writers of the Thirties*, p. 257.

37 Joad, *The Horrors of the Countryside*, pp. 17–18.

38 S. Kaye-Smith, 'Laughter in the South-East', in C. Williams-Ellis (ed.), *Britain and the Beast* (London, Dent and Sons, 1937), p. 34.

39 G. M. Boumphrey, 'Shall the towns kill or save the country?', in Williams-Ellis (ed.), *Britain*, pp. 101–2.

40 *Ibid.*

41 H. Marshall, 'The rake's progress', in Williams-Ellis (ed.), *Britain and*

the Beast, p. 172.

42 *Ibid.*, p. 173.

43 *Ibid.*, p. 164.

44 C. E. M. Joad, 'The people's claim', in Williams-Ellis (ed.), *Britain and the Beast*, p. 64.

45 D. L. North, 'Middle class suburban lifestyles and culture in England, 1919–1939', University of Oxford, unpublished D.Phil. thesis, 1988, pp. 36–7.

46 F. Hirsch, *The Social Limits to Growth*, cited in Newby, *Country Life*, p. 227.

47 Museum of Rural Life, University of Reading: Automobile Association File 78.

48 *Ibid.*

49 Museum of Rural Life, University of Reading, CPRE Files: letter from H. G. Griffin to Fryer (September 1931); letter from H. G. Griffin to H. H. Child of *The Times* (September 1931). Copies of the book went to CPRE contacts on the *London Mercury*, the *Spectator*, *Country Life*, *The Times* and the *Observer*.

50 Museum of Rural Life, University of Reading: CPRE File Motor Agents Association, 108/11.

51 Museum of Rural Life, University of Reading, CPRE File: AA Shelters and Telephone Boxes, 78/1.

52 Museum of Rural Life, University of Reading, CPRE Correspondence: The Earl of Crawford and Balcarres to H. G. Griffin, 15 February 1933.

53 Museum of Rural Life, University of Reading, CPRE File: Car Dumps, 111/11/1.

54 Public Record Office, MT 34/8.

55 W. Plowden, *The Motor Car and Politics in Britain* (Harmondsworth, Pelican Books, 1973), p. 51–2ff.

56 Royal Commission on Motor Cars, *Evidence*, Cd. 3081 (London, HMSO, 1906).

57 Plowden, *Motor Car and Politics*, p. 52.

58 R. Graves and A. Hodge, *The Long Week-End: A Social History of Great Britain 1918–1939* (New York, W.W. Norton and Co., 1963), p. 183.

59 *Autocar*, 10 May and 26 July 1919.

60 *Autocar*, 25 May 1923.

61 *Ibid.*, 15 March 1935.

62 *Ibid.*, 25 February 1938.

63 *Manchester Guardian*, 28 March 1928.

64 Graves and Hodge, *The Long Week-End*, p. 378.

65 *The Times*, 26 September 1906.

66 *Autocar*, 4 March 1932.

67 *Ibid.*, 22 April 1932.

68 J. Lowerson, 'Battles for the countryside', in F. Gloversmith (ed.) *Class, culture and Social Change* (Brighton, Harvester, 1980), pp. 268–9. The figure of 500,000 is an estimate for the 1930s.

69 Royal Commission on Motor Cars, *Evidence*, Cd. 3081 (London, HMSO, 1906), para. 1619.

70 *Ibid.*, para. 10104.

71 *Autocar*, 13 March 1931, for example, reported that the *CTC Gazette* was constantly at war with the motorist and the motoring press.

72 Royal Commission, *Evidence*, para. 7730.

73 *Pedestrians' Association Quarterly News Letter*, July 1933.

74 Plowden, *The Motor Car and Politics*, p. 52.

75 Royal Commission, *Evidence*, Para. 14180–91.

76 *Autocar*, 11 May, 1923.

77 *Autocar*, 16 August 1929.

78 *Autocar*, May 29, 1936.

79 *Austin Magazine*, April 1930.

80 Museum of Rural Life, University of Reading, CPRE File: Automobile Association, 78.

81 Museum of Rural Life, University of Reading, CPRE File: Litter, CI 24.

82 *Ibid.*

83 *Exeter Express*, 24 November 1931. *Devon Gazette*, 25 November 1931.

84 *Listener*, 1 November 1933.

85 *Autocar*, 9 June 1939.

86 A. G. Street, 'The Countryman's View', in Williams-Ellis (ed.), *Britain and the Beast*, p. 123.

87 *Autocar*, 18 August 1939.

88 Scott Report, Committee on Land Utilisation in Rural Areas, (Ministry of Works, 1943) Cd. 6378. p. 86.

89 A. G. Street, 'The inner history of camping', in *Hedge Trimmings* (London, Faber & Faber, 1933), pp. 45–51.

90 Scott Report, p. 170.

91 *Ibid.*, pp. 56–61.

92 Respondent 67, Neil Blatch: born Freshfield, near Liverpool 1917.

93 A. Armstrong, *Farmworkers: A Social and Economic History 1770–1980* (London, Batsford, 1988), p. 189.

94 Newby, *Country Life*, p. 168.

95 S. Bowden and P. Turner, 'Demand for consumer durables in the United Kingdom in the interwar period', *Journal of Economic History*, 53 (1993) 251–2.

96 *Autocar*, 3 September 1921.

97 Scott Report, p. 43.

98 *Farmer's Weekly*, 19 June 1936, 13 November 1936 and 23 December 1938.

99 *Autocar*, 23 August 1919; *Garage and Motor Agent*, 10 May 1923, reported that the Ford was employed in farm-work throughout the week and took the family to church on Sunday.

100 *Farmers Weekly*, 19 June 1936.

101 Modern Records Centre, University of Warwick, Austin Motors Board Minutes. Campbell was a celebrated racing driver and, at times, holder of the land-speed record. He also gave publicity to Austin Motors by using their cars in some of his attempts at the record.

102 This assertion is based on the information given in an advertisement for the NFU Mutual Insurance Society Ltd. which appeared in *Farmer's Weekly*, 19 June 1936.

103 *Farmer's Weekly*, 19 June 1936.

104 *Ibid.*, 30 June 1939.

105 *Listener*, 21 June 1933.

106 *Farmer's Weekly*, various issues.

107 Royal Commission on Transport, *Minutes of Evidence*, Vol. 1, Evidence of John Garton and Frederick Sabatini of the National Farmers Union, 18 December 1928.

108 *Ibid.*

109 A. W. Ashby 'The effects of urban growth on the countryside', *Sociological Review*, 31 (1940) 356.

110 *Farmer's Weekly*, 23 October 1936.

111 Ashby, 'The effects of urban growth', 351.

112 Respondent 26, Eironwy Phillips: born Neath Valley (date unknown).

113 Respondent 60, Patricia Channon: born 1915.

114 Respondent 49, Christine Paul: born Wiltshire (date unknown).

115 Respondent 57, Mary Tomkins: born USA, brought up in Shropshire, (date of birth unknown).

116 Sheila Kaye-Smith, 'Laughter in the south-east', in Williams-Ellis, *Britain and the Beast*, p. 42.

117 Royal Commission on Transport, *Minutes*, Vol. 1, para. 4384.

118 Morris, *The Country Garage*, p. 8; *Master Builder*, August 1928.

119 Museum of Rural Life, University of Reading, CPRE File: Petroleum (Consolidation) Act 1928.

120 *Report of the Committee on Land Utilisation in Rural Areas*, p. 212; Museum of Rural Life, University of Reading, CPRE File 108/6/II.

121 *Autocar*, 4 April and 25 April 1930.

122 Museum of Rural Life, University of Reading, CPRE File: Petroleum (Consolidation) Act 1928.

123 *Architect*, 1 January 1931; cited in CPRE File on Petroleum (Consolidation) Act.

124 *Report of the Committee on Land Utilisation in Rural Areas*, p. 212.

125 *Kelly's Directory of Warwickshire* (London, Routledge & Kegan Paul, 1940).

126 Town and country planning advisory committee, *Report on the Preser-*

vation of the Countryside (London, HMSO, 1938), p. 5.

127 *Ibid.*, p. 214.

128 C. E. M. Joad, *The Untutored Townsman's Invasion of the Countryside* (London, Faber & Faber, 1946), Appendix VII.

129 *Warwick Advertiser*, 2 November, 1929.

130 J. Moore, 'The Cotswolds', in Williams-Ellis (ed.), *Britain and the Beast*, p. 89.

131 Museum of Rural Life, University of Reading, CPRE File: Teashop Signs, 161/13. Letter received from vice-chairman of the Design and Industries Association, 22 September 1930.

132 E. Brunner, *Holiday Making and the Holiday Trades* (London, Oxford University Press, 1945), pp. 7–8.

133 J. A. R. Pimlott, *The Englishman's Holiday* (London, Faber & Faber, 1947), p. 242.

134 See, for example, *British Boarding House Proprietor and Private Hotelier*, July 1932 and August 1935.

6

Representations of the car

An examination of the cultural representations of the car – in literature, film and elsewhere – offers the opportunity to consider the extent
of motoring's impact on early-twentieth-century consciousness. It does
so by enabling us to trace some of the symbolic roles that the notion
of the car had come to assume. However, tracing the cultural representations of the car and motoring brings us into difficult territory. Clearly,
as the previous chapters have revealed, the car became embroiled in a
number of contentious cultural, social and political issues. These ranged
from questions in which motoring was a primary factor, such as rising
road casualties, through to its involvement in shifting class and gender
relations. Attempting to do justice to each of these areas, whilst also
offering the reader a sense of the evolving relationship between the car
and a profusion of cultural media, is a complex, exacting task. The first
difficulty is in establishing which cultural forms to investigate and,
having chosen them, then to decide which individual texts, works of
art, films and so on to analyse. To take literature as an example: is the
work of literature that was valued by contemporary critics, but scarcely
read at the time, to be treated as a profound and sage-like assessment
of the car and its role in cultural debates? Or, at the other end of the
spectrum, what of the work of the workaday novelist who produced
middlebrow or popular novels: does the formulaic structure and imagery
of many of these works make them more useful because they establish
a route into more widely held impressions of the car?

In what follows, the approach to the representation of the car will be broadly based, focusing on a series of images. By employing this thematic approach it is hoped that the cultural forms analysed will offer a true reflection of the complex and changing relationship between the car and British society in the early twentieth century. It will become clear that images of the car and motoring often had a political purpose. When depicted by enthusiasts, the car could become an emblem of the freedoms and liberties of modernity. But the car's symbolic quality also rendered it a ready-made metaphor for critics of early-twentieth-century materialism. Thus, the car became involved in long-running cultural clashes between various societal groups. The car was most favourably treated in middlebrow cultural forms, whereas it regularly received negative treatment in highbrow works. This criticism became more widespread as the twentieth century progressed, with highbrow hackles being raised by the new forms of commercialised leisure that were popular amongst the growing army of suburbanites. Thus competing aesthetic sensibilities often reflected social and economic positions. Those guardians of motoring, *Autocar* and *Motor*, were extremely aware of this development and kept regular watch on academic and artistic responses to the car. The motoring lobby was clearly aware of the importance of the representations of motoring that appeared in a variety of cultural forms. They were worried that the majority of the population, who were not car owners, were drawing their view of motoring from its depiction in literature, film and other popular media. For this reason, as we shall see, the motoring lobby was a regular critic of any portrayal of the car that it felt was unduly negative or likely to raise levels of animosity towards motoring. These intercessions were most frequent from the 1920s onwards, for a number of reasons. First, the levels of car ownership rose twentyfold during the inter-war years. Second, the ensuing rise in road casualties guaranteed the car a constant place in national debates about the negative aspects of modernity. Third, the arrival of BBC radio in 1922, with a regular programme of topical speakers, also provided motoring's advocates with frequent cause for concern.

The discussion presented here will be organised in several sections. The first of these examines the metaphorical role the car had in artistic critiques of materialism and modernity. The second section evaluates the more diverse portrayals of the car and motoring in popular culture as a whole. This section will demonstrate that cultural forms, ranging from poetry through to fairground attractions, became media through which the car, particularly its dangers, became tolerated. However, the dangers and menacing aspects of the car remained the dominant motif in depictions of motoring. The remaining sections will look at three areas in which the menacing aspect of the car was employed in cinema and literature. Thus the third section of this chapter examines the growing use of the car in cinematic crime stories, where its mobility and speed facilitated both plot direction and exciting action sequences. The fourth section examines the role of the car in a number of stories from the 1930s, some of which were transferred to the screen. Although these stories share the cultural pessimism of the anti-materialists discussed in the first section of this chapter, they do not offer direct critiques of the car. Instead they employ the car as a troubling metaphor in order to underscore points about individual characters and their role as subverters of accepted moral and social mores. The fifth and final section returns our discussion to the theme of gender for one final time. As was demonstrated in Chapter 2, the car was symbolically important in debates about the changing character of femininity and masculinity, particularly after the commencement of war in 1914. This section will explore the literary reworking of these debates in the 1920s and 1930s. In particular it will indicate that there was a conservative reaction to the gains that women made during this period and that the fictional female driver often suffered as a result.

Modernity, materialism and the critique of the car

One of the most commonly recurring symbolic roles performed by the car was in discussions about the direction and nature of modernity and materialism. In the early twentieth century a wide range of writers began to question the nineteenth-century ideal of the age of progress. A widespread disquiet about the trajectory of materialism was expressed in a variety of artistic and academic media. As car ownership spread beyond the hands of the ultra-rich, it became representative of modernity. Its speed and range provided geographical and spatial liberties to motorists and it facilitated new ways of living as well as new forms of architectural design.

The car and the motorist were regularly employed in critiques of materialism and modernity from the early twentieth century. George Sturt, whose *Change in the Village* (1912) was acclaimed by F. R. Leavis, expressed the linkage between the car and the negativity of modern materialism in a letter to a friend, written in 1911: 'I don't like England as she is – industrial, over-capitalized, where the Struggle to Live is so sordid, and success means motor-cars and insolence.'[1] This link between brash materialism and the car was frequently made in a variety of literary works. Stanley Houghton's comic play, *Hindle Wakes*, set amongst a Lancashire weaving community, was first performed in 1912. It told the tale of mill-owner's son, Alan Jeffcote, and his affair with Fanny Hawthorne, an employee in his father's weaving shed. The couple meet in Blackpool, during their town's wakes week, where their amorous exploits are facilitated by Alan's car which takes them away from the many eyes that know them to the more socially exclusive Llandudno. Ironically, Alan's father, Nat Jeffcote, had bought the car for a much less clandestine purpose: 'Why did I buy a motor-car? Not because I wanted to go motoring. I hate it. I bought it so that people could see Alan driving about in it, and say, "There's Jeffcote's lad in his new car. It cost five hundred quid."'[2] This example from Houghton's play was an early example of an important role the car frequently performed in literature. As a graphic material object its use enabled readers to create verbal photographs or repositories of information through which they could situate a story's protagonists.[3] Thus, depending on the model of car depicted, or the language through which it was described, the introduction of a car provided writers with a number of devices through which to define a character or set a mood. In particular, the car frequently became a metaphor for the shallowness of materialistic modern society.

The novel that most explicitly and coherently offered this interpretation of the car was E. M. Forster's *Howards End* (1910), the novel that established his reputation. The *Daily Mail* hailed it as that year's 'great novel'. *Punch* applauded it for introducing the reading public to the Wilcox family: 'For the Wilcoxs are England; they contain more of the essence of England even than Sunday afternoon, or Lords.'[4] *Howards End* is difficult to place in the schematic spectrum of highbrow, middlebrow and popular culture, for it offers parallel critiques of the materialistic, business world of the Wilcox family and the more ethereal,

bookish world of the Schlegel family and their Bloomsbury acquaint-
ances. The one character who escapes the novel with, it seems, the
author's full approval is Mrs Wilcox, who is the human embodiment of
the values of the English countryside, as represented by her home
Howards End. She is first set apart from her own children: 'She seemed
not to belong to the young people and their motor.'[5] Later she is
invited to dinner by Margaret Schlegel and is equally unsuited to the
company she finds herself in: 'she was not interested in … the dividing-
line between Journalism and Literature, which was started as a conver-
sational hare … Clever talk alarmed her, and withered her delicate
imaginings; it was the social counterpart of the motor-car, all jerks'.[6]
Howards End abounds with jarring references to the car such as these.

Characters are defined by their attitudes towards the car and the
diverse sensations they experience when travelling by it. Charles, the
ambitious eldest son of the Wilcox family, is seen, early in the novel,
driving through the local village. Contemplating the cloud of dust his
car had caused, which had 'percolated through the windows … whit-
ened the roses and gooseberries of the wayside gardens' and 'entered
the lungs of the villagers', Charles mutters: 'I wonder when they'll learn
wisdom and tar the roads.' The Wilcox family are energetic characters
whose only interest is in material advancement; they dismiss the contem-
plation of spiritual and intellectual matters as a waste of resources. The
intellectual Schlegel sisters, Helen and Margaret, are in turn seduced by
the simplicity and comfort of the Wilcox brand of materialism. Interestingly, when drawn to the opulence of the material world, both the
Schlegels literally sink into car seats. The outspoken and liberal Helen
is the first of the sisters to be fascinated by the energy of the Wilcoxes,
and she secretly enjoys the fact that, 'One by one the Schlegel fetiches
[*sic*] had been overthrown' by Henry Wilcox, the head of the family.
When he had said that 'one sound man of business did more good to
the world than a dozen of your social reformers', Helen 'had swallowed
the assertion without a gasp, and had leant back luxuriously among the
cushions of his motor-car.'[7] Later in the novel Margaret Schlegel
becomes even more attracted to the energetic, rawly masculine qualities
of the now widowed Henry Wilcox and she subsequently marries him.
Wilcox is showing Margaret around his London home when she is
attracted by the maroon leather chairs in which Wilcox and friends did
their after-dinner smoking: 'It was as if a motor-car had spawned. "Oh,

jolly!" said Margaret, sinking into one of them.'[8] However, it is through Margaret Schlegel that the critique of the car is repeatedly articulated. Throughout the novel her dislike of motoring is made clear. Not only does she have 'chickens and children on the brain' whenever she is in a car; she despairs about the damage motoring does to the traveller's ability to appreciate the passing landscape. Driving through Hertford-shire with Henry, he advises her: 'There's a pretty church – oh, you aren't sharp enough.' She spends the journey trying to savour the scenery, but 'It heaved and merged like porridge. Presently it congealed. They had arrived.'[9]

In inter-war Britain, as the critique of suburban culture grew shriller and motoring became increasingly popular, the assault on materialism was frequently articulated through attacks on the car. Sociologists were critical of what they labelled the mechanised life of the wireless, cinema and motoring. Henry Durant's *The Problem of Leisure*, published in 1938, discussed the largely negative impact of what he called 'the machinery of amusement' that had sprung up to replace spontaneous popular leisure amongst traditional family and community groups.[10] According to Durant, the problem was acutest amongst the middle classes, who possessed energy, time and some disposable income at the end of a working day.[11] He believed many middle-class families sacrificed every-thing in order to buy and run a car, which was then used in a not entirely positive way: 'as the main mode of recreation [the car] is the ideal form of challenging one's neighbours and at the same time main-taining one's privacy.'[12] Meanwhile Q. D. Leavis's *Radio and Fiction* iden-tified motoring with 'bad culture', locating it within a catalogue of superficial, unimaginative and philistine pursuits.[13] C. E. M. Joad, who was always to be relied upon to vent his spleen against the car, attacked what he saw as the cultureless, unsociable leisure of the suburban middle classes, who were 'cut off from the life of the spirit … without part in a community or roots in the soil, they continue to keep themselves to themselves and go out in the car on a Saturday … [in a] fantasy world of speed and physical sensation'.[14]

This mood of cultural pessimism was regularly voiced by the group of young poets who made their names in the 1920s and 1930s. Given the political postures assumed by many of these writers, it is not sur-prising that their work regularly featured anti-materialistic sentiment. Equally unsurprising is the fact that the car had a periodic role to play in these assaults on materialism. The best known single work in this vein is probably John Betjeman's 'Slough', written in 1937; with its 'bald young clerks' who do not 'know the birdsong from the radio' but 'talk of sports and motor cars in various bogus Tudor bars'.[15] Ironically, of course, at the same time Betjeman's muse was also busily engaged in waxing lyrical on behalf of the Shell series of motoring guides. A steady stream of other poets also used motoring as an unattractive metaphor of soiled materialism. In 1939 Francis Scarfe's 'Beauty, Boloney' offered a satirical reappraisal of aesthetic beauty for the modern world, in which 'True Beauty's in Nuffield and Ford/ Mussolini and Chamberlain/ they are the chosen of the Lord/ let Laureates praise them, if they can.'[16] Louis MacNeice's 'Birmingham', written in 1934, stripped away the veneer of the modern city to reveal the squalid conditions that made consumerism possible. The poem depicts a traffic policeman controlling a 'queue of fidgety machines' with 'Chromium dogs on the bonnet, faces behind the triplex screens'. The cars and their drivers leave the 'Vulcan's forges' of the slums unvisited as they head, instead, for 'half-timbered' suburban houses that have been 'seducingly rigged by the builder' and paid for, ultimately, by somebody else's 'sweated labour'.[17] This anti-materialist, anti-machine mode was also regularly taken up by D. H. Lawrence, whose own complex set of personal philosophies engendered his use of this tone. The car featured in Lawrence's poetry as a life-denying machine. In 'The triumph of the machine' he outlined this theory: 'So mechanical man in triumph seated upon the seat of his machine will be driven mad from within himself, and sightless.'[18] His poem 'Cry of the masses' pleads 'oh give us back our bodies before we die!' Humankind has become corpse-like in its adherence to the rhythm of machines, including the car: 'Trot, trot, trot, corpse-body, to work./ Chew, chew, chew, corpse-body, at the meal./ Sit, sit, sit, corpse-body in the car./ Stare, stare, stare, corpse-body at the film'.[19]

Thus criticism of the machine age regularly returned to the car as a definitive example of the coruscating effect of unchecked materialism. Osbert Sitwell went as far as to list the newly-constructed Great West Road alongside the Nazi's Nuremburg stadium as one of the evils of the age.[20] More famously, the dystopian future in Aldous Huxley's novel *Brave New World* described the 'new era', in which the pursuit of consumption was society's singular goal. This era was dated from the

8   'Cubing the circus. The inevitable impressions of metropolitan motoring experienced by a country driver.' A striking example of F. Gordon Crosby's art.

'introduction of Our Ford's first T-Model' and Christianity was replaced by the deification of Fordism. In this future, crosses have their tops cut off, so that they become Ts and the years are measured in terms of Before Ford (BF) and After Ford (AF).[21]

The motoring press was highly conscious of assaults on the car. The car's assailants were regularly dismissed as highbrows, although the lack of positive attention given to motoring by eminent artists clearly concerned the editors of *Autocar* and *Motor*. During the 1920s, *Autocar* columnist Owen John protested regularly about so-called highbrow attitudes towards the car. In 1921 he complained about 'a pig-headed section of effete high-brows' that he felt was portraying every motorist as 'a natural murderist'.[22] John was particularly concerned that the Royal Academy persistently ignored drawings and paintings of motoring subjects, believing that 'somehow art still thinks it highbrow to take no technical details'.[23] Motoring produced a number of skilled artists, not least of whom was F. Gordon Crosby whose attractive work was a regular feature of the *Autocar*. He did exhibit at the Royal Academy on three occasions, but none of the work featured was motor-related.[24] Clearly Britain's artistic establishment was not interested in the type of auto-machine themes that appeared in the work of significant continental painters such as Toulouse-Lautrec, whose 1896 lithograph *The Motorist* portrayed the artist's motoring cousin as a supercharged extension of his vehicle.

The Italian futurists, including Filippo Tommasso Marinetti and Giacomo Balla (who produced more than a hundred works which referenced the car), were the first major artistic movement to employ the car as a central metaphor of modernity from 1909. They were attracted by the 'beauty of speed' and the dynamism which they saw in the car. They were followed by the Dada school, which included Alfred Jarry, Francis Picabia and Marcel Duchamp, who parodically utilised images of the car as, for example, an analogy for sexual behaviour.[25] As was indicated in the last chapter, only the financial incentives offered by the oil giant Shell Mex could entice Paul Nash, Ben Nicholson, Graham Sutherland and others to undertake work with a motoring theme. Edward McKnight Kauffer famously began this profitable connection between Shell and the artistic world, producing a 'composite of romantic national propaganda and petrol company publicity' in a striking depiction of Stonehenge that bore the legend 'Stonehenge: See Britain First on Shell'.[26] To coincide with their advertising campaign, Shell Mex sponsored annual art exhibitions and by the fifth of these, in 1934, the critic Clive Bell claimed that the company had become a more important fosterer of art than the Royal Academy. However, as viewers of McKnight Kauffer's 'Stonehenge' will appreciate, the car was often an unseen presence in the nationalistic and pastoralist images used in the Shell Mex campaign. Indeed, the car appeared less frequently as the campaign progressed through the 1930s and as concerns about rural preservation multiplied.[27] Elsewhere in British art of the early twentieth century the car was marginalised. Indeed, its peripheral position is summed up in one of the few paintings in which a car does appear. Edward Burra's 'The snack bar' (1930), which is today owned by the Tate Gallery, depicts a heavily made-up woman customer being leered at by the café owner. Just visible in the corner of the portrait, a car stands in the street alongside a partly obscured motionless woman. The scene is seedy, suggesting solicitation and kerb-crawling. Burra's depiction of the car, like so many others, associated the car with a very unattractive form of consumption – prostitution.

With the exception of the writers and poets who used the car as a metaphor for their disapproving comments on materialism, those who would have considered themselves to be the literary elite followed the example of their artistic contemporaries and largely ignored motoring. Indeed one unidentified literary critic went so far as to claim that 'motoring is the antithesis of literature' because 'it dulls all spiritual activity except the drowsy pleasure of motion'.[28] With such sentiments widely held amongst so-called highbrow thinkers, it was left to the purveyors of middlebrow and popular culture to provide more frequent, naturalistic images of the car.

'When you cross the road by day or night, beware of the dangers that loom in sight': learning to live with the car

In much of what might be designated as middlebrow or popular culture, the car was assigned a more varied series of attributes than was the case in the anti-materialist works discussed above. From Rudyard Kipling's poems and short stories through to Will Hay's comic films, the car certainly received less disparaging treatment than at the hands of some of the writers already cited. Whilst at the hands of film-makers, the darker side of motoring was generally subsumed by its potential for comic or exciting spectacle. Kipling was an early convert to the car. In October 1899 Alfred Harmsworth of the *Daily Mail* took Kipling out for his first drive.[29] Kipling promptly bought his own car and later wrote that, 'In three years from our purchase, the railway station had passed out of our lives.'[30] He became an avid motorist, keeping notes on road and hotel conditions and passing on reported defects to the Automobile Association.[31] Motoring themes quickly entered Kipling's writing, an early example being the 1904 collection of poems 'The muse among motors', which was first published in the *Daily Mail*. Between 1900 and 1930, Kipling wrote many poems with motoring references. These poems do not make for inspiring reading, although several of those from the 1904 collection experiment with poetic forms, imitating a range of great writers including Chaucer, Shakespeare and Byron. The poems dealt with the range of contradictory attitudes towards and possibilities offered by the car. This mood was best summed up in the poem 'Contradictions', where a carrier on a quiet country road is disturbed by the 'howl, a hoot, and a yell' from a passing car, which is likened to 'a blast from the mouth of Hell.' But reading on we learn that the car is a doctor's car, rushing to the aid of an anxious mother. For her, the hum of the car is like 'the beat of an angel's wing'; and Kipling concludes that the car and the carrier's van, when 'properly understood', are 'neither evil nor good'.[32]

As befitted someone with close links to the AA, the issue of speed traps became a recurring theme in Kipling's writing. His poem 'The tour' described 'the Dogberry and the Waterbury' bringing a motorist to justice for allegedly reaching the speed of 50 m.p.h.. The allusion to Shakespeare's comic constable, Dogberry, being a satirical comment on the speed limit.[33] However, Kipling's best known contribution to the debate on speed traps was represented by his short story of 1913 'The village that voted the earth was flat'. In this tale, magistrate Sir Thomas Ingell MP arranges a speed trap near the village of Huckley, a trap in which the narrator and his party of politicians and journalists are caught. Ingell then presides over their case, ridiculing them and labelling them as cads. Annoyed by what they see as the contrived nature of their detection and treatment at the hands of the Huckley Bench, the motorists conceive an elaborate plot through which to exact their revenge on Ingell and the village of Huckley. Using their various newspaper columns, they initiate antiquarian correspondence about the village. Having placed Huckley in the national consciousness they then bus in a troop of musical-hall performers to the village who take part in an election that decides that the earth is flat. This event is publicised in the press, in a musical hall song – 'The village that voted the earth is flat' – and a dance called the 'Gubby'.[34] Nora Crook, a Kipling expert, believes that a central theme in his work was the notion that excessive control encourages lawlessness.[35] In reiterating Kipling's opposition to the authorities' attitude towards speeding motorists, his view of the car certainly conforms with his general apprehension about restrictions on individual liberty. In this case, his feelings were shared by a growing number of car owners. By lampooning the inhabitants of Huckley, Kipling by association also ridiculed the police, the magistrates and their use of speed traps.

This was not the last time the speed trap was parodied. In Will Hay's 1939 film *Ask a Policeman*, the popular comedian played an inept police sergeant who has not made an arrest for many years.[36] Pressed by a new chief constable to improve his performance, Hay and his companions decide that a speed trap will prove the simplest form of achieving some arrests. Their efforts descend into the expected farce when they decide not to charge a speeding motorist because Hay and his constables are confused by the fact that the culprit has no driving licence. Police relations with motorists were also regularly satirised in cartoon form, in newspapers and magazines such as *Punch*. Thus a variety of media comically reflected the tensions that developed between law enforcers and the middle classes as car ownership grew. There was also a growing tendency for road accidents to be seen in a humorous light. Commenting on the car's impact on California, historian Ashleigh Brilliant has argued that much of the humour surrounding the car involved death and violence. He believes that this served as a release of fear, frustration and guilt, to which it was impossible, or undesirable, to give direct expression. Thus a feeling of powerlessness may have led to a willingness to laugh at the destruction the car could produce.[37]

The first British examples of the phenomenon described by Brilliant are to be found in early cinematic portrayals of motoring, which revelled in the novelty value of the new technologies of the car and film. Early films regularly featured motorists receiving what many contemporary film-watchers might have felt was their come-uppance. The 1900 film *How it Feels to be Run Over*, directed by Cecil M. Hepworth, was a comedy that involved a speeding car running into a cart. Particles from the crash float onto the screen to reveal the words 'Oh, Mother will be pleased'.[38] In the same year, Hepworth continued this grotesque imagery in *Explosion of a Motor Car*, in which four motorists are blown into pieces by an explosion which is witnessed by a note-taking police-man.[39] The twin themes of the car and disembodiment appeared once again in the 1902 film *How to Stop a Motor Car*, during which a police-man attempts to halt a motorist but is knocked into pieces. Miraculously reassembled, he is instructed by his inspector that to stop a car he should turn his back and bend over, so that the car will bounce off him.[40] The 1903 film *Car Ride* was another that experimented with camera trickery to engineer a series of dramatic and dangerous motoring scenes, before concluding with a crash.[41] Little is known about the 1905 film *The Motor Hooligans*, but its title suggests that it may have reflected popular antagonism towards motorists at that juncture.[42] Certainly the 1906 film *Motor Mad* did reflect the belief that motorists were selfish to the point of representing a danger to the rest of society. *Motor Mad* was the comic story of a motorist who instructs his chauffeur to shoot a police constable who has curtailed his motoring jaunt. The motorist is committed to a psychiatric hospital, where in the final scenes he is pictured continuing his motoring obsession in a motorised bath chair.[43] In these earliest motoring films, it was usually the car or the motorist who bore the brunt of the joke. Within a few years, however, cinematic depictions of motoring were becoming more equivocal. *The Motorist's Dream*, released in 1915, appears to have been the first film to offer the audience a car owner's perspective. The film involved a dream sequence in which the motoring protagonist avenges himself on a traf-fic policeman with whom he had been in dispute.[44]

Kenneth Grahame's children's story *The Wind in the Willows* (1908) illustrates Brilliant's thesis, as well as an argument made in our earlier chapter on road safety. The book dealt comically with the disastrous motoring exploits of Toad, a faddish, pompous character who persist-ently becomes engrossed in expensive hobbies only to rapidly tire of them. Disaster strikes when he is almost run over by a passing car. It immediately captures Toad's imagination and he begins to dream of 'the dust-clouds [that] shall spring up behind me as I speed on my reckless way!'[45] He destroys a series of expensive cars, styles himself the 'Terror of the Highway' and regularly finds himself in trouble with the police.[46] His friends, Badger, Rat and Mole try to cure him of his dangerous obsession by imprisoning him in his own home, Toad Hall. He manages to escape and comes across a car which he steals, becoming, at its wheel, 'Toad at his best and highest, Toad the terror,

Toad the traffic-queller, the Lord of the lone trail, before whom all must give way or be smitten into nothingness and everlasting night'.[47] He is subsequently arrested and sentenced, in a farcical court-room scene, to nineteen years' imprisonment. He escapes once more, however, and crashes yet another car, before, at the end of the tale, becoming a changed, more mature animal. The story fits Brilliant's theory in that Toad is a figure of fun rather than a character that is censured by the tale. His obsession is dangerous, but no one is ever seriously injured through his motoring misdemeanours. *The Wind in the Willows* also helped propagate the idea that the dangers of motoring arose primarily through the behaviour of road hogs, rather than through the inherent threat posed by the car itself.

After the 1914–18 war, jokes about road safety issues were regularly offered up in British cinema. As has already been noted, the enormously popular film comedian Will Hay lampooned speed traps in his film *Ask a Policeman*. The film also included a number of comic/dramatic road chases, some of which were filmed at the Brooklands race track, with Hay driving the wrong way around the track in a bus whilst a motor race was taking place. This last stunt had previously been undertaken by comedians Flanagan and Allen in their 1935 film *A Fire Has Been Arranged*.[48] In his 1938 film *Convict 99*, during which Hay is mistakenly made the governor of a tough prison, the car was also used as a comic device. Whilst being driven to his new appointment, Hay and his driver both manage to become intoxicated. Once he has sobered up and arrived at his new post, Hay meets a prisoner known as 'The Mole' because he is renowned for digging tunnels, albeit unsuccessfully. He tells Hay that he plans to build a tunnel that will see him emerge on the main road alongside the prison. Hay warns him that he will be run over, unless he surfaces on a pedestrian crossing. In a further, running, joke Hay manages to damage the assistant governor's car on two occasions.[49]

A variety of other sources also regularly satirised motoring accidents. Brilliant's thesis would appear to be supported by the fact that this trend became more marked as the accident figures climbed in the inter-war period. Importantly, this was also a period of rapidly increasing ownership and a concomitant rise in the numbers of people with actual experience of motoring. The magazine *Punch*, for example, published frequent cartoons about motoring accidents and dilemmas, but national and local newspapers also regularly ran similar comic drawings. Another typical example of the trend to satirise the dangers brought by the car was Osbert Lancaster's *Progress at Pelvis Bay*, which was published in 1936. The book introduced readers to the fictional seaside resort of Pelvis Bay whose attractions included the 'Hearts are Trumps' road-house, an old farmhouse which had been reconstructed in the Tudor style by Elizabethan Enterprises Ltd. As well as offering the motorist ample garage space and petrol facilities, the Hearts are Trumps provided food in its 'Olde Englishe Grille and The Restaurant Fleurie' or jazz in its American bar. The management had also thoughtfully provided an 'excellently equipped first-aid station together with a small operating-theatre with a doctor and nurses in constant attendance on the premises' and there were plans to 'install an up-to-date funeral parlour'.[50]

Even the arcade games in 1930s' Blackpool can be added to the list of cultural artefacts that provided a comic safety valve for tensions raised by road casualties. At Blackpool a particular target of comic aggression was not the car as such but the increasing regulation of pedestrians by road-safety legislation in the 1930s. Thus Mass Observation's reports on Blackpool reveal the popularity of humour at the expense of Belisha beacons. One arcade game, called 'Belisha beacons', encouraged revellers to throw balls at various traffic signs. Attendants encouraged participation with the cry: 'Come on … Have a whack at one. You must have wanted to do it. Here's your chance. Have a bang at the ruddy things.'[51]

Clearly, Brilliant has a point in suggesting that much of the humour surrounding the car acted as an unconscious safety valve for fears about the dangers brought by motoring. However, we also need to be aware that as well as having an almost subliminal appeal to motorists and others, this use of humour was also something that was orchestrated by the motoring lobby. As was outlined in Chapter 4, by the 1930s the motor lobby was keenly aware of the valuable role of propaganda in establishing the dominance of their view of motor traffic issues. In 1935 *You Have Been Warned*, by Fougasse and McCullough, was published with funds from the National Safety First Association.[52] Taking its lead from *Punch*, it satirised *The Highway Code*, through cartoons and epigrams, becoming a best seller which reached a fifth edition within two months of its launch.[53] By March 1936 the book's sales were approaching the 100,000 mark and Fougasse and McCulloch had written a pamphlet, at

TURN LEFT, WHITTINGTON

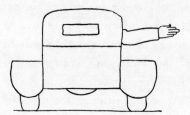

No. 2. " I am going to TURN to my RIGHT."

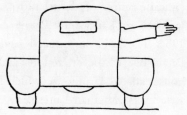

No. 2b. " The rain is OFF, I think."

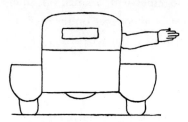

No. 2a. " I am going to TURN to my RIGHT, and when I discover that it 's the wrong turning, I am going to TURN BACK again just in time to give you the FRIGHT of your LIFE."

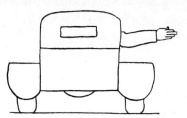

No. 2c. " The house over there with the GREEN door is where our cook's MOTHER lives."

9   Satirising the *Highway Code*.

the behest of the NSFA, which was given away with newly issued driving licences from August of that year.[54] A series of cartoons from *You Have Been Warned* is reproduced here as Figure 9. This use of humour appealed to the road lobby, for whom such an approach was clearly preferable to what they believed to be the 'gruesome safety publicity' deployed in the USA and France at that time.[55] From this perspective, humour offered the potential for road-safety education, whereas blunter references to the grim reality of road accidents were likely to cause increased animosity towards motorists.

The NSFA also encouraged the use of song as part of its road-safety education strategy. Appropriately enough, Gracie Fields, whose films such as *Sing As We Go* advocated national consensus rather than class conflict, recorded the road-safety song *Look to the Left, and Look to the Right*, which was aimed primarily at school children.[56] Fields was an enthusiastic motorist herself. The song, recorded in 1936, included the following lyrics:

> Listen little children, I've a tale to tell,
> All you little boys and little girls as well.
> When you leave the schoolroom, when you're at your play,
> Don't run into danger, think of what I say.
>
> (*Refrain*)
> When you cross the road by day or night,
> Beware of the dangers that loom in sight.
> Look to the left, and look to the right,
> Then you'll never get run over.[57]

Between 1937 and 1939 residents of Lancashire were treated to renditions of Fields' song through the auspices of police loudspeaker vans, which also offered listeners speeches on road safety by Minister of Transport Leslie Hore-Belisha, and racing driver Sir Malcolm Campbell.[58] Two years before Fields' lyrical contribution to road safety, her male counterpart, George Formby, offered a more barbed comment on the privileged position of the private motorist in his 1934 musical film *Off the Dole*. Formby played a work-shy character who was forced to seek work. The apparent bitterness of the lyrics were lessened by Formby's usual jaunty delivery, but the fact that the car was seen as a symbol of privilege and of another social class was unmistakable:

> Who has to live in houses
> You could cut them with a knife?
> Who is it builds your motor cars
> That last you all your life?
> And who was to the fore in the great world war?
> Why, the poor old working man![59]

There is no record of anyone representing the motoring lobby objecting to Formby's lyrics, but there is a plethora of evidence reflecting its general disquiet with the BBC's coverage of motoring. The motoring press became particularly critical of the BBC in the early 1930s, a period which coincided with widespread national debate about road safety. The BBC carried regular talks on road safety by racing drivers, which, as has been seen, were the subject of criticism from the Pedestrians' Association. However, this concession was not enough for the motoring press, who were at times scathing about the corporation. A regular objection raised by the motoring press, was with the BBC's policy of announcing in 'hushed tones' the weekly road death and accident statistics. In 1934, *Motor* protested that these transmissions left the listener with the impression that the car was to blame for all the accidents.[60] The following year the same magazine asked: 'when did the BBC last have a good word for the motorist?' The source of displeasure on this occasion was a radio comedy called 'Advanced Sparks', which had included what *Motor* called 'scintillating witticisms' such as 'remember that all roads lead to the infirmary'. The programme was called 'depressing and typical of the BBC'.[61] In reality, such jokes were no worse than those featured in the NSFA-funded *You Have Been Warned*, which was extremely favourably received by both *Autocar* and *Motor* in the same year that 'Advanced sparks' caused such offence. It would seem highly likely that the role of the BBC in keeping road casualties in the news was the fundamental cause of the motoring lobby's attacks on the corporation. Thus early in 1936, a *Motor* editorial accused the BBC of 'abusing a monopolistic privilege' because its review of 1935 included an estimate of how many listeners might die on the roads in 1936.[62] *Motor* led the motoring lobby's attacks on the BBC, but others also pressurised the corporation to offer what they felt was more favourable coverage of motoring. For example, the Automobile Association archives include a file marking its disapproval of a BBC radio play, broadcast in 1935. The AA objected to the heated discussion between pedestrians, cyclists and motorists which took place in the programme.[63] *Autocar* also recorded its disapproval of this BBC offering, claiming that it glorified antagonism between road users.[64]

The BBC appears to have experienced some concern about this periodic criticism from motoring sources. From 1935, motoring features appeared in the corporation's programming schedules with greater regularity. In that year, listeners could tune in to what was the first of many series of motoring nostalgia called 'Motoring then and now'.[65] In 1936, the motoring nostalgia continued with coverage of the fortieth London–Brighton run.[66] In 1936 the BBC covered the London–Exeter trial by entering a car of its own. In 1938 a young Richard Dimbleby was Alan Hess's co-driver in the RAC rally.[67] In the same year, BBC television covered the motor show for the first time and its presentation kept within gender stereotypes. The programme was fronted by Alan Hess, who tried the driving seat of several cars, whilst his co-host Penelope Sims tested the back seats for comfort.[68] In winning this type of coverage from Britain's only national broadcaster, the motoring lobby scored a significant victory in its fight to secure a favourable portrayal of the car in the media. In backing comic depictions of road dangers, such as those by Fougasse and McCulloch, they also took part in a movement that, in effect, checked some of the animosity that would otherwise have risen to even greater levels around the car. This brand of humour was born out of a growing sense of fatalism and powerlessness surrounding the car. Thus the promotion of this response to the dangers of the car helped avert more passionate and less car-friendly reactions.

The car and crime: the case of British cinema

Humour was not the only outlet through which tensions concerning the dangers of the car were released. Another safety valve – and popular entertainment – was presented by the involvement of the car in action and crime stories and films. It is possible to chart the increasing regularity with which the car was used to inject excitement and facilitate plot development in popular British feature films. In fact, the cinematic linkage between the car and crime was based on the fact that the dangers of motoring were as alluring as they were repelling. As we have seen, the earliest cinematic depictions of the car tended to be grotesquely comic. The car was also put to a number of other uses in the Edwardian cinema. In 1905, Arthur Cooper directed *The Motor Highwayman*, which featured motor-cycling thieves holding up a car.[69] By 1912 cinema-goers had been introduced to their first motorised bank robbers in *The Motor Bandits*.[70] By the 1920s the car was frequently involved in crime films, reflecting its growing utilisation in actual crime and its detection. By this point, organised criminals were taking advantage of the speed and mobility offered by the car and in 1919 the Metropolitan Police responded to a growing problem by forming the motorised Flying Squad.[71] The press quickly found an all-embracing label for motorised criminals, calling them motor bandits. A favourite crime of the motor bandits was the smash-and-grab raid, for which a car provided a swift means of departure. Larry Rankin, whose joyriding escapades were described earlier, also stole cars for use in the smash-and-grab raids that he and other members of Glasgow's Beehive Boys gang undertook in surrounding towns such as Kilmarnock.[72]

In 1922 the Pathe Freres serial *Hurricane Hutch* featured its hero jumping from one moving car to another to save the story's heroine.[73] Also in the 1920s the 'Pixie at the wheel' series of films – *Miles against Minutes*, *Speeding into Trouble* and *Peacetime Spies* – featured the crime-solving duo of a female American reporter and a motorist.[74] By 1928, what was to become familiar cinematic terrain, the Brooklands race circuit, was used for the filming of *Smashing Through*. The film's plot was also to become a familiar one, dealing with a villainous attempt to steal the technical secrets of a successful racing car. *Smashing Through* was one of many films which served to confuse non-car owners with ludicrous technical references. One scene, in which the villains took it in turns to probe the car's secrets by patting and stroking its casing, was particularly preposterous.[75] By the 1930s, the increasing popularity of Hollywood gangster movies provided a further incentive for domestic film producers to continue exploiting the theme of criminality and the car. During the 1930s crime films made up approximately a quarter of British cinematic output, partly because they were far cheaper to produce than alternatives such as costume dramas. They also drew upon important cultural roots, the British public having a long-standing taste for crime and detective stories that had been fostered by Wilkie Collins, Dickens, Conan Doyle, Christie and many other writers.[76] The serial *Lloyd of the CID* (1932) featured a heavy dose of motoring action. So, too, did another of that year's offerings, the feature film *Footsteps in the Night*, which featured a mobile policeman, a villain and a Bentley-driving heroine.[77] By 1934 a young Ralph Richardson was using a Bentley to fight crime in *The Return of Bulldog Drummond*.[78]

Although many of these British films were fairly unremarkable, the British cinema did make at least one landmark contribution to the history of the car in film. Alfred Hitchock's film *Young and Innocent* (1938) was arguably the original road movie, despite claims that the cinematic genre was spawned by the 1950s' Beat Generation.[79] Furthermore, the film's heroine, Erica Burgoyne (Nova Pilbeam), anticipated *Thelma and Louise*, usurping the authority of her chief-constable father to take the side of a murder suspect, Robert Tisdell (Derrick de Marney), who she drives around in search of his alibi. Being a British road movie, the distances travelled do not compete with later American examples of the genre, fifty miles being the longest single stretch of motoring undertaken by the fugitive couple. The centrality of the car in the film facilitated the use of familiar Hitchcockian themes. *Young and Innocent* resembled Hitchcock's earlier film *The 39 Steps* in its plot structure; the hero is wrongly accused of murder and his bid to prove his innocence is aided, reluctantly at first, by the heroine. Battling against the strictures of time and space, the couple gradually become romantically linked, the romance being ultimately sanctioned by the hero's exoneration in the final scenes.[80] Interestingly, given the later popularity of the American road movie, *Young and Innocent* proved to be, in the American market, the most commercially successful of Hitchcock's British-made films.[81]

The car as menacing presence

The menacing side of the car also surfaced in non-crime films and literature. A particularly striking example of this is to be found in the early writing of Grahame Greene. In fact, his short story 'A drive in the country' is another instance of a British artistic response to the car that predated later American cinematic and literary existential tales of doomed, motoring anti-heroes. The story is a simple one. An unnamed young woman, who despises her father because of his conservative and suburban lifestyle, decides to run away with her boyfriend Fred. The young woman's family disapprove of Fred because he has been unemployed for years despite the fact that he appears to come from a reasonably affluent background. When the lovers meet, the woman is surprised and pleased to see that Fred has managed to obtain a car in which they can make good their disappearance. The woman is attracted to Fred by the 'odd reckless quality of [his] mind'. The pair set off without any particular destination, the car adding to the sense of freedom, for the young woman at least. However, we soon learn that Fred does not intend to travel very far and that he has stolen the car. He pulls the car into a field, where it becomes apparent that he has a gun with which he suggests they kill each other in a suicide pact following a night of sex. Suddenly, the young woman is frightened by the traits she found attractive in Fred: 'She had admired his conceit; he had always carried his unemployment with a manner. Now you could no longer call it conceit; it was a complete lack of any values.'[82] The story concludes with the young woman running away from the doomed Fred, who commits suicide alone. The young woman hitches a lift home with a motorist, who propositions her before dropping her off. All in all, the story leaves the reader with an unsettling and seedy picture of the car.

In other examples, the threatening nature of particular fictional characters was transmitted by references to their cars. Such individuals were often social parvenus who had made money through means that the audience was encouraged to condemn. In these cases their possession of such a prized commodity as a car could be seen as illegitimate. The 1939 film version of A. J. Cronin's novel *The Stars Look Down* is a case in point. It was directed by Carol Reed and featured Michael Redgrave in the lead role of Davie Fenwick, with Margaret Lockwood as Jenny Sunley.[83] The story is set in the Northeastern mining community of Sleascale. Davie Fenwick is the bookish son of a miner's union leader, who has the chance of building a life outside mining by taking up a place at Tynecastle University. As the story begins Davie's father is seen urging the local miners to come out on strike because the coal seam they are being asked to work is vulnerable to flooding. He claims to have seen plans revealing this danger many years earlier. Mr Barras, the mine owner, denies that any such plans or danger exist; nevertheless a lengthy strike ensues and places the community in dire poverty. After some months, tensions have grown and when the local butcher insultingly refuses credit to a desperate woman his shop is ransacked by a group of locals. Their actions are depicted sympathetically, in a manner that is redolent of historical essays on the moral economy of the crowd. However, one young man, Joe Garlen, oversteps the mark by stealing the money from the butcher's till. This opportunism and recklessness is Garlen's hallmark. When next seen he has become a bookmaker who is affluent enough to travel everywhere by taxi. He is amorously involved with his landlady's manipulative and selfish daughter, Jenny Sunley, but is keen to jilt her because he wants to move on to better things, as he has secured a job with a coking company and is also having an affair with his new employer's wife. Before departing the scene, Joe introduces Jenny to Davie Fenwick, who by this point is doing well at university. With Joe gone, Jenny decides marriage to Davie is her next-best option. She persuades him to give up his university course to take up a teaching post for 45 shillings a week. Once settled in their new home, equipped with furniture obtained by hire-purchase, Davie finds it difficult to cope with the financial demands of his new wife, who is seen to be a very poor household manager. While Davie is out at work, Jenny is seen eating shop-bought cake, drinking port and contemplating a budget-draining evening's entertainment in Tynecastle. Furthermore, Davie's mother points out that Jenny uses a private laundry rather than do her own washing. Their financial situation becomes so perilous that Davie is forced to take on an extra job, tutoring the despised mine owner's son.

At this point Joe Garlen reappears, complete with a shiny new sports car, on which the camera significantly lingers. Joe visits Davie and Jenny, arriving just as they are engaged in a heated argument about money. Jenny opens the door to her former boyfriend and casts an appraising glance at him and his car before informing him that her husband will be going out later that evening. Later, when he returns unexpectedly, Davie sees Joe's car and discovers his wife's infidelity. He also spots Joe's car outside the mine owner's home and realises that his company has invested in the mining of the dangerous seam, which is by this point proceeding. In fact, the viewer learns that Joe himself has £2,000 invested in this risky scheme. The inevitable happens and flooding strikes the seam, killing several miners. The film ends with a voice-over declaring that some day man will overcome greed. In *The Stars Look Down* the character of Joe Garlen represented the economic (and sexual) attractions and dangers of greed and recklessness. His flashy sports car provided the film-makers with the means of transmitting this message in a form of visual shorthand.[84]

Walter Greenwood's novel *Love on the Dole*, and its subsequent film adaptation, also made metaphorical usage of the car's menacing side. Greenwood's story is also set in a desperately poor working-class area. The only car owner is Sam Grundy, described in the novel as 'the gross street-corner bookmaker', who is 'a small fat man, with beady eyes, an apoplectic complexion'. Grundy's unattractive characterisation is completed by the description of the 'preposterous-sized diamonds' worn on his 'thick fingers', together with the 'collection of gold pendants, spade guineas and Masonic emblems' that hang 'heavily across his prominent stomach'.[85] Grundy's illegal activities enable him to enjoy a lifestyle beyond the dreams of all the other characters in the fictionalised Hanky Park. Like many Labour Party activists, Greenwood was frustrated by the popularity of gambling in working-class communities. The character of Sam Grundy reflected Greenwood's animosity towards bookmakers, whom he saw as parasites. Despite Grundy's grossness, his money provides him with influence and power with the police and other local officials. It also enables him to pluck a succession of young women from the poverty of Hanky Park to establish them in a house in Wales where 'his mistress of the moment resided'.[86] Despite the heroine Sally Hardcastle's love for the socialist Larry Meath, Grundy pursues her and hopes to make her his latest conquest. The pursuit is facilitated by his ever-lurking car, and we learn that he has previously used its glamour to woo young women. At one point, he is confronted by the thuggish Ned Narkey, who is angry at the loss of a lover to Grundy: 'Kate Gayley was mine when Ah'd a pocket full o' dough … Shuts bloody door i' me face sin' you tuk her out in y' car.'[87] Grundy's car, a mobile symbol of his wealth and power, literally enables him to stalk Sally outside her home, her work or wherever she may be. Sally constantly rejects his offers of a drive in his car and it is made obvious that should she accept a lift she will be surrendering her respectability, if not her body, to Grundy. One evening, for example, he hails her from his car: '"Hey, Sal," he cried, winking: "Wharra bout a little ride, eh?" he nodded and winked again: "Ah'll get y' back, early … Go on … What'j'say, eh?" Another grin and a wink.'[88] On this occasion Grundy is rejected by Sally, who swears at him and then ignores his continued entreaties. However, after the death of Larry Meath, with her parents struck by unemployment and her young brother married with a young child and also without work, Sally begins to succumb to Grundy's advances. To begin with, she needs to borrow £5 to cover funeral expenses and other debts. In Hanky Park only one person, Grundy, could possibly have such a sum of money. He readily agrees to Sally's request for a loan, but again fails to persuade her to enter his car to 'talk business where no one can hear', Sally replying firmly: 'Ah want t' borrow five pounds. Ah want no drives in no cars.'[89]

Significantly, the passage where Sally finally decides to become Grundy's mistress commences with her finally entering his car in order to race quickly to her brother's lodgings where his wife is giving birth. By this point Sally is thoroughly dispirited and exhausted, her hopes ended by Larry's death. Larry was dead 'and so was Sally Hardcastle'. Armed with a fatalistic attitude, her thoughts turn to Sam Grundy: 'He had everything to offer; she had nothing to offer. He had money. Money to change life. Money, the fast conveyance in the search of forgetfulness.' In the street outside, Grundy waits to take Sally away from poverty in his fast conveyance. In the film version, Sally is seen being driven away whilst the neighbours exchange knowing glances.[90]

Love on the Dole and *The Stars Look Down* impart a clear sense of unease through the car ownership of Sam Grundy and Joe Garlen, both of whom have acquired the trappings of middle-class status through questionable means. Furthermore, Grundy and Garlen, with the aid of their flashy cars, both subvert the social and moral codes of Hanky Park and Sleascale. However, the theme of car ownership causing changes in morality and social conduct was strongest when the subject of changing gender relations was broached.

Gender and the car in cinema and literature

The symbolic role of the car in contested notions of gender was regularly employed in the cinema and literature of the early twentieth century. In this context, it featured most consistently in those novels of the 1920s and early 1930s that addressed the issue of the post-1918 reconstruction of gender relations. A typical example of the car's metaphorical use in this respect can be found in the scores of novels where a modern emancipated heroine was readily identified by her position in the driver's seat. The most successful and infamous novel of the early 1920s was Michael Arlen's *The Green Hat*. Its content ensured that it was seen as vulgar by many critics, but, despite this, the novel went through seventeen editions between June 1924 and August 1926. His novel made Arlen a celebrity and inspired a number of literary spoofs, a fashion in green hats and a film – *A Woman's Affairs* – which starred Greta Garbo.[91] *The Green Hat* was essentially the story of its heroine, the stylish but tragic Iris Storm, and her complicated love life. The twin themes of style and tragedy were consistently symbolised in the novel by motoring references. After the narrator, the first character met by the reader is Iris Storm's yellow Hispano-Suiza, which 'shone like a battle chariot and 'charmed the eye'. The narrator informs the reader that 'I am one of those who are affected by motor-cars.' So, of course, were readers for whom the romantically described Hispano-Suiza, added glamour to the story. However, even at this first meeting with Iris's elegant car, there was a reminder of its potential menace, the narrator indicating that the car's distinctive mascot could indicate to passers-by that 'they have just escaped death beneath the wheels of a Hispano-Suiza'.[92] Later the reader is told that her car 'was like a great yellow beast with shining scales, and Iris, tall and gentle and white, the lovely princess of the tale who has enslaved the beast'.[93] But *The Green Hat* was not a fairy tale and Iris Storm did not live happily ever after, for the novel concludes with her committing suicide by deliberately crashing the elegant car rather than eloping with her married lover. This and virtually every other key moment in the novel are facilitated by the mobility and speed provided by the car. The novel implies that this mobility has loosened morals, particularly female ones. Hilary Townshend, one of the older male characters in the story, provides this perspective through a discussion of the younger generation of women. This generation 'have motors and telephones and wireless with which to lose [their] sense of the stabilities', whereas in the past people couldn't 'get about so quickly'. By the 1920s 'if a woman has kicked through every restraint of caste and chastity there's the whole world open for her to play the mischief in, there's every invention in the world to help her indulge her intolerable little lusts'.[94]

The novels of Gilbert Frankau constantly return to the control of the car by women as a metaphor for changing gender relations in inter-war Britain. He wrote a succession of moderate-to-best-selling novels such as *Peter Jackson Cigar Merchant* (1919), which had sold 150,000 copies by 1930. Frankau was a self-appointed interpreter of national taste, and as a champion of middlebrow sentiment he relentlessly campaigned against the subversive in literature. One onslaught on BBC radio in 1927 inspired Leonard Woolf's essay 'Hunting the highbrow'. Frankau associated the highbrow with amorality, a factor which moved him to explore the so-called 'new morality' in his own novels.[95] Today, his best known work is probably *Christopher Strong* (1932) because it became a Hollywood movie, starring Katharine Hepburn. The plot of novel and film involves the steady life of Member of Parliament Christopher Strong being transformed when his car crashes with that of Lady Cynthia Darrington. Lady Cynthia, we read, is a chance-taking emancipated woman, an aviator as well as a motorist. Strong and Lady Cynthia embark on an affair which comes to a melodramatic conclusion when the pregnant Lady Cynthia commits suicide by deliberately plunging from the skies in her aeroplane. So, rather like Iris Storm in *The Green Hat*, which also attracted the Hollywood film-makers, Darrington is a modern woman who pays the ultimate price for her emancipation.

Another of Frankau's novels, *Martin Make-Believe* (1930), employs even more conspicuously the metaphor of the female motorist as destabilising influence in society. The novel is set in the years during and after the Great War. The main protagonist, Martin Kenterton, is first encountered fighting on the western front. His wife, Jill, spends the war acting as a chauffeur in London. The liberation she achieves through her work has its corollary in the sexual liaison Jill has with Martin's friend and commanding officer Harry. Jill's infidelity towards her husband sets the tone for a misogynistic streak which perforates the novel, such as the caustic comment that women were being splendid in the war: 'Why – its in all the papers.'[96] There are several hackneyed references to Jill having been tempted and having fallen, and her emancipated character is compared unfavourably to the girlish and compliant Sylvia, whom Martin falls in love with after separating from Jill. The car is used to suggest the dangers of shifting gender relations. At the end of the novel, Martin is wrongly imprisoned for fraud. On his release, Sylvia is waiting for him. Tellingly, Martin is disorientated and frightened as he returns to the outside world, so Sylvia takes the wheel of the car. As they drive along, Sylvia uncharacteristically offers to be Martin's mistress, but he insists that they should marry. A relieved Sylvia admits that she is happy with his answer because she is not really 'modern', but was simply pretending to be. With traditional morality successfully defended, Martin takes to the driving seat and 'normal' gender relations are resumed as the happy couple drive off at the novel's denouement.

Radclyffe Hall's novel *The Well of Loneliness* was another notorious 1920s' novel that featured women at the driving wheel. The novel's infamy arose because of press reaction to its portrayal of lesbian characters and the subsequent obscenity trial. The *Daily Mail*'s editor, James Douglas, colourfully informed his readers that, 'I would rather give a healthy boy or a healthy girl a phial of prussic acid than this novel. Poison kills the body, but moral poison kills the soul.'[97] Based on a mixture of her own real-life experiences and those of her friends, Hall's novel centres on the lesbian Stephen Gordon. Stephen experiences unhappiness throughout the novel because of her sexuality and society's negative attitude towards it. She is most contented during the war when her ability to drive enables her to work with an all-female ambulance unit. The novel implies that the majority of these women share Stephen's sexual orientation.[98] The obscenity trial was widely reported in the national press and must only have served to reinforce many of the deeply rooted feelings, held by many people, about gender and the car. That is, that it was somehow natural for men to drive, but questionable, even unsettling for some, to see a woman at the wheel. With that point in mind, it is interesting to note that the car-driving heroines of all the novels discussed here are ultimately unhappy despite their show of independence.

Other novels, with equally unsympathetic attitudes towards the changing position of women in inter-war Britain, naturalised the male role of car driver. They did so by underscoring the rejuvenation of masculinity that male characters experienced when they took the wheel. In R. Denne Waterhouse's *Week-end Ticket* (1934) the main protagonist Lois travels from her farm home near Worcester to visit family and friends in London. Whilst her friend from pre-war days, the ex-suffra-gette Jennifer, is depicted as a rather shrill communist, the group of motor-sports enthusiasts that Lois meets enliven her weekend with their passion for life. Their cars are an invigorating influence on them. One of these characters, Bumps, is portrayed at the wheel, where he 'was a man transfigured. It was as if the starting motor had set him as well as the engine in motion. His lackadaisical manner disappeared, his movements became quick and certain, and his face looked definitely intelligent.' [99] In John C. Moore's novel *The Walls are Down* (1933), the heroine Audrey Sanderson is forced, through a downturn in her bour-geois family's fortunes, to find work. During her short career she finds herself in the employ of a number of unsympathetically portrayed characters; one is a crudely sketched lesbian and two others are wealthy, but gauche, social climbers. Audrey is troubled and unnerved by the world away from her home, and she only finds security when she returns. Once again normality is represented through a scene where Audrey's boyfriend Harry Lampeter takes her out in his car and his masculinity is reassuringly accentuated: 'he always had the appearance of being half-asleep except when he was … climbing a rock-face, or driving a car. Then he became taut and eager suddenly: a fighting-man all over … Audrey was glad these men of hers did things.'[100]

Conclusion

In terms of the literary representations of the car and gender, it is accurate to conclude that much of what was written on this theme in the 1920s and 1930s provides support for Rebecca West's claim that anti-feminism was 'strikingly the correct fashion' amongst inter-war writers.[101] In this respect motoring metaphors were regularly deployed to represent conservative desires for the return of 'traditional' – that is pre-1914 – gender relations. This conservatism was paralleled by the treatment of the car and motoring in many other cultural forms. The clearest example of this was seen in the work of British artists. For the most part the car was ignored, the influence of futurism and Dadaism having less of an impact on British art than traditional 'English' themes. When the car was finally depicted by British artists, it was situated in a comfortable pastoral context. Furthermore, this work, sponsored by Shell Mex, failed to address the contradictions inherent in the encounter between modernity and heritage. In doing so, it protected and promoted the commercial interests of its patron. Indeed, the motoring lobby, from the AA and motoring magazines through to the NSFA, was very busily engaged in monitoring the cultural representations of the car. These champions of the car welcomed the emergence of a number of cultural responses to it that offered to reify the position of motoring rather than challenge it. Chief amongst these was the comic depiction of the car that acted as form of release for concerns about its alarming safety record.

However, despite this development, an analysis of the images of the car that were not welcomed or sponsored by the motoring lobby makes it apparent that the car, and modernity in general, had a troubling, unsettling impact on early-twentieth century consciousness. The frequency with which images of danger, death and the car appeared alongside each other in film and literature reflected motoring's real and imagined perils. As has been seen, these ranged from its threat to life and limb, to its role in the despoliation of the countryside, through to its impact on sexual behaviour and, more fundamentally, on class and gender norms.

Notes

1 Cited in M. Wiener, *English Culture and the Decline of the Industrial Spirit 1850–1980* (London, Penguin, 1992), p. 61.

2 S. Houghton, *Hindle Wakes* (London, Sidgwick and Jackson, Ltd, 1919), p. 28.

3 K. Flint, 'Fictional Suburbia', in P. Humm (ed.), *Popular Fictions* (London, Methuen, 1986), p. 120.

4 P. N. Furbank, *E. M. Forster: A Life, Volume 1 1879–1914* (London, Secker & Warburg, 1977), pp. 188–90.

5 E. M. Forster, *Howards End* (Harmondsworth, Penguin, 1986), p. 23.

6 *Ibid.*, p. 78.

7 *Ibid.*, p. 25.

8 *Ibid.*, p. 173.

9 *Ibid.*, p. 209.

10 H. Durant, *The Problem of Leisure* (London, Routledge, 1938), p. 21.

11 *Ibid.*, p. 66.

12 *Ibid.*, p. 60.

13 Cited in D. L. North, 'Middle class suburban lifestyles and culture in England, 1919–1939', D.Phil. thesis, Oxford, 1988, p. 317.

14 *Ibid.*

15 R. Skelton, *Poetry of the Thirties* (Harmondsworth, Penguin, 1987), p. 75.

16 *Ibid.*, p. 76.

17 *Ibid.*, p. 80.

18 D. H. Lawrence, 'The triumph of the machine', in *The Complete Poems of D. H. Lawrence*, Vol. 2; cited in H. Williams, *Autogeddon* (London, Jonathan Cape, 1991), p. 105.

19 D. H. Lawrence, 'Cry of the masses', in *The Complete Poems of D. H. Lawrence*, Vol. 2 (London, Heinemann, 1964), pp. 584–5.

20 V. Cunningham, *British Writers of the Thirties* (Oxford, Clarendon Press, 1988), p. 400.

21 A. Huxley, *Brave New World* (St Albans, Triad/Panther Books, 1977), p. 51.

22 *Autocar*, 3 September 1921.

23 *Ibid.*, 20 February 1925.

24 P. Garnier, *The Art of Gordon Crosby* (Hamlyn, London, 1978), p. 12.

25 G. D. Silk, 'The image of the automobile in American art', in D. L. Lewis and L. Goldstein (eds), *The Automobile in American Culture* (Ann Arbor, University of Michigan Press, 1983), pp. 207–9.

26 D. Mellor, 'British art in the 1930s', in F. Gloversmith (ed.), *Class, Culture and Social Change*, (Brighton, Harvester, 1980), p. 195.

27 M. Bommes and P. Wright, 'Charms of residence: the public and the past', in R. Johnson (ed.), *Making Histories* (London, Hutchinson, 1982), p. 282.

28 *Ibid.*, 15 November 1935.
29 C. Carrington, *Rudyard Kipling: His Life and Work* (London, Macmillan, 1955), p. 367.
30 *Ibid.*, p. 368.
31 *Ibid.*, p. 496.
32 R. Kipling, *Rudyard Kipling's Verse: Definitive Edition* (London, Hodder & Stoughton, 1977), p. 683.
33 Kipling, *Rudyard Kipling's Verse*, pp. 681–2.
34 R. Kipling, 'The village that voted the earth was flat', in *A Diversity of Creatures* (London, Macmillan, 1917).
35 N. Crook, *Kipling's Myths of Love and Death* (London, Macmillan, 1989), p. 51.
36 *Ask a Policeman* (1939), dir. Marcel Varnel.
37 A. Brilliant, *The Great Car Craze: How Southern California Collided with the Automobile in the 1920s* (Santa Barbara, CA, Woodbridge Press, 1989). pp. 97–9.
38 R. Holman, National Film Archive, Federation Internationale Des Archives Du Film, *Cinema 1900–1906: An Analytical Study by the National Film Archive (London) and the International Federation of Film Archives* (Brussels, FIAF, 1982), F14.
39 *Ibid.*, F10.
40 *Ibid.*, F53.
41 D. Gifford, *The British Film Catalogue 1895–1985: A Reference Guide* (London, David & Charles 1986), no. 00752.
42 *Ibid.*, no. 01034.
43 *Ibid.*, no. 01330.
44 *Ibid.*, no. 05594.
45 K. Grahame, *The Wind in the Willows* (London, Heinemann Educational, 1988), p. 26.
46 *Ibid.*, p. 78.
47 *Ibid.*, pp. 86–8.
48 *Motor*, 10 September 1935.
49 *Convict 99* (1938), dir. Marcel Varnel.
50 O. Lancaster, *Progress at Pelvis Bay* (London, Murray, 1936), pp. 67–8.
51 G. Cross (ed.), *Worktowners at Blackpool: Mass-Observation and Popular Leisure in the 1930s* (London, Routledge, 1990), p. 126.
52 K. Fougasse and W. D. H. McCullough, *You Have Been Warned: A Complete Guide to the Road* (London, Methuen, 1935)
53 University of Liverpool, D266/2/29.
54 *Autocar*, 13 March 1936.
55 *Autocar*, 29 May 1936.
56 *Autocar*, 13 March 1936.
57 Reprinted in Major C. V. Godfrey, *Roadsense for Children* (London, Oxford University Press, 1937), p. 59.

58 Manchester Police Museum, Chief Constable of Lancashire, Home Office Report on Experimental Motor Patrol Scheme (1937–1939); cited in S. Dunne, 'The motoring revolution: the impact of the car on the police 1918–1939', BA Dissertation, University of Liverpool, 1997, p. 29.

59 P. Miles and M. Smith, *Cinema, Literature and Society: Elite and Mass Culture in Interwar Britain* (London, Croom Helm, 1987), p. 27.

60 *Motor*, 4 September 1934.

61 *Ibid.*, 6 August 1935.

62 *Ibid.*, 21 January 1936.

63 Automobile Association Archive, Pedestrians Association File.

64 *Autocar*, 1 February 1935.

65 *Ibid.*, 1 February 1935.

66 *Autocar*, 13 November 1936.

67 A. Briggs, *History of Broadcasting in the United Kingdom: The Golden Age of Wireless* (Oxford, Oxford University Press, 1965), p. 120.

68 *Autocar*, 14 October 1938.

69 Gifford, *The British Film Catalogue*, no. 01010.

70 *Ibid.*, no. 03437.

71 R. Murphy, *Smash and Grab: Gangsters in the London Underworld 1920– 1960* (London, Faber & Faber, 1993), p. 48.

72 For full discussion of Larry Rankin's story, see A. Davies, 'Street gangs, crime and policing in Glasgow in the 1930s: the case of the Beehive Boys', *Social History* (October 1998).

73 *Autocar*, 14 January 1922.

74 Gifford, *The British Film Catalogue*, nos 07851–4.

75 *Autocar*, 17 August 1928.

76 T. Ryall, *Alfred Hitchcock and the British Cinema* (London, Croom Helm, 1986), p. 75.

77 *Autocar*, 15 January 1932 and 11 March 1932.

78 *Autocar*, 12 January 1934.

79 T. Manning, 'Driving along in my automobile', *New Statesman and Society*, 14 April 1995, made this claim. His assertion was disputed in the 21 April issue by a correspondent, John Fletcher, who pointed out the existence of *Young and Innocent*.

80 *Young and Innocent* (1938), dir. Alfred Hitchcock.

81 R. Durgnat, *The Strange Case of Alfred Hitchcock* (London, Unwin, 1975), p. 141.

82 G. Greene, 'A drive in the country', in *Collected Short Stories* (Harmondsworth, Penguin, 1986), p. 87.

83 *The Stars Look Down* (1939), dir. Carol Reed.

84 *Ibid.*

85 W. Greenwood, *Love on the Dole* (London, Vintage, 1993), pp. 24, 113.

86 *Ibid.*, p. 136.

87 *Ibid.*, p. 116.
88 *Ibid.*, pp. 142–3.
89 *Ibid.*, p. 220.
90 *Love on the Dole* (1941), dir. John Baxter.
91 B. Melman, *Women and the Popular Imagination in the Twenties* (London, Macmillan, 1988), ch. 4.
92 M. Arlen, *The Green Hat* (Bury St Edmunds, St Edmundsbury Press, 1983), p. 4.
93 *Ibid.*, p. 101.
94 *Ibid.*, p. 66.
95 B. Melman, *Women and the Popular Imagination in the Twenties* (London, Macmillan, 1988).
96 G. Frankau, *Martin Make-Believe* (London, Hutchinson, 1930), p. 80.
97 Cited in M. Baker, *Our Three Selves: The Life of Radclyffe Hall* (London, Hamish Hamilton, 1985), p. 223.
98 R. Hall, *The Well of Loneliness* (London, Falcon Press, 1949).
99 R. Denne Waterhouse, *Week-end Ticket* (Bristol, Arrowsmith, 1934), p. 96.
100 *Ibid.*, p. 236.
101 S. M. Gilbert, 'Soldier's heart: literary men, literary women, and the Great War', in M. R. Higonnet et al. (eds), *Behind the Lines: Gender and the Two World Wars* (New Haven, CT, Yale University Press, 1987).

Conclusion

Society's choices between possible technological developments are highly indicative of patterns of political, social and economic power. Employing insights from recent historical and sociological work on class, gender, consumption and technology, this study has investigated the complex processes by which social relations shaped the design, marketing and uses of the car. In turn, it has been maintained that the car, and the legal and physical frameworks which developed in its wake, were extremely expressive of class and gender relations. The years between 1896 and 1939 have provided the focus for this analysis because it was during this period, when the car as a technology was still emerging and therefore open to contestation, that British car culture was defined. The car's increasing usefulness for middle-class Britons, both as a utilitarian tool (for work or travel) and as a symbolic one (to express social status and taste, or to travel to places which expressed both of these factors) saw influential sections of opinion swing against significant restrictions on motoring. This account has also demonstrated how the pro-motoring lobby was instrumental in shaping road-safety discourse and policy. Whereas the Edwardian press featured regular attacks on 'selfish' car owners, by the 1930s the motoring lobby had succeeded in ensuring that road-safety debates were conducted in a language suffused with notions of *laissez-faire* and 'Englishness'. As a result, the slim possibility that private motoring could have been subject to legislative restrictions disappeared as technical experts, planners and successive governments began to develop road-safety education schemes along-side schemes for the segregation of road users. Thus, a combination of commercial and middle-class self-interest influenced the evolution of new road-transport policies which began a process of accommodation towards the car. Even by the 1930s, this involved a transfer of social relations into geographical space, pedestrians being channelled, symbolically, into subways to allow the smoother transit of motor traffic. In return for the freedoms brought by the private car, successive governments, together with rising numbers of actual and aspiring car owners, were willing to accept the social costs, in terms of death and injury, brought by this form of transport. The regulations contained in the Road Traffic Act of 1934 remain as the basis of road-safety policy.

The history of transport policy following the Second World War has been one of Conservative and Labour governments promoting motoring through economic support for the motor industry and heavy expenditure on road building.[1] Two-thirds of British households now own a car; a factor that increasingly damages our quality of life, particularly that of the remaining third of households who cannot afford to run a car, do not drive or choose not to do so.[2] In fact, average distances walked per person in Britain fell by a fifth between 1975–76 and 1993–95, with the largest decrease amongst children. Furthermore, a higher proportion of Britain's passenger traffic travels by car than is the case in any other European Union country.[3] As a result, congestion in large cities such as London reduces average car speeds to as little 7 m.p.h.[4] News reports constantly inform us that consumers have begun to question the nature of car ownership. In particular, its contribution to environmental damage has been an increasing cause of concern in recent years. But these reports also indicate that the problem is that the average person wants everyone else to lessen their dependency on the car rather than do so themselves. This study has provided an account of the historical roots of such ambivalent attitudes. From its inception, there have been a cluster of conflicting perspectives on the car. The disquiet about its negative impact was greatest in the area of road safety and in debates about its role in rural Britain. However, at the same time, flexibility and freedoms brought by the car ensured that it held many attractions. The ambivalence towards the car, produced by its competing attractions and dangers, was vividly seen in the cultural representations of motoring produced by writers, artists and film makers before 1939.

The important and numerous roles that ideologies of femininity and masculinity had in the design and consumption of the car have also been related. Most significantly, the car was identified as a masculine technology, a process which alienated many women from seeking a place at the driving wheel. Others who sought to take the driver's seat were often denied it for reasons clearly founded in gender ideology. Only 12 per cent of private driving licences were held by women in 1933, and even by the mid-1960s only 13 per cent of women held a driving licence, in comparison with 56 per cent of men. By the 1990s the gap has narrowed, but there are still significant differences within specific age groups. Thus a study by Stephen Potter and Peter Hughes of the Open University found that in the 30–59 age group, 32 per cent of women drive cars, compared with 58 per cent of men. However, in the 65-plus age group, only 7 per cent of women drive cars, significantly fewer than the 36 per cent of their male counterparts who still take a seat at the driving wheel.[5] This account does not offer a story of brutish men denying women their freedom, although women's autonomy and mobility were limited in these cases. What has been explained is the role played by gender ideology in the normative regulation of femininity and masculinity within the context of motoring. This process involved men and women in regulating the behaviour of others of the same gender as well as that of the other gender. To a large extent, manufacturers and dealers shared this outlook. They adopted conventional ideas about women as consumers which were not always appropriate. At times this led to angst-ridden meditation on the negative effects some faddish female consumers might have on the car.

On another level, such thinking allowed men to divert attention away from developments in automotive technology that did not fit well with dominant ideas of masculinity. In the process, women became associated with an almost frivolous side of the car, being most frequently held responsible for developments in comfort or aesthetics. The involvement of men in these aspects of the car was therefore denied as they were viewed as, by nature, serious motorists who understood how a car worked and appreciated the intricacies of its engineering. These attitudes have not been dissipated by time. Thus, despite the fact that a third of all new cars sales in 1995 were to female buyers, many women still find that 'chauvinism stalks the [motor] showroom' and that they are 'intimidating places to visit'. In particular, women resent the condescending attitudes of the salesmen who 'still think women buy cars because of their colour'.[6] Furthermore, the myth of the woman driver still persists, and they are often depicted as poorer drivers than men, when statistics have always shown that a typical female driver is less likely than a typical male driver to be involved in an accident. For example, a poll of *Manchester Evening News* readers, conducted in 1997, found that 40 per cent of respondents thought that women were dangerous drivers.[7] For men, the legacies of motoring's early years are just as significant. For the majority of young men, the car continues to play a central role in the expression of their masculinity. This is true in the case of the importance attached to the model of car selected, the way it is driven, and the technical knowledge about the car which male drivers are expected to possess as opposed to their female contemporaries. But it most clearly surfaces on the subject of attaining a driving licence, which, in our society, has become a rite of passage for young men. So much so, that it is possible to claim that 'The greatest shame for a grown man is to admit he cannot drive a car.'[8]

In following the car's journey from the factory to the motor show-room, out onto the open road and even into the artistic imagination, this book has attempted to offer a rounded account of the consumption of one of this century's most iconic consumer items. Its crucial position as a medium through which individuals and families signalled social position, taste, status and gender identity has been detailed. These factors, together with the powerful economic role of the motor industry, shaped the state's response to a technology which has produced enormous social costs as well as massive material benefits. In the process an abundance of material about the car and motoring has been revealed. It is hoped that this empirical evidence, together with the analysis herein, will significantly advance our understanding of the car and its impact on British society. If it also encourages further research, that would be a most welcome outcome. The history of the car since 1945, in particular, awaits, and requires, thorough analysis.

Notes

1 J. Adams, *Transport Planning: Vision and Practice* (London, Routledge & Kegan Paul, 1981), p. 263.
2 Office for National Statistics, *Key Data* (London, HMSO, 1996), Table 12.5.

3 *Social Trends 27* (London, HMSO, 1997), p. 199.
4 P. Freund and G. Martin, *The Ecology of the Automobile* (Montreal, Black Rose Books, 1993), p. 7.
5 *Guardian*, 11 May 1993.
6 *The Times*, 6 July 1996.
7 *Manchester Evening News*, 1997.
8 *Sunday Times Magazine*, 18 February 1990.

Select bibliography

Manuscript sources

National repositories

Public Records Office, Kew
MT 33 – 168/171/173/174/177/178/211/261/410
MT 34 – 2/18/19/34/65/76/112/142/180/184/227/242/248/322/331/
356/638
MT 39 – 144/619/620/739
MT 900
HLG 51 – 919/920
HLG 52 – 545/547

Local repositories

Museum of Rural Life, University of Reading
Campaign for the Preservation of Rural England (CPRE) Files:
Motor Agents' Association
CPRE file: Automobile Association, 78
CPRE file: AA Shelters and Telephone Boxes, 78/1
CPRE file: Car Dumps, 111/11/1
CPRE file: Litter, CI 24
CPRE file: Report of the Committee on Land Utilisation in Rural Areas,
108/6/11
CPRE file: Petroleum (Consolidation) Act 1928
CPRE file: Teashop Signs, 161/13
CPRE file: Car Dumps, 111/11/1
CPRE file: Motor Agents Association, 108/11

Modern Records Centre, University of Warwick
Austin Board Minutes
Morris Board Minutes
Rover Board Minutes
The Tofahn papers

The Automobile Association Archive, Basingstoke
Various papers

The Royal Automobile Club Library, London
Various papers

Archives and Special Collections, University of Liverpool
Archives of the Royal Society for the Prevention of Accidents: National
    Safety First Association File

Newspapers and periodicals

Acton Gazette and Express
Advance (Wolseley dealers' journal)
Advertiser's Weekly (all issues 1918–39)
Architect
Austin Magazine
Autocar (all issues 1900–39)
Blackpool Gazette and Herald
British Boarding House Proprietor (later *British Boarding House Proprietor* and
    finally *Hotel*: all issues 1932–39)
Bulletin of the Riley Register
City News
Daily Dispatch
Daily Express
Daily Herald
Daily News
Daily Telegraph
Devon Gazette
The Economist
Evening Chronicle
Exeter Express
Farmers' Weekly (all issues 1918–39)
Ford Owners' Journal
The Garage and Motor Agent (all issues 1918–39)
Good Housekeeping (all issues 1922–39)
Hansard, House of Commons Debates
Hansard, House of Lords Debates

Listener
Manchester Evening News
Manchester Guardian
Modern Motoring
Morris Owner (all issues 1924–39)
Motor
Motor Trader (all issues 1910–39)
News Chronicle
On the Road
Popular Motoring (official organ of the Singer Motor Club)
Practical Motorist
Quarterly Newsletter (Pedestrians' Association publication – all issues)
Standard Car Review
The Times (all issues 1896–39)
Warwick Advertiser
Yarmouth Independent

Primary printed sources

Official publications

Committee on Consumer Credit, *Consumer Credit: Report of the Committee* (London, HMSO), Cmnd. 4596.

Department of the Environment and the Department of Transport, L. Pickup, *Housewives' Mobility and Travel Patterns*, TRRL. Report LR 971 (Crowthorne, Transport and Road Research Laboratory, 1981)

Department of Transport, *Road Accidents, Great Britain* (London, HMSO, 1991)

Home Office, *Return showing by Police District, the Number of Persons dealt with for Motoring Offences During the Period July to December 1928* (London, Home Office 1929).

House of Lords, Select Committee on Road Traffic Accidents, (Compensation for Accidents) Bill and Road Traffic (Emergency Treatment) Bill: *Report and Evidence* (1933)

House of Lords Select Committee on Prevention of Road Accidents, *Report and Evidence*, HL 35, 192 (1937–38); *Report and Evidence*, HL2 (1938–39)

Ministry of Transport, *Report on Fatal Road Accidents which occurred during the year 1933* (HMSO, 1934)

Ministry of Transport, *National Travel Survey 1964: Part One – Household Vehicle Ownership and Use* (1964)

Royal Commission on Motor Cars, *Report*, Cmnd. 3080; *Evidence*, Cmnd. 3081 (1906)

Royal Commission on Transport, *Evidence*, 3 vols (Ministry of Transport, 1928–30)

Scott Report, Committee on Land Utilisation in Rural Areas (Ministry of Works, 1943), Cmnd. 6378.

Town and Country Planning Advisory Committee, *Report on the Preservation of the Countryside* (London, HMSO, 1938)

Books

Arlen, M., *The Green Hat* (Bury St Edmunds, St Edmudsbury Press, 1983)

Autocheques Ltd, *Autocheque Handbook 1937* (London, Autocheques, 1937)

Automobile Association, *The Automobile Association Handbook 1935–6* (London, Automobile Association, 1935)

Calvert, W. R., *Family Holiday: A Little Tour in a Second-hand Car* (London, Putnam, 1932)

Denne Waterhouse, R., *Week-end Ticket* (Bristol, Arrowsmith, 1934)

Evans, C. W. and D.S. Dannreuther, *Law for the Private Motorist* (London, Pitman, 1936)

Forster, E. M., *Howards End* (Harmonsworth, Penguin, 1986)

Fougasse, K. and W. D. H. McCullough, *You Have Been Warned* (London, Methuen, 1935)

Frankau, G., *Martin Make-Believe* (London, Hutchinson, 1930)

Freeston, C. L., *Continental Touring* (n.d.)

Godfrey, C. V., *Roadsense for Children* (London, Oxford University Press, 1937)

Grahame, K., *The Wind in the Willows* (London, Heinemann Educational, 1988)

Greenwood, W., *Love on the Dole* (London, Vintage, 1993)

Hall, R., *The Well of Loneliness* (London, Falcon, 1949)

Haworth, D., *Figures in a Bygone Landscape* (London, Methuen, 1986)

Haworth, D., *Bright Morning: Images of a Lancashire Boyhood* (London, Methuen, 1990)

Henslowe, L., *Buying a Car?* (London, Hutchinson, 1930)

Huxley, A., *Along the Road* (London, Chatto & Windus, 1925)

Huxley, A., *Brave New World* (London, Triad/Panther Books, 1977)

Joad, C. E. M., *The Horrors of the Countryside* (London, Hogarth Press, 1931)

Joad, C. E. M., *The Untutored Townsman's Invasion of the Countryside* (London, Faber, 1946)

Levitt, D., *Woman and Her Car: A Chatty Little Book for Women Who Motor or Want to Motor* (London, Lane, 1909)

Long, G., *English Inns and Roadhouses* (Newcastle-upon-Tyne, W. Laurie, 1937)

Lucas, A. R., *Motor Dealing* (London, Willowbrooke Press, 1922)

Masterman, C. F. G., *The Condition of England* (London, Methuen, 1909)

Ogilvie, F. W., *The Tourist Movement: An Economic Study* (London, P. S. King, 1933)

Prioleau, J., *Motoring for Women* (London, Geoffrey Bles, 1925)

Prioleau, J., *Car and Country: Week-End Signposts to the Open Road* (London, Dent, 1929)

Redmayne, P. and H. Weeks *Market Research* (London, Butterworth, 1931)

Reeves, E. H., *The Riley Romance* (Coventry, The Riley Motor Co. 1930)

Rittenberg, M., *Direct Mail and Mail-Order* (London, Butterworth, 1931)

Society of Motor Manufacturers and Traders, *The Motor Industry of Great Britain* (London, SMMT, Annual)

Strachey, R., *Careers and Openings for Women* (London, Faber, 1937)

Street, A. G., *Hedge Trimmings* (London, Faber, 1933)

Thomas, M. W., *Out on a Wing* (London, Michael Joseph, 1964)

Tracey, H., *Father's First Car* (Chatham, Routledge & Kegan Paul, 1966).

Tripp, H. A., *Town Planning and Traffic* (London, Arnold, 1942)

Williams-Ellis, C. (ed.), *Britain and the Beast* (London, Dent & Sons, 1937)

Wilman, C.W., *Camping by Caravan* (London, Cassell, 1929)

Secondary printed sources

Books

Adeney, M., *The Motor Makers: The Turbulent History of the British Car Industry* (London, Fontana, 1988)

Andrews, P. W. S. and E. Brunner, *The Life of Lord Nuffield: A Study in Enterprise and Benevolence* (Oxford, Basil Blackwell, 1954)

Armstrong, A., *Farmworkers: A Social and Economic History 1770–1980* (London, Batsford, 1988)

Bagwell, P., *The Transport Revolution From 1770* (London, Batsford, 1974)

Bardou et al., J. P., *The Automobile Revolution* (Chapel Hill, University of North Carolina Press, 1982)

Barker, T. (ed.), *The Economic and Social Effects of the Spread of Motor Vehicles* (London, Macmillan, 1987)

Barty-King, H., *A History of the Automobile Association* (Basingstoke, Automobile Association, 1980)

Beddoe, D., *Back to Home and Duty* (London, Pandora, 1989)

Belasco, W. J., *American on the Road: From Autocamp to Motel 1910–45* (Cambridge, MA, MIT Press, 1979)

Beetham, M., *A Magazine of Her Own?: Domesticity and Desire in the Woman's Magazine, 1800–1914* (London, Routledge, 1996)

Benson, J., *The Rise of Consumer Society in Britain 1880–1980* (London, Longman, 1994)

Bishop, G., *The Age of the Automobile* (London, Hamlyn, 1977)

Bourdieu, P., *Distinction: A Social Critique of the Judgement of Taste* (London, Routledge, 1986)

Bourdieu, P., *The Logic of Practice* (Cambridge, Polity Press, 1992)

Breward, C., *The Culture of Fashion: A New History of Fashionable Dress* (Manchester, Manchester University Press, 1995)

Briggs, A., *History of Broadcasting in the United Kingdom: The Golden Age of Wireless* (Oxford, Oxford University Press, 1965)

Brilliant, A., *The Great Car Craze: How Southern California Collided with the Automobile in the 1920s* (Santa Barbara, CA, Woodbridge Press, 1989)

Brunner, E., *Holiday Making and the Holiday Trades* (London, Oxford University Press, 1945)

Buchanan, C. D., *Mixed Blessing: The Motor Car in Britain* (London, Leonard Hill, 1958)

Bunce, M., *The Countryside Ideal: Anglo-American Images of Landscape* (London, Routledge, 1994)

Chapman, A. L., *Wages and Salaries in the United Kingdom 1920–1938* (Cambridge, Cambridge University Press, 1953)

Church, R., *Herbert Austin: The British Motor Car Industry to 1941* (London, Europa, 1979)

Church, R., *The Rise and Decline of the British Motor Industry*, Studies in Economic and Social History (London, Macmillan, 1994)

Collett, P. and P. Marsh, *Driving Passions: The Psychology of the Car* (London, Jonathan Cape, 1986)

Colls, R. and P. Dodd (eds), *Englishness: Politics and Culture 1880–1920* (London, Croom Helm, 1986)

Cooke, S., *This Motoring* (London, Automobile Association, 1931)

Cosgrove, D. E., *Social Formation and Symbolic Landscape* (London, Croom Helm, 1984)

Cross, G., *Worktowners at Blackpool: Mass Observation and Popular Leisure in the 1930s* (London, Routledge, 1991)

Cross, G., *Time and Money: The Making of Consumer Culture* (London, Routledge, 1993)

Cunningham, V., *British Writers of the Thirties* (Oxford, Oxford University Press, 1988)

Davies, A., *Leisure, Gender and Poverty: Working-Class Culture in Salford and Manchester, 1900–1939* (Milton Keynes, Open University Press, 1992)

Davis, D. F., *Conspicuous Production: Automobiles and Elites in Detroit, 1899–1933* (Philadelphia, Temple University Press, 1988)

Davis, R., *Death on the Streets: Cars and the Mythology of Road Safety* (Hawes, Leading Edge Press, 1993)

Dean, J. S., *Murder Most Foul* (London, Allen & Unwin, 1947)

Demaus, A. B., *Motoring in the Twenties and Thirties* (London, Batsford, 1979)

Demaus, A. B., *Motor Sport in the 20s* (Gloucester, Alan Sutton Publishing, 1989)

Demaus, A. B. and J. C. Tarring *The Humber Story 1868–1932* (Gloucester, Alan Sutton, 1989)

Dettelbach, C. G., *In the Driver's Seat: A Study of the Automobile in American*

Literature and Popular Culture (Westport, CT, 1976)

Douglas, M. and B. Isherwood, *World of Goods* (London, Lane, 1980)

Drackett, P., *The Story of the RAC International Rally* (Yeovil, Haynes Foulis, 1980)

Durant, H., *The Problem of Leisure* (London, Routledge, 1938)

Elbaum, B. and W. Lazonick (eds), *The Decline of the British Economy* (Oxford, Clarendon Press, 1986)

Flink, J. J., *The Car Culture* (Cambridge, MIT Press, 1975)

Foreman-Peck, J., S. Bowden and A. McKinlay, *The British Motor Industry* (Manchester, Manchester University Press, 1995)

Freund, P. and G. Martin, *The Ecology of the Automobile* (Montreal, Black Rose Books, 1993)

Garnier, P., *The Art of Gordon Crosby* (London, Hamlyn 1978)

Gartman, D., *Auto Opium: A Social of American Automobile Design* (London, Routledge, 1994)

Gervais, D., *Literary Englands: Versions of 'Englishness' in Modern Writing* (Cambridge, Cambridge University Press, 1993)

Gifford, D., *The British Film Catalogue 1895–1985: A Reference Guide* (London, David & Charles, 1986)

Graves, R. and A.Hodge, *The Long Week-End: A Social History of Great Britain* (New York, W. W. Norton, 1963)

Grazia, V. de, and E. Furlough (eds), *The Sex of Things: Gender and Consumption in Historical Perspective* (Berkeley, University of California Press, 1996)

Hamer, M., *Wheels Within Wheels: A Study of the Road Lobby* (London, Routledge & Kegan Paul, 1987)

Holman, R., *Cinema 1900–1906: An Analytical Study by the National Film Archive (London) and the International Federation of Film Archives* (Brussels, FIAF, 1982)

Howkins, A. and J. Lowerson, *Trends In Leisure, 1919–1939* (Falmer, University of Sussex/Social Science Research Council, 1979)

Humphries, S., *A Secret World of Sex* (London, Sidgwick & Jackson, 1988)

Humphries, S. and P. Gordon, *Forbidden Britain: Our Secret Past 1900–1960* (London, BBC Books, 1994)

Jackson, A. A., *Semi-detached London: Suburban Development, Life and Transport* (London, Allen & Unwin, 1973)

Jackson, A. A., *The Middle Classes 1900–1950* (Nairn, David St John Thomas, 1991)

Johnson-Davies, K.C., *The Practice of Retail Price Maintenance: With Particular Reference to the Motor Industry* (London, Iliffe & Son, 1955)

Kellet, J. R., *The Impact of the Railway on Victorian Cities* (London, Routledge & Kegan Paul, 1969)

Levy, J., *Retail Trade Associations: A New Form of Monopolist Organisation in Britain* (London, Kegan Paul, Trench, Trubner and Co., 1942)

Lewchuck, W., *American Technology and the British Vehicle Industry* (Cambridge, Cambridge University Press, 1987)

Lewis, D. L. and L. Goldstein (eds), *The Automobile in American Culture* (Ann Arbor, University of Michigan Press, 1983)

Light, A., *Forever England: Femininity, Literature and Conservatism between the Wars* (London, Routledge, 1991)

Ling, P., *America and the Automobile* (Manchester, Manchester University Press, 1992)

Little, J., L. Peake and P. Richardson, *Women in Cities: Gender and the Urban Environment* (London, Macmillan Educational, 1988)

MacKenzie, D. and J. Wajcman (eds), *The Social Shaping of Technology* (Milton Keynes, Open University Press, 1985)

McShane, C., *Along the Asphalt Path: The Automobile and the American City* (New York, Columbia University Press, 1994)

Magde, C. and T. H. Harrison, *Britain by Mass Observation* (Harmondsworth, Penguin, 1939)

Mass Observation, *Meet Yourself on Sunday* (London, Falcon Press, 1949)

Maxcy, G. and A. Silbertson, *The Motor Industry* (London, Allen & Unwin, 1959)

Melman, B., *Women and the Popular Imagination in the Twenties* (London, Macmillan, 1988)

Miles, P. and M. Smith, *Cinema, Literature and Society: Elite and Mass Culture in Interwar Britain* (London, Croom Helm, 1987)

Miller, D., *Material Culture and Mass Consumption* (Oxford, Blackwell, 1989)

Miller, D. (ed.), *Acknowledging Consumption: A Review of New Studies* (London, Routledge, 1995)

Mitchell, B. R. and P. Deane, *Abstract of British Historical Statistics* (Cambridge, Cambridge University Press, 1962)

Mitchell, D., *Women on the Warpath: The Story of Women in the First World War* (London, Cape, 1966)

Montague of Beaulieu, Lord, *The British Motorist: A Celebration in Pictures* (Bristol, Queen Anne Press, 1987)

Moorehouse, H. F., *Driving Ambitions: An analysis of the American Hot Rod Enthusiasm* (Manchester, Manchester University Press, 1991)

Morris, L. E., *The Country Garage* (Worcester, Shire Publications, 1983)

Murphy, R., *Smash and Grab: Gangsters in the London Underworld 1920–1960* (London, Faber & Faber, 1993)

Nevett, T. R., *Advertising In Britain: A History* (London, Heinemann, 1982)

Newby, H., *Social Change in Rural England* (Madison, University of Wisconsin Press, 1979)

Newby, H., *Country Life: A Social History of Rural England* (London, Weidenfeld & Nicolson, 1987)

Nicholson, T. R., *The Vintage Car 1919–1930* (London, Batsford, 1966)

Nicholson, T. R., *Wheels on the Road: Road Maps of Britain 1870–1940* (Norwich, Geo Books, 1983)

Overy, R. J., *William Morris* (London, Europa, 1976)

Perkin, H., *The Age of the Automobile* (London, Quartet Books, 1976)

Pimlott, J. A. R., *The Englishman's Holiday* (London, Faber & Faber, 1947)

Pinney, R. G., *Britain – Destination of Tourists?* (1944)

Plowden, W., *The Motor Car and Politics in Britain* (Harmondsworth, Pelican Books, 1973)

Political and Economic Planning, *Motor Vehicles* (London, PEP, 1950)

Preston, H. L., *Automobile Age Atlanta* (Athens, Georgia University Press, 1979)

Pugh, M., *Women and the Women's Movement in Britain 1914–1959* (London, Macmillan Educational, 1992)

Rae, J. B., *The American Automobile Industry* (Cambridge, MA, MIT Press, 1984)

Richards, T., *The Commodity Culture of Victorian England: Advertising and Spectacle 1851–1914* (London, Verso, 1991)

Richardson, K., *The British Motor Industry 1896–1939: A Social and Economic History* (London, Macmillan, 1977)

Robson, G., *Motoring in the Thirties* (Cambridge, Stephens, 1979)

Sachs, W., *For the Love of the Automobile: Looking Back into the History of Our Desires* (Oxford, University of California Press, 1992)

Scharff, V., *Taking the Wheel: Women and the Coming of the Motor Age* (New York, Free Press, 1991)

Schivelbusch, W., *The Railway Journey: Trains and Travel in the Nineteenth Century* (Oxford, Berg Publishers, 1980)

Scott, J., *Gender and the Politics of History* (New York, Columbia University Press, 1988)

Scott, R., *The Female Consumer* (London, Associated Business Programmes, 1976)

Sedgewick, M., *Cars of the 1930s* (London, Batsford, 1970)

Sheail, J., *Rural Conservation in Interwar Britain* (Oxford, Clarendon Press, 1981)

Skelton, R. (ed.), *Poetry of the Thirties* (Harmondsworth, Penguin, 1987)

St Clair, D. J., *The Motorization of American Cities* (New York, Praeger Publishers, 1986)

Stedman Jones, G., *Outcast London: A Study in the Relationship between Classes in Victorian Society* (Oxford, Clarendon Press, 1971)

Stone, J. R. N. and D. A. Rowe, *Consumer Expenditure in the United Kingdom 1920–1938* (Cambridge, Cambridge University Press, 1966)

Sutton, R., *Motor Mania: Stories from a Motoring Century* (London, Collins & Brown, 1996)

Tripp, H. A., *Road Traffic and its Control* (London, Arnold, 1938)

Tripp, H. A., *Town Planning and Road Traffic* (London, Arnold, 1942)

Urry, J., *The Tourist Gaze* (London, Sage, 1990)

Veblen, T., *The Theory of the Leisure Class* (London, Allen & Unwin, 1970)

Wajcman, J., *Feminism Confronts Technology* (Cambridge, Polity Press, 1991)

Walvin, J., *Leisure and Society 1830–1950* (London, Longman, 1978)

Weiner, M., *English Culture and the Decline of the Industrial Spirit 1850–1980* (Harmondsworth, Penguin, 1992)

Whiteman, W. M., *The History of the Caravan* (London, Blandford Press, 1973)

Williams, R., *The Country and the City* (London, Chatto & Windus, 1973)

Worthington-Williams, M., *From Cyclecar to Microcar* (London, Beaulieu Books, 1981)

Worthington-Williams, M., *Automobilia* (London, Batsford, n.d.)

Wyatt, R. J., *The Motor for the Million: The Austin Seven, 1922–1939* (London, McDonald, 1968)

Zweig, F., *The Worker in an Affluent Society* (London, Heinemann, 1961)

Essays in edited collections

Blaich, F., 'Why did the pioneer fall behind? Motorisation in Germany between the wars' in T. Barker (ed.), *The Economic and Social Effects of the Spread of Motor Vehicles* (London, Macmillan, 1987)

Bommes, M. and P. Wright, 'Charms of residence: the public and the past', in R. Johnson (ed.), *Making Histories* (London, Hutchinson, 1982)

Bowden, S., 'The new consumerism', in P. Johnson (ed.), *Twentieth Century Britain: Economic, Social and Cultural Change* (London, Longman, 1994)

Church, R., 'The marketing of automobiles in Britain and the United States before 1939' in A. Okochi and K. Shimokawa (eds), *The International Conference on Business History 7: The Development of Mass Marketing* (Tokyo, University of Tokyo Press, 1981)

Church, R. and M. Miller, 'The big three: competition, management, and marketing in the British motor industry, 1922–1939', in B. Supple (ed.), *Essays in British Business History* (Oxford, Clarendon Press, 1977)

Church, R. and C. Mullen, 'Cars and corporate culture: the view from Longbridge 1905–1989', in B. Tilson (ed.), *Made in Birmingham: Design and Industry 1889–1989* (Studley, Brewin, 1989)

Dawson, G., 'The blond bedouin: Lawrence of Arabia, imperial adventure and the imagining of English-British masculinity', in M. Roper and J. Tosh (eds), *Manful Assertions: Masculinities in Britain since 1800* (London, Routledge, 1991)

Flink, J. J., 'The car culture revisited' in D. L. Lewis and L. Goldstein (eds), *The Automobile in American Culture* (Ann Arbor, University of Michigan Press, 1983)

Flint, K., 'Fictional suburbia', in P. Humm (ed.), *Popular Fictions* (London, Methuen, 1986)

Foreman-Peck, J., 'Death on the roads: changing national responses to motor accidents', in T. Barker (ed.), *The Economic and Social Effects of the Spread of Motor Vehicles* (London, Macmillan, 1987)

Friedenson, P., 'French automobile marketing 1890–1979', in A. Okochi and K. Shimokawa (eds), *The International Conference on Business History 7: The Development of Mass Marketing* (Tokyo, University of Tokyo Press, 1981)

Friedenson, P., 'Some economic and social effects of motor vehicles in France since 1890' in T. Barker (ed.), *The Economic and Social Effects of the Spread of Motor Vehicles* (London, Macmillan, 1987)

Gatrell, V. A. C., 'Crime, authority and the policeman state' in F. M. L. Thompson (ed.), *The Cambridge Social History of Britain, 1750–1950*, 3 vols (Cambridge, Cambridge University Press, 1990), vol. 3

Gilbert, S. M., 'Soldier's heart: literary men, literary women, and the Great War', in M. R. Higonnet et al. (eds), *Behind the Lines: Gender and the Two World Wars* (New Haven, CT, Yale University Press, 1987)

Lewchuk, W., 'The origins of Fordism and alternative strategies: Britain and the United States, 1880–1930', in S. Tolliday and J. Zeitlin, *Between Fordism and Flexibility, the International Motor Industry and its Workers* (Oxford, Clarendon Press, 1985)

Lewchuk, W., 'The motor vehicle industry', In B. Elbaum and W. Lazonick (eds), *The Decline of the British Economy* (Oxford, Clarendon Press 1986)

Lowerson, J., 'Battles for the countryside', in F. Gloversmith (ed.), *Class, Culture and Social Change: A New View of the 1930s* (Brighton, Harvester, 1980)

Mellor, D., 'British art in the 1930s', in F. Gloversmith (ed.), *Class, Culture and Social Change* (Brighton, Harvester, 1980)

Miller, M. and R. Church, 'Motor manufacturing', in N. K. Buxton and D. H. Aldcroft (eds), *British Industry Between the Wars* (London, Scolar Press, 1979)

Pickup, L., 'Hard to get around: a study of women's travel mobility', in J. Little, L. Peake and P. Richardson (eds), *Women in Cities: Gender and the Urban Environment* (London, Macmillan, 1988)

Tolliday, S., 'Management and labour in Britain, 1896–1939', in S. Tolliday and J. Zeitlin (eds), *The Automobile Industry and its Workers: Between Fordism and Flexibility* (Cambridge, Polity Press, 1987)

Tolliday, S., 'The failure of mass production unionism in the motor industry, 1914–39', in C. Wrigley (ed.), *A History of British Industrial Relations*, vol. 2 (Brighton, Harvester, 1987)

Widdowson, F., '"Educating teacher": women and elementary teaching in London, 1900–1914', in L. Davidoff and B. Westover (eds), *Our Work, Our Lives, Our Words* (London, Barnes & Noble, 1986)

Journal articles

Ashby, A. W., 'The effects of urban growth on the countryside', *Sociological Review*, 31 (1940) 345–69

Barker, T. C., 'Slow progress: forty years of motoring research', *Journal of Transport History* 14 (1993) 142–65

Berger, M. L., 'Women drivers!: the emergence of folklore and stereotypic opinions concerning feminine automotive behaviour', *Women's Studies International Forum*, 9, 3 (1986) 257–63

Bowden, S. M., 'Demand and supply constraints in the inter-war UK car industry: did the manufacturers get it right?', *Business History* 33 (1991) 241–67

Bowden, S. M. and M. Collins, 'The Bank of England, industrial regeneration, and hire purchase between the wars', *Economic History Review* XLV (1992) 120–36

Bowden, S. and P. Turner, 'Some cross-sectional evidence on the determinants of the diffusion of car ownership in the inter-war UK economy', *Business History*, 35 (1993) 55–69

Bowden, S. and P. Turner, 'Demand for consumer durables in the interwar period', *Journal of Economic History*, 53 (1993) 244–57

Brownell, B. A., 'A symbol of modernity: attitudes toward the automobile in Southern cities in the 1920s', *American Quarterly*, 24 (March 1972)

Cherry, G. E., 'Town planning and the motor car in twentieth century Britain', *Journal of High Speed Ground Transportation*, 4, 1 (1970)

Church, R., 'Markets and marketing in the British motor industry before 1914', *Journal of Transport History* 3 (1982) 1–20

Corley, T. A. B., 'Consumer marketing in Britain 1914–60', *Business History*, 29 (1987)

Davies, A., 'The police and the people: gambling in Salford, 1900–1939', *Historical Journal*, 34 (1991) 87–115

Emsley, C., '"Mother, what did policemen do when there weren't any motors?" The law, the police and the regulation of motor traffic in England, 1900–1939', *The Historical Journal* 36 (1993) 357–81

Flink, J. J., 'Three stages of American automobile consciousness', *American Quarterly* (October 1972) 451–73

Koerner, S., 'The British motor-cycle industry during the 1930s', *Journal of Transport History*, 16 (1995) 55–76

Ling, P., 'Sex and the automobile in the jazz age', *History Today* (November 1989) 18–24

Miller, S., 'Land, landscape and the question of culture: English urban hegemony and research needs', *Journal of Historical Sociology*, 8 (1995) 94–107

Mort, F. and P. Thompson, 'Retailing, commercial culture and masculinity in 1950s Britain: the case of Montague Burton, the 'Tailor of Taste'', *History Workshop*, 38 (1994)

Olney, M. L., 'Credit as a production-smoothing device: the case of automobiles, 1913–1938', *Journal of Economic History*, 49 (1989) 377–91

Overy, R. J., 'Cars, roads and economic recovery in Germany, 1932–1938', *Economic History Review*, 28 (1975) 466–82

Reekie, G., 'Impulsive women, predictable men: psychological constructions of sexual difference in sales literature to 1930', *Australian Historical Studies*, 24 (1991) 359–77

Samuel, R., 'Middle class between the wars', *New Society* (January–June 1981)

Saul, S. B., 'The motor industry in Britain to 1914', *Business History* 5 (1962) 22–44

Shand, J. D., 'The Reichsautobahn: Symbol for the Third Reich', *Journal of Contemporary History* (1984) 189–200

Stearns, P. N., 'Stages of consumerism: recent work on the issues periodization', *Journal of Modern History*, 69 (1997) 102–17

Westall, O. M., 'The invisible hand strikes back: motor insurance and the erosion of organised competition in general insurance, 1920–38', *Business History*, 30 (1988)

Winner, L., 'Do artifacts have politics?', *Daedalus*, 109 (1980) 121–36.

Unpublished theses

Greenfield, J., 'From "angels in the house" to the "craft workers of today": women's roles and the ideology of domesticity in popular women's magazines in the 1930s', MA dissertation, University of Warwick, 1991

North, D. L., 'Middle-class suburban lifestyles and culture in England, 1919–1939', D.Phil. thesis, University of Oxford, 1988

O'Connell, S., 'The social and cultural impact of the car in interwar Britain', Ph.D. thesis, University of Warwick, 1996

Index